The Political Imagination in History

J.G.A. Pocock is the greatest political historian of our time. His studies belong to a tradition in the humanities that has looked to the research university as its sign and symbol. But the power of his vast erudition and of his hermeneutic—put to reconstructing crucial political aspects of the British and European past—have made him an institution unto himself.

This volume throws into relief Pocock's procedures and concerns. While focusing in particular on his masterworks, *The Ancient Constitution and the Feudal Law* (1957), *The Machiavellian Moment* (1975), and *Barbarism and Religion* (1999–2005), and on his methodological claims, it offers a full-scale appraisal of his writings. The contributing essayists work in diverse fields in history and literature: Glenn Burgess, Jonathan Clark, D.N. DeLuna, J.A.W. Gunn, Robert D. Hume, Michael McKeon, Gordon Schochet, and J.G.A. Pocock himself.

The Political Imagination in History

Essays concerning J.G.A. Pocock

Edited by

D.N. DeLuna

Assisted by

Perry Anderson and Glenn Burgess

OWLWORKS

Cataloguing information for this volume is available from the Library of Congress.

ISBN: 1-934084-02-6
Owlworks is an imprint of The Archangul Foundation.

Typesfaces: Janson MT
Printed by Thomson-Shore, Inc., Dexter, MI

Acknowledgements

The editor wishes to thank Jonathan Clark, John Irwin, Richard Macksey, John Morrill, Norris Pope, Gordon Schochet, Quentin Skinner, Hayden White, and Steven Zwicker for helpful criticisms and support. Deepest thanks go to Perry Anderson and Glenn Burgess.

Contents

Notes on Contributors   VII

Abbreviations   IX

Editorial Introduction   I

Part One   Contexts

1   The "Ancient Constitution" as Necessary
Interpretative Trope   II
GORDON SCHOCHET

2   Pocock's Contextual Historicism   27
ROBERT D. HUME

Part Two   Political Language

3   Civic Humanism and the Logic of Historical
Interpretation   59
MICHAEL MCKEON

4   Republican Virtue Reconsidered, or a Sop
to Cerberus   101
J.A.W. GUNN

5   Topical Satire Read back into Pocock's
Neo-Harringtonian Moment   129
D.N. DELUNA

6 Pocock's History of Political Thought, the Ancient
Constitution, and Early Stuart England 175

GLENN BURGESS

Part Three   Ancient or Modern

7 Barbarism, Religion and the History of
Political Thought 211

JONATHAN CLARK

8 Propriety, Liberty and Valour: Ideology,
Rhetoric and Speech in the 1628 Debates
in the House of Commons 231

J.G.A. POCOCK

Index

Notes on Contributors

PERRY ANDERSON is Professor of History and Sociology at the University of California, Los Angeles, and editor of the *New Left Review*. His numerous books include *Lineages of the Absolutist State* (1974), *Passages from Antiquity* (1974), *Arguments within English Marxism* (1980), *English Questions* (1992), *A Zone of Engagement* (1992), *Spectrum* (2005), and *Extra Time* (forthcoming).

GLENN BURGESS, Professor of History at the University of Hull, is author of *The Politics of the Ancient Constitution* (1992) and *Absolute Monarchy and the Stuart Constitution* (1996). He is currently at work on a biography of James I.

JONATHAN CLARK is Hall Professor of Humanities at the University of Kansas. His principal publications include *The Dynamics of Change* (1982), *English Society, 1660–1832* (2000 [1985]), *Revolution and Rebellion* (1986), *The Language of Liberty* (1994), and *Samuel Johnson* (1994). He is recently editor of *Edmund Burke: Reflections on the Revolution in France* (2001) and author of *Our Shadowed Present* (2003). He is now at work on a monographic study, "Providence, Chance and Destiny."

D.N. DELUNA, Visiting Lecturer in letters at The Johns Hopkins University, is completing a first book, "Defoe and the Business of Politics."

J.A.W. GUNN is Sir Edward Peacock Professor Emeritus of Political Studies at Queen's University. His principle books include *Politics and the Public Interest in the Seventeenth Century* (1969), *Factions No More* (1971), *Beyond Liberty and Property* (1983), and *Queen of the World* (1995).

Robert D. Hume is Professor of English at Pennsylvania State University. His many books include *The Development of English Drama in the Late Seventeenth Century* (1976) and *Reconstructing Contexts: The Aims and Principles of Arhaeo-Historicism* (1999). He is recently co-author of the multivolume *Italian Opera in Late Eighteenth-Century London* (1995–2001) and coeditor of the Oxford Buckingham (forthcoming).

Michael McKeon is Board of Governors Professor of Literature at Rutgers University. Distinguished author of *Politics and Poetry in Restoration England* (1975) and *The Origins of the English Novel* (2002 [1987]), his most recent book is *The Secret History of Domesticity: Public, Private, and the Division of Knowledge* (2005).

J.G.A. Pocock is Harry C. Black Professor Emeritus of History at The Johns Hopkins University, and previously Professor of Political Science at the University of Canterbury. His major works are referenced in the Abbreviations, below.

Gordon Schochet, Professor of Political Science at Rutgers University, is author of *Patriarchalism in Political Thought* (1975) and a co-founding director of the Folger Center for the History of British Political Thought. His recent publications include his coedited *Questions of Tradition* (2004), *Political Hebraism in the Early Modern Period* (forthcoming), and his *Rights in Context* (forthcoming).

Abbreviations — Titles by J.G.A. Pocock

ACFL:

The Ancient Constitution and the Feudal Law: A Study of English Historical Thought in the Seventeenth Century: A Reissue with a Retrospect (Cambridge UP 1984 [1957])

PLT:

Politics, Language, and Time: Essays on Political Thought and History (Chicago UP, 1989 [1971])

MM:

The Machiavellian Moment: Florentine Political Thought and the Atlantic Republican Tradition (Princeton UP, 2003 [1975])

PWJH:

The Political Works of James Harrington (Cambridge UP, 1977)

VCH:

Virtue, Commerce, and History: Essays on Political Thought and History, Chiefly in the Eighteenth Century (Cambridge UP, 1985)

BR 1:

Barbarism and Religion, Volume One: The Enlightenments of Edward Gibbon, 1737–1764 (Cambridge UP, 1999)

BR 2:

Barbarism and Religion, Volume Two: Narratives of Civil Government (Cambridge UP, 1999)

BR 3:

Barbarism and Religion, Volume Three: The First Decline and Fall (Cambridge UP, 2003)

BR 4:

Barbarism and Religion: Volume Four: Barbarians, Savages and Empires (Cambridge UP, 2005)

DI:

The Discovery of Islands: Essays in British History (Cambridge UP, 2005)

Editorial Introduction

J.G.A. Pocock's writings show the talents and energies of a consummate research scholar. His influential work on civic humanism began in 1967 and culminated in *The Machiavellian Moment* of 1975. Yet he is the author of a series of benchmark works that also centrally includes *The Ancient Constitution and the Feudal Law* (1957) and *Barbarism and Religion* (1999–2005). At points in tandem there appeared the essays of his *Politics, Language, and Time* (1971); his edition of *The Political Works of James Harrington* (1977); his provocative essays on historical method; his articles on the historian's craft; the essays of his *Virtue, Commerce, and History* (1985); and his works on the polities of New Zealand and the British archipelago, most recently *The Discovery of Islands* (2005). The contributors to the present volume interpret and interrogate Pocock's writings from a variety of historical and literary perspectives. The result is a comprehensive appraisal of his oeuvre.

As all of his readers know, to confront this corpus is to deal with books and essay that are educational *Gymnasia*: where we encounter argumentative structures that are notoriously elaborate, in which is secreted the learning of a historian of political thought who simply knows too much. And bound up with these provisions is Pocock's literary style, by turns histrionic, whose earmarks are narrative finesse, half-controlled explicative furor, oblique statement, swanky metaphors and allusions, and the timed labyrinthine sentence. But the characteristic of Pocock's writings which is most importantly arresting is that of metascholarly thought; so much of his work is pregnant with serious reflections on the enterprise of historical scholarship itself.

In fact, all of his major studies are at one level vehicles for expressing his distinctive view of the working relations between political moralism and erudite learning—it might be called 'the Pocockian paradigm.' Each of his masterworks tenders the precept that such political effort risks failure if the best erudite powers of historical study are not tapped in support of its stated truths. *The Ancient Constitution and the Feudal Law* builds to the concluding narrative of the unfortunate Whig lawyers of 1680–82. Unlike their Tory polemical opponent, the triumphant Dr. Robert Brady, these constitutional thinkers followed Sir Edward Coke in alleging parliamentary rights prescribed by ancient legal custom, paying no regard to the late scholarly reconstructions of the feudal origins of English law. In *The Machiavellian Moment*, Pocock maintains that the construct of legislative sovereignty based on republican principles was raised to a compelling ideology in seventeenth-century England by a line of political idealists who cultivated historical argument—beginning with James Harrington. *Barbarism and Religion* unfolds to the dramatic climax of Edward Gibbon imagined in the throes of casuistic agony over his historicist resolve about treating the spread of Christianity in chapters 15 and 16 of the *Decline and Fall*; because in taking an inherently secular evidentiary approach, rather than recurring to Providentialist explanation, Gibbon was forced to compromise his otherwise staunch politico-ecclesiastical commitment, thereby publicly undermining establishmentarian interests.[1]

What is also noteworthy about Pocock's paradigm is its autobiographical significance. For his precept was laden with special pertinence to the academic context in which his own career took shape. Indeed, this precept precisely specified the lines along which advanced humanistic study in the Anglophone world was tensely fissured during the postwar years through the 1950s, divided between college educationists and publishing researchers. By and large, such study remained politicized throughout that period, since still it was widely conceived and practiced as a pedagogy for fashioning civilization's future governors through ethical discipline. Accordingly, its professors continued to teach canonical works by authors considered to be paragons of moral sagacity. And its new leading exponents—the heirs of Sir Arthur Quiller-Couch and Irving Bab-

---

1. Forthcoming in *BR 4*; but see Pocock, "The Ironist," *London Review of Books* 24 (14 November 2002): 13–17.

bitt—still claimed enthusiastically that itwas an ongoing revival of the educational programme of Renaissance humanism.

In the US, a number of these exponents—notably Austin Warren, Norman Foerster, Russell Kirk, and Richard M. Weaver—openly declared against devoted humanist research scholars, whom they denounced as pedagogically unfit and protested their incursion into colleges and universities. For example, in 1956 Russell Kirk republished Babbitt's *Literature and the American College* (1908) in order to satirize distinguished émigré romance philologists who had fled Germany and Eastern Europe during the past two decades. Babbitt in this work had fulminated against the rise at universities of a "philological syndicate," gloomily warning of its compulsive "heaping up of volumes of special research" primed by "all the *strengwissenschaftliche Methode*" "from the German incubus."[2] Nevertheless, humanist research scholars were a minority in the world of higher education at midcentury.

This academic context, with its divided cultures, impinged on Pocock's consciousness early on, when he was a graduate student. In 1948 he left a post of teaching assistant at the University of Canterbury to pursue doctoral work in history at Cambridge, where the milieu he there found himself in would later typify graduate training-grounds in the humanities. It was one in which young faculty and students were newly alive with professional aspirations for their scholarship and in a heightened degree apprehended at the level of experience that their discipline was a technology—that is, a practiced art whose mastery required expert method and specialized knowledge. Pocock gave expression to this alternative understanding of humanistic study in his dissertation, completed in 1951, which became *The Ancient Constitution and the Feudal Law*. His recovered train of erudite medievalists from Henry Spelman to Sir William Dugdale figure as its very incarnations, while the zealous Whig constitutionalists are failed versions of the type—defective historians, as methodologically unscrupulous as they are un-erudite.

Pocock's teachers, Sir Herbert Butterfield and Peter Laslett, had both in more neutral terms reflected on the complicated relationship between Whig ideology and historiographic bias. For Pocock, however, the problem of 'Whig interpretation' of the past is one of unprofessional complacence, involving a sacrifice of the properly distinct and independent

---

2. Russell Kirk, ed. Irving Babbitt, *Literature and the American College* (1956 [1908]), pp. 133, 149. 153.

vocational sphere of research scholars.[3] Some forty years later, he with undisguised autobiographical reference expressed his conviction of their rightful autonomy in his valedictory lecture at Johns Hopkins University in 1994: "The duality of school and guild is inseparable from the duality of teaching and research…At bottom I believe that we are not educational functionaries, carrying out policies which society has decided meet its current needs. We are members of a guild, practicing a great art and training those who have apprenticed to it. Our loyalty is to the great art, however you define it." Earlier in this lecture, he recalled that during his undergraduate days "Karl Popper spent the years of the Second World War at Canterbury in the post of a senior lecturer in education—a circumstance for which I don't think he ever quite forgave those who had given him asylum."[4] Among other things, Pocock was again rehearsing his technocentric conception of humanistic learning, the scholarly fruits of which he did not wish confused with the operational needs of educationist political moralism.

In the case of his own work of the 1960s and 70s, on historical method and civic humanism, these fruits were even an aggressive means of discrediting the old pedagogical humanists by exposing their scholarly deficiencies. With these writings, Pocock aimed to assert and model his rather singular conviction that historical research scholars had superior claims on truth. But his interventionism was, too, part of a collaborative enterprise, comprising teamwork with Quentin Skinner, Peter Laslett, John Dunn, and John Wallace in the venture of the 'Cambridge school' of political history. Whereas the pedagogical humanists had sought to uphold ethical standards, Pocock and his fellow 'Cambridge' workers promoted methodological standards in the study of Western civilization, while as well sponsoring and conducting studies in early modern English political discourse.

Pocock's manifesto "Languages and Their Implications" (1971) opened by remarking the frankly confrontational stance of the Cambridge School toward "men under the old regime" whose reference-point is the classical canon, wherein major works stand "isolated by academic tradi-

---

3. Consult Pocock on the debt of his thesis-work to Herbert Butterfield and Peter Laslett in the Preface to the 1987 edn. of *ACFL*, pp. vii–xii.

4. Pocock, "The Owl Reviews his Feathers: A Valedictory Lecture," in *J.G.A. Pocock's Valedictory Lecture: Presented at The Johns Hopkins University, 1994* (Baltimore: Archangul, 2006), pp. 11, 20–21.

tion" and the communications of its authors are "arbitrarily defined as philosophy." Throughout the essay, Pocock then proceeded to catalogue the reasons as to why they had typically failed to produce historically correct interpretations of documents. For instance, he cited their insufficient attention to "what *eigentlich* happened or—the special form which this takes in the history of thought—what *eigentliche* was meant." Their neglect of the fact that many of the selected authors had, in addition to indulging philosophical interests, "practiced disciplines as diverse as theology, jurisprudence, history, economics or aesthetics," "and that here and there the startled face of a Florentine diplomat or a Cromwellian soldier peered out of the *galère*." Their guiding assumption of this canon's enshrined legacies of "effective communication between the dead and the living" as revealed in the regime's spate of textbooks and commentaries. Yet those publications—Pocock announced—must now be relegated to substandard status in the face of more proficient scholarship in Western intellectual history from 1500–1800, such as studies raised upon the discoveries with which the Cambridge School practitioners are currently engaged:

That Machiavelli's political vocabulary is strikingly continuous with the language of debate in the Florentine *practiche*; that Puritan thinking was organized around eschatological and apocalyptic concepts largely discountenanced by Calvin, and that the apocalyptic mode was as often employed by ruling structures as by rebellions; that Hobbes's *Leviathan* can be located as a contribution to the Engagement debate of 1649–51; that the significance of Locke in eighteenth-century political discussion requires complete reassessment; that the conservative style of the mid-eighteenth century was anti-historical rather than Burkean; that the American revolutionaries and founding fathers were obsessed by the fear of Machiavellian corruption.[5]

Hereafter emerged *The Machiavellian Moment*, then Quentin Skinner's *Foundations of Modern Political Thought* of 1978—works heavily indebted to the formidable scholarship of Hans Baron and Oskar Kristeller, respectively. They not only clinched the warrant for Pocock's pronouncement. They, additionally, exposed with a vengeance the inadequate historical erudition of the educationist exponents, who had presumed to know of what they spoke in proclaiming an authentic revival of the political agenda of Renaissance humanistic learning.

---

5. Pocock, "Languages and Their Implications," in *PLT*, pp. 4, 5, 7, 26–27.

The present volume is the product of an academic world that, since the 1970s, has seen the balance of its cultural forces shift considerably. The contributors are historians and literary specialists who thankfully recognize the almost iconic significance of Pocock's professional magnitude. Nonetheless, they undertake expert appraisal of his writings unconstrained by any genre of courtesy. The essays represent a diverse range of interests, while a welcomed essay from Pocock himself performs as a coda. The project of a full-scale assessment of his writings is long overdue. Happily this volume comes to fruition on the fifty-year anniversary of *The Ancient Constitution and the Feudal Law*. To date, Pocock's writings continue in full flood.

The essay contributions are grouped under three sections. Part One contains a set of broadly conceived pieces that examine Pocock's writings through evaluative frameworks of vision—political theory, political hermeneutics in history, and 'archaeo-historicism.' Gordon Schochet's essay is on the significance of *The Ancient Constitution and the Feudal Law*. Schochet early on interjects comparative clarifications that distinguish Pocock's approach to history from his own instrumental approach, namely, that of a political theorist trained in Cambridge School method. His essay begins with a memorial reconstruction of the intellectual formation of the first 'Cambridge' practitioners. Robert D. Hume treats the subject of context recovery in Pocock's practice as a historian. He looks at a wide variety of relevant materials dealing with Pocock's methods and results in general to try to determine the validity of his contextualist procedural principles.

In Part Two, the theme of political language is broached in essays by Michael McKeon, J.A.W. Gunn, and D.N. DeLuna, who undertake critical appraisal of Pocock's study of the tradition of civic humanism as presented in *The Machiavellian Moment*. Topics taken up in the discussions include: Pocock's theory of successive and controlling linguistic paradigms in the history of political thought, the compatibility of his account of civic humanism as the dominant political language in England after the Civil Wars with the advance of rights-based populism, the evidence for normative connotations in his historical narrative, the challenge posed to monarchical sovereignty by opposition 'Country' partisans in English polemical debate at the turn of the eighteenth century. The language of ancient constitutionalism in the reign of James I is revisited by Glenn Burgess. He reconstrues it as rhetoric seized on by contemporary parliamentarians and political writers who felt threatened by the prospect of Anglo-Scottish union. In making his argument, Burgess draws on conceptual resources in Pocock's writings on New Zealand politics—i.e., the 'new British history.'

Essays by Jonathan Clark and J. G. A. Pocock in Part Three share a concern with the problem of obtruded anachronism in studies of English politics and society from the sixteenth through the nineteenth centuries. In recent years, Pocock has declared that Cambridge School publications of the 1960s and 70s willfully factored theology out of the effort to historicize political thought. Moreover, he has noted with critical thrust that the historical "journey into political theology" so powerfully initiated by Jonathan Clark's "revolutionary—or rather counter-revolutionary revelation" about the 'ancient' ecclesiastical regime of England before Reform (1832) is refused in Quentin Skinner's ongoing work.[6] Clark in his essay lends support to these statements through, first, a presentation of a new genealogy of the 'Cambridge' association and, second, an exhibition of the 'counterrevolutionary' steerage dared in *Barbarism and Religion*. Pocock's own essay focuses on the debates in the House of Commons in 1628, on eve of the Petition of Right. While intimating that historiographic work on 'early modern' libertarianism from J.H. Hexter to Quentin Skinner commits the fallacy of proleptic distortion, Pocock re-examines the 'languages' of liberty and property in these proceedings in order to recover their complexities of meaning in contemporary parliamentary culture. The debaters, he argues, possessed constitutional sensibilities which were "palaeo-gothic": keyed to an ancient moral universe in which a gentleman's inviolable tenure of estate and virtuously 'free' political personality were perceived as coextensive conditions, and as such were thought to embody the timeless essence of English legal monarchy. It is only surprising to students of modern political thought that 'propriety' and 'property' were interchangeable words, Pocock suggests intriguingly.

D.N. DeLuna

---

6. Pocock, Afterword to *MM*, p. 568, and his "Quentin Skinner: The History of Politics and the Politics of History," *Common Knowledge* 10 (2004): 546.

Part One: Contexts

1. The "Ancient Constitution" as Necessary Interpretative Trope

GORDON SCHOCHET

I once introduced John Pocock as someone who had had two and one half or three ideas in his life, which, I quickly added, was at least one and one half or two more than the collective accomplishment of almost any gathering of scholars. Those ideas were "the ancient constitution," "republicanism," and "political language"—which was then still in the process of development and was my possible half; to these now must be added "enlightenments" (with an emphasis in this last case on their plurality). To be thrice a hedgehog is quite an accomplishment, all the more so in a world that seems committed to the production of foxes. But to have had four ideas is virtually unheard of.

This essay discusses the first of those ideas, the "ancient constitution"; my intention is not to reappraise that concept or the book to which it gave a name,[1] but to address the question of the value of the idea itself from the perspective of a political philosopher/political scientist concerned with the history of political thought. I should note, however, that it is a mark of the singular and continuing significance of the book and its central theses that it continues to draw praise and criticism.[2] In a recent search

---

1. I.e., Pocock, *The Ancient Constitution and the Feudal Law*, 2nd edn. subtitled "A Reissue with a Retrospect."

2. Some of which are addressed by Pocock in Part II of the "reissue" of the book in 1987, thirty years after its original publication. Subsequent discussions

on Lexis-Nexus, I found more than a hundred law review citations in the period since 1995.

Although my perspective is importantly shaped by my interest in the history of political thought, my history is conceived not as the *historian's* history: Pocock is interested in history per se, in getting the story relatively straight. While I am hardly indifferent to accuracy and thoroughness, I, in contradistinction to proper historians, want rather more to *use* history than to *do* it. Pocock's history is prospective, and cumulative; it follows time's arrow in its movement *from* "factor" — I dare not call it "cause" — to result (which is a weaseling way of avoiding "causes"). My history is retrospective and archaeologically subtractive; it seeks to reverse the flow of time, moving backward from "effects" to their "causes," terms my procedure allows me. And because I am self-conscious about the problems inherent in my version of history — and especially when it is contrasted with the *real* history of the *real* historians — and believe that I can both account for and avoid them, perhaps by draping them in Mandrake's cloak,[3] my secondary concern is with various aspects of the philosophy of history. Both of these perspectives tend to place me somewhere toward the fringes *of right membership* of this volume's contingent of historians.

There is an irreducibly personal quality to the tenor of my discussion, which is best explained by stressing my inspiration by, and general sympathy with, "Cambridge historicism." Thus my perspective is tied to this context. Cambridge University was a very exciting place to be in the 1960s for one interested in political theory and especially in the history of political thought, and when I arrived in 1962, Peter Laslett's edition of Locke's *Two Treatises* was not quite two years old; its impact still lay a few — but very few — years in the future. Macpherson's *Possessive Individualism* had just been published to almost universal Cambridge scorn; and Quentin Skinner and John Dunn were beginning the researches that

---

are to be found in Corinne C. Weston, "England: Ancient Constitution and Common Law," in *The Cambridge History of Political Thought: 1450–1700,* ed. J. H. Burns and Mark Goldie (Cambridge: Cambridge UP, 1991), ch. 13; Glenn Burgess, *The Politics of the Ancient Constitution: An Introduction to English Political Thought, 1603–1642* (University Park, PA: Pensylavania State UP, 1992); *The Roots of Liberty: Magna Carta, Ancient Constitution, and the Anglo-American Tradition of Rule of Law,* ed. Ellis Sandoz (Columbia, MO: U of Missouri P, 1993).

3. "Mandrake the Magician" was a popular us comic strip of the mid-twentieth century; among Mandrake's tricks was the donning of a magic cloak that rendered him invisible.

would lead to their important publications. There was not at that time in the United States an academic subject called "political theory" that was conceived of as independent of the various sorts of chronological narratives, however simplistic, that went by the name "history of political thought." Recall that in 1956, Laslett, in a well-turned and what came to be oft-quoted proclamation, had pronounced political philosophy "for the moment anyway...dead,"[4] and Leo Strauss had declared in 1959, "Today, political philosophy is in a state of decay and perhaps putrification, if it has not vanished altogether...We hardly exaggerate when we say that...political philosophy does not exist any more, except as a matter of burial, i.e., for historical research, or else as a theme of weak and unconvincing protestation."[5] But only a few years later, in 1962, just before I was to take up my residence in Cambridge, Isaiah Berlin would reverse the verdicts of those coroners' inquests and insist with the Enlightenment zeal that would become his identifying trademark that political theory could never die so long as humans disagreed about the ends of life; and he did not foresee a termination to such disagreements. Berlin's remarks, directly in reply to Laslett, were made in his contribution to the second series of Laslett's *Philosophy, Politics and Society.*

When I showed up in Cambridge, I found myself surrounded by genuine historians who called themselves "political theorists" and "historians of political thought." They insisted that the only way to understand political theory was to situate its concerns—I am, for present purposes, intentionally avoiding such terms as "texts," "works," and "books"—thoroughly in the political and historical circumstances that had nurtured them, to which they were responses, and which they inevitably and unavoidably reflected. I was puzzled by the fact that none of them was a "political scientist," and had it not been for the fact that I had taken a good many history courses both as an undergraduate and as a graduate student, I probably would have felt severely handicapped in that crowd. At least I knew what they were talking about and was more or less in sympathy with their methodological objectives. After all, I had come to work with Peter Laslett, who, three years earlier, had given me the pageproofs of his forthcoming edition of Locke—the introduction to which

---

4. Peter Laslett, introduction to *Philosophy, Politics and Society*, 1st ser., ed. Peter Laslett (Oxford: Blackwell, 1956), p. vii.

5. Leo Strauss, *What Is Political Philosophy and Other Studies* (Glencoe: Free Press, 1959), p. 17.

I virtually committed to memory — permitting me to scoop my fellow graduate students as well as my teachers.

What I did not fully appreciate at the time was that I was in the midst of what we might now call a conceptual revolution that would occasionally turn into some approximation of an academic shooting war. That same second series of *Philosophy, Politics and Society* contained an essay by Pocock that is certainly a claimant to the status of having been the original manifesto of the newly-emerging practice that is now thought of as "Cambridge historicism."[6]

In that essay, which remains relatively unknown because he never republished it in English, Pocock set forth an early version of the conceptual notion of "public language" that was long to be at the center of his work, and he deplored the tendency of the history of political thought to become "philosophy." His reliance upon what he called a "tradition of intellectualizing," as he acknowledged, was reminiscent of Burke and Oakeshott. The essay itself is a forceful but rather mild defense of his historicism, not nearly so strident in its criticisms of rival practices as the articles published a few years later by Dunn and especially Skinner would be. Pocock left room for other ways of proceeding and of using the materials with which he was concerned, so long as those other commentator-scholars did not poach on his turf. Dunn and Skinner, on the other hand, launched lethal fusillades against the purveyors of "influence," "anticipation," and even "development," and their insistences upon historically recoverable "intentions" as the only possible interpretative ways into texts was a virtual "take no prisoners" response to *all* the "great books" conceptions of political philosophy, political theory, and especially the history of political thought.

I

In the 1920s, *The Nation* ran a regular column entitled "Books that Changed Our Minds," and I have often thought about what books I would include in such a category: one that always comes to mind is *The Ancient Constitution and the Feudal Law*, which I first read as a beginning

---

6. Entitled "The History of Political Thought: A Methodological Enquiry" (in *Philosophy, Politics and Society*, Laslett [ed.]), it is, so far as I can determine Pocock's first published overt discussion of "the functions within a political society of what may be called its language (or languages) of politics" (p. 183).

graduate student in 1959, two years after it was published. It was, in fact, the third book I bought from Blackwell's after my account was established,[7] which was a considerable and almost heady rite of passage for burgeoning scholars in North America in those days.

Substantively, *The Ancient Constitution* permanently altered our understanding of English political thought in the early-modern period. It is today virtually impossible — and certainly unwise — to embark upon a study of that subject without addressing the development of England as a "legitimatist" or juridical state. The politics of the seventeenth century were increasingly the overt stake in the political battle between crown and Parliament. By 1640, many of the extra-legal mechanisms of control and sources of order were so fractured and dispersed that law appeared to be the only possible foundation for unity. Ultimately, it was the collapse of the constitutional accommodation of "king-in-parliament" that led to the conflict that is variously known as the English Civil War or "Revolution" or the Puritan Revolution. Among the most substantial reasons for the failure of that accommodation were irreconcilable differences about the law, differences that, in the first instance, were to have been resolved by recourse to history. But history itself turned out to be no more tractable than the law to which it gave force.

Conceptually, it was from *The Ancient Constitution*, more than any other work, that I learned one of the fundamental tools of my trade, how to read "old books." Pocock taught me — confirming what now seems like a natural predisposition toward what is loosely and old-fashionedly called "the sociology of knowledge" — the inescapability of historical context. More specifically, the message I took from that work was that one should read *from* tracts, pamphlets, and minor writings *to* the "important" and philosophical treatises, not the other way round. The clues to the "character of an age," as it were, and to the interpretation of its most substantive political writings are to be sought in the first instance not in the major books themselves — books that we have subsequently learned to call "canonical" — but in the larger worlds they inhabited. One ought not attempt to understand the history of political thought by reading its

---

7. The first two were Peter Laslett's edition of Filmer and the initial volume of what was to become his *Philosophy, Politics and Society* series. Indeed, it was at the suggestion of Laslett — whom I had met in the spring of 1959 — that I read and then bought *The Ancient Constitution*. The next year, he urged on me Pocock's 1960 *Historical Journal* article, "Burke and the Ancient Constitution," which I read with the zeal of the convert that I was.

basic "texts" as if they had just rolled off the presses, by isolated and protracted immersion in them, and/or by presuming that there is a recoverable conversation across the ages among a collection of major thinkers
and philosophers about a series of "enduring" questions.

It was a far more complex and ultimately contentious claim than I
realized at the time, and many of us—not the least Pocock himself—
have devoted considerable energies to working out those complexities
and reining in some of that contentiousness over the past forty plus years.
But it is difficult and almost strange to realize that "historicist contextualism" of this sort was, in the not very distant past, something new that
had to be learned and then refined.

The Ancient Constitution was published toward the middle of an artificial decade that I think of as beginning in 1953 with Leo Strauss's per-
versely anti-contextual *Natural Right and History* and ending in 1962 with
C.B. Macpherson's idiosyncratically contextual *Political Theory of Possessive
Individualism*, both of which purported to deal with portions of the same
period addressed by Pocock. 1953 was also the year in which Ludwig Wittgenstein's *Philosophical Investigations* and T.D. Weldon's *Vocabulary of Politics*
were published along with Strauss, and E.H. Carr's *What is History?* and
Thomas Kuhn's *The Structure of Scientific Revolutions* were partnered with
Macpherson in 1962.[8] And, as we know, it was in1956—the year before

---

8. Other works of significance for political theory and the history of political thought published in that ten-year span include Clinton Rossiter's *Seedtime
of the Republic* (1953), Perez Zagorin's *History of Political Thought during the English
Revolution* and Wolfgang von Leyden's translation and edition of Locke's *Essays
on the Law of Nature* (both 1954), J.W. Gough's *Fundamental Law in English Constitutional History*, Louis Hartz's *The Liberal Tradition in America*, and John Yolton's
John Locke and the Way of Ideas (these, 1955), the first of Laslett's *Philosophy, Politics
and Society* volumes (1956), Howard Warrender's *Political Philosophy of Hobbes*, Bertrand de Jouvenal's *Sovereignty: An Inquiry into the Political Good*, and William
Dray's *Law and Explanation in History* (1957), Hannah Arendt's *The Human Condition*,
Isaiah Berlin's *Two Concepts of Liberty*, Peter Winch's *The Idea of a Social Science*,
John Rawls' "Justice as Fairness," the theoretical foundation of *A Theory of Jus-
tice*, and the first volume of *NOMOS* (titled *Authority*), the annual publication
of the American Society for Political and Legal Philosophy (1958), J.H. Salmon's
French Wars of Religion in English Political Thought, Caroline Robbins' *The Eighteenth-
Century Commonwealthman*, Arnold Brecht's *Political Theory*, and Stanley Benn and
Richard Peters' *Social Principles and the Democratic State* (1959), Laslett's edition
of Locke's *Two Treatises* and Sheldon Wolin's *Politics and Vision* (1960), H.L.A. Hart's
Concept of Law, the third edition of George Sabine's *A History of Political Theory*,
and Christopher Hill's *A Century of Revolution* (1961), and the second series of Las-

The Ancient Constitution—that Peter Laslett so memorably informed us in his introduction to the first of his *Philosophy, Politics and Society* volumes, "For the moment, anyway, political philosophy is dead"—therein reflecting not only on the impact of logical positivism but, as well, on the ideological exhaustion that followed in the wake of the Second World War and the optimism of American social science.[9]

The value of that claim some forty-five years later when it is not so easily accepted is that it reminds us of the theoretical distance that had to be traveled to reach the contemporary over-abundance of political theory and helps us begin the process of trying to understand the relationship among the history of political thought, political theory proper,[10] and conceptualizations of how the two subjects are to be analyzed and "done." This is all the more dramatic and vital when *The Ancient Constitution* is made part of the mix.

On its face, the book is more than an analytic chronicle of a strain of political theory than it is a work of theory *per se*. But as Pocock knew then

---

lett's *Philosophy, Politics and Society*, Michael Oakeshott's *Rationalism in Politics*, a collection that included his 1951 address, "Political Education," and J.L. Austin's *How to Do Things With Words* and *Sense and Sensibilia*, reconstructions of his lectures (1962).

Important works of that same period that might be less familiar to successive generations of students of Anglophone political history include Gilbert Ryle's *Dilemmas* and Richard Brandt's *Hopi Ethics* (1954), John Ladd's *The Structure of a Moral Code* (1957), Kurt Baier's *The Moral Point of View* (1958), and Ernest Gellner's *Words and Things*, Brandt's magisterial textbook *Ethical Theory*, P.F. Strawson's *Individuals*, and Stuart Hampshire's *Thought and Action* (1959).

9. Laslett's analysis was something of an echo of the "end of ideology" thesis of the 50s, memorialized by Daniel Bell's book of that name and, ironically perhaps, partook of the same outlook as Leo Strauss' anguished pronouncement in 1959 on the non-existence of political philosophy. For the "end of ideology," see *The End of Ideology Debate*, ed. Chaim I. Waxman (New York: Funk and Wagnalls, 1968).

The works cited in the previous note invite the inference that Laslett's "moment" was already ending when he wrote. The second series of *Philosophy, Politics and Society*, published in 1962 and co-edited by Laslett and W.G. Runciman, opened with an attempted refutation of the death thesis of Isaiah Berlin, and the entire volume is something of a testimony if not to Berlin's claim at least to Laslett's own suggestion that what he now termed a "resurrection" might be underway.

10. See Raymond Plant, *Modern Political Thought* (Oxford: Blackwell, 1991), pp. 3–22, for a parallel discussion.

— although many historians today still seem not to know — the selection, reporting, and "translation" that are part of all historical scholarship require an "explanatory framework" as we might be inclined to call it, in short a *theory*. This insistence upon the unavoidability of theory is especially important to the various historical enterprises that deal with the abstractions or "ideas" or "thought" and their relationships to "action," cultural practices, and/or material institutions, for part of what the historian is after may include theoretical accounts of precisely those relationships. However implicit (or even unconsciously applied)[11] or elementary this methodological or conceptual theory may be, it is the general basis on which historians figure out what people were and presumably thought they were up to as well as a micro or specific theory about the particular set of phenomena under study. All this, I claim, is necessary to *The Ancient Constitution*, but it is not presented in the book itself.

---

11. Practitioners of an activity — in this case, historians — need not consciously *know* and be able to articulate the theoretical bases of what they do in order to accomplish their objectives (but they are arguably better at it if they are fully aware of the framework within which they operate). See, for instance — in addition to the anthropological literature on culture — Michael Polanyi, *Personal Knowledge: Toward a Post-Critical Philosophy*, 2nd ed. (Chicago: U of Chicago P, 1962); his *The Tacit Dimension* (New York: Doubleday, 1966); Polanyi and Harry Prosch, *Meaning* (Chicago: U of Chicago P, 1975); Phillip Pettit, *The Common Mind: An Essay on Psychology, Society, and Politics* (Oxford: Oxford UP, 1993); Stephen Turner, *The Social Theory of Practice: Tradition, Tacit Knowledge, and Presuppositions* (Chicago: U of Chicago P, 1994) — and, of course, Thomas Kuhn, *The Structure of Scientific Revolutions* (Chicago: U of Chicago P, 1962).

One of the functions of the philosophy of science is to bring implicit operating assumptions to the fore, but, as we know, the logic of explanation applied to someone else often leads to conclusions the explainee vehemently rejects. Historians are especially prone to this kind of theoretical contentiousness, for the discipline itself continues to harbor suspicions toward theory, perhaps but not exclusively because it retains some of the older views of academic history as purely descriptive. Contrast the "pragmatic relativist" response to post-modernist attacks by Joyce Appleby, Lynn Hunt, and Margaret Jacob, *Telling the Truth About History* (New York: Norton, 1994), a work by historians, with the philosophic "realism" of Martin Bunzl, *Real History: Reflections on Historical Practice* (London: Routledge, 1997), esp. ch. 6; and see discussion of *Telling the Truth* by Bunzl, Bonnie G. Smith, and John Higham with a response by Appleby *et al* in the *Journal of the History of Ideas* 56 (1995): 651–80. Also relevant but more overtly concerned

Pocock's specific historical intention was to demonstrate the important role played by historical thinking—thinking about the nature and place of the past—in seventeenth-century English politics and political thought.[12] Historical consciousness of this sort, he argues, represented something of a new departure; as it turned out, it was part of what can be called a growing cultural awareness of and commentary on the very existence of the English political nation as something that continued to exist over time. The primary vehicle of this persistence was the law, more specifically the peculiarly English common law.[13]

But the relationship of a culture's past to its present is not a uniquely English problem; nor are the awareness and political expression of that relationship especially English.[14] The persistence over time of a culture and its practices—institutions, conventions, traditions, habits—is irreducibly historical; a substantial part of what identifies and unites a culture and holds it together is the tangle of phenomena—real and invented, palpable and imagined—that comprise its history. At some point and in an indeterminate and possibly undeterminable but profoundly complex

---

with post-modernism is the work of historian Alun Munslow, *Deconstructing History* (London: Routledge, 1997).

12. See now, D.R. Woolf, *The Idea of Historical Thinking in Early Stuart England: Erudition, Ideology, and "The Light of Truth" from the Accession of James I to the Civil War* (Toronto: U of Toronto P, 1990), for an appreciative but rather different presentation and without detailed attention to law and to what historians of political thought would recognize as political theory. Woolf comments on and is a useful guide to works by historians—contributions to the British component of an emerging field that could be called "the history of historiography"—published between *The Ancient Constitution* and his own book.

13. For more recent and strikingly different appraisals of the distinctiveness of the common law and its role in "constituting" England, see Donald R. Kelley, *The Human Measure: Social Thought in the Western Legal Tradition* (Cambridge, MA: Harvard UP, 1990), ch. 10 ("English Developments: The Common Law"); Richard Helgerson, *Forms of Nationhood: The Elizabethan Writing of England* (Chicago: U of Chicago P, 1992), ch. 2 ("Writing the Law"); J.W. Tubbs, *The Common Law Mind: Medieval and Early Modern Conceptions* (Baltimore: Johns Hopkins UP, 2000).

14. Stephen Toulmin and June Goodfield, *The Discovery of Time* (New York: Harper and Row, 1965), provides a considerably different but not incompatible account of the development of temporal consciousness on a cultural scale; see esp. pp. 55–170. But for a passing reference to "legal humanism" (p. 106), Toulmin and Goodfield appear to be indifferent to law and politics; their perspectives are rather more cosmology, philosophy, and natural science.

manner, that history becomes an overt part of the culture's politics and
helps provided its internal coherence. History thus conceived also provides the standards to which justificatory appeals are made. Changes are
defended or attacked as they are asserted to be consistent with or vio-
late the requirements of history. "This is — or is not — the way we have
done things" stands as a justifying claim.

While we are not able to determine with any precision how this
historical consciousness comes about, we can talk about its operation.
Generally speaking, we predicate self-conscious history on all more or
less united people of whom we are willing to say something like "They
know [or 'have a sense of'] who they are"; such a description is even more
appropriate if their public interactions are superintended by a recognizable "state."15 In the modern, legitimatist (or "juridical") state, the *law*,
conceived both concretely and as an abstraction, is one of the principle
means by which past and present are united and the historical identity
of a culture is asserted and preserved. As a consequence of rapid, international communication, economic globalization, and the internation-
alization of appeals to human rights, even authoritarian states today
generally pay lip-service to the rule of law and unavoidably incorporate
historical awareness into their politics. It is of the essence of the rule of
law that it provides continuity and predictability. Outside the law and
morally prior to it is the even more abstract standard of justice, but it has
been characteristic of the legitimatist state that it either claims to have
incorporated justice into its practices and laws or denies the relevance

----

15. Or — but somewhat less apparently — by the *desire for* and proclaimed
entitlement to such a state (as asserted, for example, by modern Albanian Koso-
vars, Iraqi and Turkish Kurds, and Québecois separatists), by the cultural *memory* of such a state that no longer exists (eighteenth- and nineteenth-century Poles;
Soviet-ruled Lithuanians, Latvians, and Estonians; and contemporary Arminians,
Palestinians, and Scottish Nationalists), or by the *imagination* (also a kind of cultural memory) of a state that never actually existed (although it is difficult to
find examples of this phenomenon, it is readily conceivable). The legitimacy of
a state of "one's own" — self-government broadly conceived as an attribute of identifiably distinct cultural groups — has become the nearly universal rallying cry
of "cultures," "peoples," and "nations" (however self-styled those designations
may be) who find themselves under the domination or "alien rule" of others. On
the concept of "alien rule," which seems not to have informed recent discussions
of nationalism and "post-colonialism," see the little-known work by J.P. Plamenatz,
On Alien Rule and Self-Government (London: Longmans, 1960).

if not the existence of universal criteria of justice; in either case, such a state is functionally indifferent to external standards.

Broadly speaking, Pocock determined that the political discourse of Stuart England was dominated by what was conceived by the participants as an historical debate about whether English governmental and political institutions and practices originated in an "ancient" or immemorial constitution that preceded all law or in the acts or grants of medieval or feudal rulers. On the one side, the argument was that Parliament and all its entitlements and protections were embedded in a network of what we might now call "foundational" practices that were older than and were the legitimating bases of all existing laws and institutions; while on the other, it was insisted that the whole of English politics could be traced back to specific grants by identifiable kings and that these grants had led to various conventional arrangements, practices, and laws.

The former view shares some conceptual space with "natural" or "higher" law arguments and appeals to justice and, superficially at least, is at the base of traditional "populist" doctrines. The opposing position is close to the early-modern version of the doctrine of sovereignty; it resembles the modern, positivist understanding of law as the "command of the sovereign" and is often regarded as supporting absolutist politics.[16] In both cases, what was at stake was the location and possession of the "fundamental law" of the kingdom.

II

We stand here, with Pocock and Coke, with Davies and Selden, and later with Spellman and Brady, relatively early in what is recognizably the prehistory of the early-modern constitutionalism. We are on the verge of a transition from a previous conception of *the* constitution and constitutionalism as parts of a vaguely comprehended amalgam of the characteristic conventions, accumulated customs, and political traditions of a

---

16. Which, in point of fact, it often did. For the most part, proponents of the feudal law doctrine were supporters of monarchical absolutism, and there is a wonderful instancing of the closeness of these positions in Sir Robert Filmer's having endorsed Hobbes' conclusions while rejecting the non-Biblical and conventional bases of his doctrine. See Filmer, *Reflections on the Originall of Government* (1648), reprinted in his *Patriarcha and Other Political Works*, ed. Peter Laslett (Oxford: Blackwell, 1949), p. 239.

people. Springing as they have from and reflecting as they do the people's essence, according to the older or traditional notion of constitutionalism, these customs are somehow both constitutive and representative of the people's essence and are the principles on which their political and social order is based.

Modern constitutionalism, on the other hand, is about the need to place enforceable limits on governmental power. It arises from the failures of traditional constitutional appeals to historical practice to achieve that goal and from the need to find non-military solutions to political conflicts. It looks not to vagaries of history but to the precision of specific rules and to the mechanics of political structures.[17]

Inherent in the older conception of constitutionalism is the "traditionalist" or Burkean dictum — found as well in Francis Hutcheson, David Hume, Adam Ferguson, and Adam Smith — that additions to this cumulation must be in accord with what already exists. Ultimately, this would expand into a sociological and putatively descriptive claim that inconsistent or inappropriate additions would lead to disruptive failures. But all that is a later chapter in the development of British historical consciousness.

The constitution as it was conceived in seventeenth-century England and elsewhere depended on a series of compromises and accommodations as well as on a predisposition to self-restraint on the part of the governors. But when, for whatever reasons, that accommodation persistently failed and it was widely believed that the governors were not exercising self-restraint, the entire system could break down. On most tellings, this is precisely what occurred in England in the 1640s, with one side standing on the ancient and irrevocable rights of the people as the "fundamental law," while the other asserted the equally inviolable fundamental prerogatives of the monarchy.[18] Here, at least, Clausewitz was right.

---

17. For an earlier discussion of the differences between "traditional" and "modern" constitutionalism, see my "Constitutionalism, Liberalism, and the Study of Politics," *NOMOS XX: Constitutionalism* (1979), ch. 1.

18. Before the final collapse occurred, both sides searched for ways of preserving the government and the state. The Parliamentary story is frequently told; for a brief account with an emphasis on the ideological threat and political possibility of "dissolution," see Pocock and Schochet, "Interregnum and Restoration," in *The Varieties of English Political Thought*, ed. Pocock, Schochet, and Lois G. Schwoerer (Cambridge: Cambridge UP, 1994), esp. pp. 146–61, and Schochet, "The English Revolution in the History of Political Thought," in *Country and Court: Essays in Honor of Perez Zagorin*, ed. Bonnie Kunze and Dwight Brautigam, ch. 1.

For the commentator, the preoccupation with historical continuity that is central to traditional constitutionalism lends a kind of crudely whiggish air to the entire enterprise. The past—any past, all pasts collectively—has become the present, however varied and various the presents may be; that's an irrefutable statement about the way the world actually works. But the past is not history. All pasts must be reported and thereby *constructed* in order to achieve or come into conceptual existence. Before it (or they) is (or are) reported and *transformed* into history, the past is the undifferentiated and inaccessible chronology of *everything*; it is a series of stories waiting not to be told but to be made up.

We know this retrospectively, and it is part of the very meaning of the present that it is the successor to its own past, and the way we relate them is through history. In the abstract, retrospective history could not claim that any specific present is the *unavoidable* consequence of its past: things *could have* turned out differently but they *did not*. Accordingly, one of the issues any explanatory account of any present must confront is how and why it became what it did. Retrospective history thus will invariably take on a whiggish hue.

Did Pocock's seventeenth-century antiquarians and lawyers know all this? Did they understand that they were fabulators and myth-makers and that rival accounts could be given of what purported to be the same phenomena? Did they realize that their quests for the origins of the practices they were defending and attacking were more matters of political rhetoric and persuasion than discoveries of truths? The most likely answers to all these questions are "No," for we are here very near the beginnings of modern historical consciousness. These historians did grasp the fundamental truth of chronology, that the present had emerged from the past, but probably little more than that. So we are required, non-judgmentally, to attribute a degree of naivety to these Stuart historians if we are to comprehend what would have been for them the "logic" of their positions. But part of that "logic" is that they were not historians in the sense that John Pocock is; they were rather closer to me. They were up to something political. (It is somewhat amusing in this respect to compare the genealogy of modern historical scholarship to that of astronomy, which has its roots in astrology.)

(Rochester: U of Rochester P, 1992), ch. 1. The royalist version is considerably less familiar; however, see David L. Smith, *Constitutional Royalism and the Search for Settlement, c. 1640–1649* (Cambridge: Cambridge UP, 1994).

III

One of the significant advantages *real* historians have over the likes of me is that they are not encumbered by the specious presentism that haunts social scientists. For instance, it is perfectly clear to me that *positive* law is ultimately arbitrary. Law, in the partial truths of Thomas Hobbes and John Austin, is the expression of the determinate interests (or will) of an authority, backed by some legitimate, coercive power, and accompanied by an inclination to obey on the part of those at whose conduct it is directed. It is not some — I am inclined to say mysterious — embodiment of the customs that comprise the ancient constitution. It is no less clear to me that the operational differences between the common law and the civil or Roman law are fewer and less important than their similarities. Both need to be interpreted and applied, and past instances — precedents or glosses — are guides to that application. Both ultimately rest on acceptance of some sort or another. Both are among the primary vehicles that transform the past into (a particular kind of) history and facilitate its incorporation into the present.

I remain puzzled about how people like Coke and his successors could not have seen and understood this, about how they could have *believed* that a dedication to the common law and the ancient constitution it manifested would save and preserve England. I sometimes envy the historian who need not confront any such puzzle, but may report the facts of that "ignorance," as it were, and leave the tasks of explanation to others.

But it is not a problem that has gone away in the high-minded and conceptually sophisticated twenty-first century. One of the debates that recurs throughout us constitutional interpretation is that between those who feel bound by the "intentions of the framers" ("originalists," they are sometimes called) and those who believe that the Constitution should be interpreted in ways that correspond to contemporary circumstances, limited, of course, by precedent and the doctrine of *stare decisis*. The criticism of these latter interpreters is that they are unconstrained by tradition and history and would permit themselves the freedom to make the Constitution mean whatever they thought appropriate. And it can be added to this criticism that precedent is sufficiently contradictory to permit diverse outcomes. On the other side, it is often asserted that it is notoriously difficult to determine "original intent"; the historical record is no more univocal on that score than it is on the matter of precedent.

From the perspective of *The Ancient Constitution and the Feudal Law* it is instructive to see how the grounds have shifted. In the seventeenth century, it was the defenders of individual rights and liberties who looked to immemorial principles and practices for protection against law made by the will of the sovereign. Today, it is that sovereign will rather than mythologized history that affords protections. The important difference is that today's sovereign will is alleged to be *vox populi*, not that of a remote, indifferent ruler bound only by his allegiance to and possible fear of divinity. But it is no less true today than it was in seventeenth-century England that the sovereign will often needs to be restrained. History, unfortunately, and the fear of divinity, two of the traditional sources of restraint, both seem to have fallen into the wrong hands.

2. Pocock's Contextual Historicism

ROBERT D. HUME

John Pocock is generally viewed as a 'historian of ideas' (specifically political ideas) whose concern with 'languages' as they were used and understood at particular times has made him one of the foremost practitioners of contextualist methods in his fields. Pocock has always sturdily proclaimed himself a 'working historian' rather than a theorist, and his richly
particular books support that characterization. He has, however, published
methodological essays and thrown out some hints of underlying principles in his books—and, given his longstanding association with Quentin
Skinner and the 'Cambridge School' of intellectual history, Pocock's work
gets both hailed and denounced for its methodological practice. My aim
here is to examine his work from 1957 through 2006 with an eye to his
explicit and implicit aims and the theoretical principles on which he seems
to be working. My concerns are almost entirely with method: Pocock is
unquestionably one of the major intellectual historians of the later twentieth century, but while agreement (or disagreement) with his particular conclusions is one measure of his ultimate contribution, our assessment of the validity and future utility of his methodology is another.

Pocock has done quite different sorts of scholarship over half a century
of publication (and counting). *The Machiavellian Moment* (1975) and *Bar-*

For useful advice and criticism of this essay, I am indebted to Eve Tavor Bannet,
Clement Hawes, Kathryn Hume, Judith Milhous, and David J. Twombly.

barism and Religion (1999–) are markedly different in *modus operandi*, even though their author might legitimately maintain that they represent similar sorts of enterprises in underlying principle. The first traces the use of an 'idea' through many writers and over decades or centuries; the other attempts to recapture a sense of what one writer was doing over the span of a couple of decades. The nature of the *connectivity* of a single–author-centred study is very different from that of a multi-person investigation, and more so when long timespans are involved in the latter. We may fairly say, however, that Pocock's historical practice has remained true to principles he enunciated relatively early in his career. How well have they worn? Contextualizations of the sort Pocock has produced are open to a variety of doubts and objections, but I believe that the essential nature of his scholarly enterprise remains highly persuasive.

A personal disclaimer is probably in order at this point. I am a theatre historian, not a 'historian of ideas,' and certainly not a political scientist. For one interested in the heights of proscenium arches, performers' salaries, box-office receipts, the cost of costumes, and the amount of light provided during performances, any form of *Begriffsgeschichte* has to seem alarmingly nebulous. If anything, my specialty inclines me to skepticism in the realm of ideas. As a theorist of context reconstruction, my concerns tend to be more with the dismal practicalities of handling unsatisfactory evidence (and dealing with lack of evidence) than with more abstract issues.[1] I find, nonetheless, that the methods and assumptions employed by Cambridge School historians of political theory have quite a lot in common with mine. I find, further, that precisely because I am *not* particularly knowledgeable about Machiavelli, Harrington, *et al.*, I am the less inclined to quarrel over particulars and conclusions. I have read extensively in the debates about Cambridge School methodology, and I have read a lot of reviews of Pocock's (and Skinner's) books, some of them sharply critical and some absolutely hostile, but I can contemplate the objections with no personal stake in the disagreements. Disputes over Aristotle's republican thought and the speech-act theory wars seem deeply fascinating to those in the trenches, but not to me.

This is an analysis of Pocock, not a celebration, and I shall not hesitate to query, challenge, and admit doubts. I shall largely ignore his particular results, which experts in various fields can evaluate more credibly than I can. A crucial issue is the nature of those results, the degree

---

1. Robert D. Hume, *Reconstructing Contexts: The Aims and Principles of Archaeo-Historicism* (Oxford: Oxford UP, 1999).

to which they can be tested or 'proven,' and whether they are replicable. What are Pocock's foundational assumptions, what do his methods consist of, and what do they produce?

The Working Historian

We might approach Pocock's multitudinous publications in any of several ways. Chronological analysis would invite attention to the evolution of his interests and methodologies. One could certainly make a case for jumping off from his most celebrated theoretical piece, the essay on "Languages and Their Implications" that constitutes the opening chapter of *Politics, Language, and Time* (1971). One might concentrate on *Barbarism and Religion*, trying to demonstrate its antecedents and innovations in Pocock's work. I have chosen, however, to adopt a more eccentric (but I hope ultimately more revealing) strategy. I propose to start with two relatively late statements about method and aims, taking them as profound indicators of Pocock's commitments and interests. I shall then devote a short section to more technical concepts of 'method' as Pocock and Skinner have pronounced on the subject, and another to theoretical issues connected with intentionalism.[2] From there I will proceed first to an examination of various criticisms that have been directed at Pocock in particular and the Cambridge School more generally and then to a consideration of their enterprise in comparison with *Begriffsgeschichte*. And finally, I shall offer a brief working analysis of the sort of contextual historicism Pocock has long practiced, with some evaluation of its potentialities and limitations.[3]

In 1985 Pocock published a 750-word sketch of his views on 'intellectual history.'[4] He almost immediately printed a fuller statement of his position under the very Pocockian title," A New Bark Up an Old Tree."

---

2. By 'intentionalism' I mean the assumption by Pocock and Skinner that they can construct and appeal to the aims, motives, and designed meanings of the authors whose texts they analyse as a crucial part of reading those texts in their genetic contexts. On objections and justifications concerning such a process, see the third section of this essay.

3. 'Historicism' is a term with a vexed and contradictory history. What I mean by it is simply commitment to reconstruction of the meaning of a text at the time of its composition and initial and subsequent reception.

4. Pocock, "What is Intellectual History?" *History Today* 35 (1985): 52–53.

Obviously fed up with factional and definitional squabbles, he called himself a "historian of intellectual activity," observing that

I now call myself 'a historian of political discourse' (rather than 'of political thought,' though I may still use the term); I do not necessarily call myself 'a historian of ideas' or 'an intellectual historian,' and when I encounter the writings of those who call themselves by these names, I often find them engrossed in problems to which I do not have to address myself.

An "intellectual activity," he says, "is one in which human intelligence is applied not only to the practice of the activity, but to the ways in which it is itself applied to the activity and its practice. We cannot say this without introducing the concept of 'theory.'" So for Pocock, "this kind of historian is a historian of activities involving theory: not just the practice of the activity, but the discussion of the activity and the discussion of the discussion of the activity." Politics is the human activity which generates the theory he studies, and he differentiates such study from "philosophy considered as the theory of theory."

In a key passage late in this little essay, Pocock sharply distinguishes two varieties of the practice of this sort of history. The one is essentially theoretical, the other practical and particular.

It is possible to define 'intellectual history' as the pursuit by the 'intellectual' of an attitude towards 'history,' and to write it as a series of dialogues between the historian himself, as intellectual, and his probably French or German intellectual predecessors, in the attempt to arrive at a 'philosophy of history' or something to take the place of one. Such 'intellectual history' will be meta-history, meaning that it will be reflection about 'history' itself.

Pocock raises no objection to such a pursuit, but his obvious preference is for a more specific and down-to-earth form of investigation.

But it is also possible to imagine a 'working historian' who desires to be a historian but not (in this sense) an intellectual, who desires to practise the writing of history but not to arrive at an attitude towards it, and who does not look beyond the construction of those narrative histories of various kinds of intellectual activity which she or he knows how to write. Such a historian will not be a 'historian of ideas' or of 'great traditions,' unless these turn out to be the empirical facts of the situation with which he or she is dealing; merely a historian of those intellectual actions and activities which she or he has chosen to study.[5]

---

5. Pocock, "A New Bark," *Intellectual History Newsletter* 3 (1986): 3–9.

This gives us, in plain, clear language, a sense of the enterprise Pocock is committed to (if not much idea of what history is for). Without claiming pure factuality or objectivity or any other such chimera, he is opting both for greater particularity/less abstraction and for an enterprise less liable to encourage the investigator to impose conceptual predispositions on large bodies of material.

What "A New Bark" does *not* do is offer much sense of how the particularist investigation actually works. Any reader familiar with *Politics, Language, and Time* or *The Machiavellian Moment* well understands Pocock's lifelong commitment to intentionalist readings of particular texts in the contexts of their writers and reception. By way of a more recent window on Pocock's sense of historical practice, let us look at a passage buried deep in Volume I of *Barbarism and Religion*. He is talking here not about himself but about Gibbon's method as it was evolving in his *Essai sur l'étude de la littérature* (1761), but I am prepared to argue that it vividly represents Pocock's sense of his own procedures.

What had begun as an enquiry into *belles-lettres* became an enquiry into *littérature*, but to us it is abundantly evident that the study it advocated was a study of history. The words histoire and historien recur in its text; but more importantly, the study of literature becomes more and more a matter of anchoring texts in their historical contexts, as we should say; the context of past states of society and culture, recovered by philosophy and erudition, the exercise of the imagination and the judgment. Without this texts can barely be understood; with its aid their understanding is enriched, and the mind knows itself better in its capacity so to understand them. To us this is what 'history' means. (*BR 1*, p. 238)[6]

Pocock has never believed that the meaning of a text is purely verbal or that its contextual significance can be established in mechanical ways. He continues:

The understanding of a text in its historical context was a task for the imagination. It was necessary to situate oneself in the world of Virgil and Augustus — se donner les yeux des anciens — in order to understand how the *Aeneid*

---

6. Eve Tavor Bannet points out that this quotation could easily describe the method of Richard Hurd's *Letters on Chivalry and Romance* (1762), and the next could be used to define Bolingbroke's position in *Letters on the Study and Use of History* (1752). Pocock definitely applies eighteenth-century ideas of context in his study of the period.

and the *Georgics* had been written, heard or read by inhabitants of that world. Imagination entailed judgment: the critical judgment needed to authenticate a text, a taste needed to evaluate it, and finally the civil, political and philosophical judgment needed to choose between or combine the various probable explanations of an event, the various causes that could plausibly be assigned to it. Judgment was an education in probability...and in the last analysis in irony, for Gibbon...there is no pleasure equal to that of watching, and understanding, behaviour which is anomalous and ambiguous. (*BR 1*, pp. 238–39)

I am inclined to appropriate this analysis of Gibbon as a legitimate description of Pocock's own convictions and *modus operandi*. His readings depend heavily on a deeply cultivated imagination, a trained judgment, a sense of historical taste, all of which help him see through other eyes. If the result is simultaneously (a) sympathy for the historical individuals who are studied and (b) a distanced understanding of their circumstances, then small wonder if a dry and teasing irony is the style in which this comprehension is characteristically expressed. Like Gibbon, Pocock enters deeply into his subjects' mindsets and renders his explanations and judgments with a cool assurance that delights some readers and sets others' teeth on edge. Like the style or hate it, the method is crucially based on contextual reading executed by a highly experienced specialist.

Méthode and *Système*

I draw my terms here (with perhaps a smidgeon of irony) from Pocock's discussion of "Erudition and Enlightenment in the Académie des Inscription" (*BR 1*, ch. 7). My concern is to start to elaborate some of the particulars in Pocock's historical practice, and a foundatonal point is his commitment to a set of working procedures (ie, method) and his absolutely consistent refusal to appeal to any general theory as a source of explanation for the particulars he is investigating (i.e. system).[7] So far as I can de-

---

7. I must emphasize here that rejecting 'general theory' as a 'source of explanation for particulars' is entirely different from pretending that historical practice requires no theorized objectives or consciously critiqued methodology. In the first chapter of *Virtue, Commerce, and History*, Pocock says that "Though the present volume is intended as a contribution to the practice, not the theory, of its branch of historiography, it is necessary to introduce it with a statement of where it stands in the process of change regarding the history of political thought" (*VCH*, p. 1) — and devotes 34 pages of small print to doing so.

termine, Pocock entirely agrees with Quentin Skinner's blunt statement on this subject: "I have no general theory about the mechanisms of social transformation, and I am somewhat suspicious of those who have."[8]

This brings me to an awkward practical problem in the present investigation. To what extent are we entitled to appeal to Skinner's abundant and explicit pronouncements on theory and method in trying to make sense of the work of Pocock? Our subject's disinclination to stray into these realms, and his overt contempt for some of the scholars who have challenged his procedures, leave us somewhat in the dark as to his theoretical justifications for his modus operandi. Commentators on the Cambridge School have often regarded the two as a sort of Hopbridge or Po-Skin conflation and treated them as interchangeable, but even a casual reading of their major books reveals considerable differences in their practice. For my present purposes I am going to quote Skinner freely where his views seem pertinent and where (as best I can judge) he is sketching positions with which Pocock's practice is generally conformable.

In Pocock's classic and much-quoted 1971 essay on "Languages and Their Implications"—which strikingly anticipates recent fascination with 'discourse'—he cites Skinner's celebrated 1969 article on "Meaning and Understanding in the History of Ideas" and insists on the importance of "historical explanation of what the author meant to say" as opposed to "philosophical explanation of how the ideas in a system are related to one another.[9] He vigorously opposes the imposition of "coherence" and insists —years ahead of the boom in 'reader-response theory'—on the inescapable diversity of individual readings and the potential plurality of "meanings" at any time (*PLT*, pp. 6, 29). His belief that we can learn things from a text that were not intended by the author or understood at the time of writing and publication now seems thumpingly obvious, but caused a surprising amount of *angst* in the first two decades after the appearance of this essay. The assertion (made specifically in respect to the next chap-

---

8. Quentin Skinner, *Regarding Method*, in *Visions of Politics*, 3 vols. (Cambridge: Cambridge UP, 2002), 1:180 ("Retrospect").

9. Pocock, "Languages and Their Implications," in *PLT*, p. 9; hereafter cited parenthetically. Pocock's appeal to Kuhn and paradigm theory in this article, though sensibly hedged, seems to me unnecessary and largely unproductive. It was almost immediately challenged by Richard Buel Jr., in a friendly review-essay in *History and Theory* 12 (1973): 251–64. I tend to agree with Iain Hampsher-Monk's comment that the use of Kuhn was no more than a "fashionable flirtation." See his generally sympathetic review article, "Political Languages in Time—The Work of J.G.A. Pocock," *British Journal of Political Science* 14 (1984): 90–116 at 104.

ter, on "Apparent Political Meanings of Ancient Chinese Philosophy") that his "reconstruction is testable as a historical hypothesis" (*PLT,* p. 31) is not thoroughly explored, but implies a commitment to the replicability of results. The "Essays on Political Thought and History" that constitute the rest of *Politics, Language, and Time* apply the method — basically, localized contextual reading — to such subjects as "Civic Humanism and its Role in Anglo-American Thought," "Machiavelli, Harrington and English Political Ideologies," and "Time, History and Eschatology in the Thought of Thomas Hobbes."

The principal points of Skinner's 1969 "Meaning and Understanding" essay seem essentially congruent with Pocock's aims and methodology. He disavows dateless wisdom and universal ideas, denounces the enforcement of 'coherence' and insists on seeking to understand both the text and the circumstances in which the text was composed and initially received. A key point is the realization that concepts are not stable universals. Such notions as "state," "justice," and "nature" should not be treated as "contributions" to allegedly perennial debates. Here as in many other places, Skinner expresses his skepticism "about the value of writing histories of concepts or 'unit ideas'" (A. O. Lovejoy's term), insisting that "The only histories of ideas to be written are histories of their uses in argument."[10] Both Pocock and Skinner are deeply (and in my view, rightly) resistant to the notion that 'ideas' in intellectual history exist outside particular exemplifications of them.

Denial of enforced 'coherence' is a point that requires a brief excursus and clarification. Pocock scrupulously refrains from trying to see his subject authors as internally consistent and non-contradictory. Neither does he push towards simplistic meta-narratives or insist that concepts relate tidily to one another either across time or at a single point in history. Pocock savours complexity and elaborates its permutations and puzzles with the air of one relishing a fine single malt — a taste that obviously irritates political scientists of a different bent who want utility and present-day application. If, however, 'histories of the uses of ideas in argument' is a fair description of much of Pocock's work, then we must admit that this formulation carries strong methodological implications regarding the material and situations he chooses to analyse. If he is, for example, looking at the mid–seventeenth-century ideas of James Harrington and their recurrence in neo-Harringtonian form circa 1675, 1700,

---

10. Skinner, "Meaning and Understanding in the History of Ideas" (1969); I am quoting the revised version of 2002 in Skinner, *Regarding Method,* p. 86.

and 1775, then the selectivity and connectivity imposed by his choices very definitely create a form of coherence. Pocock's scrupulous concern for the subtlety and complexity of the ideas he traces and the internal contradictions of his authors is one thing; the logic and coherence that he seeks and creates in his own narratives quite another.

So far, so good, but we arrive now on more treacherous ground. If the historian is addressing an essentially static system, or one comprising a relatively short period of time, then we have one situation. If hu is dealing with many writers, most especially if they span decades or centuries, then serious problems of consistency and connectivity arise. In *Barbarism and Religion* Pocock invokes the concepts of *peinture* (essentially static depiction) and *récit* (narrative description). The former is "the depiction of a historical world," the latter "in the narrative sense an intellectual history" (*BR 1*, p. 10). In the course of his career, Pocock has done quite a lot of both. *The Machiavellian Moment* does not tell a 'story,' but it does examine a 'problem' (the point at which a republic becomes conscious of its instability in time) across multiple countries and centuries.[11] The difficulties are definitely queasy-making—or should be. Lovejoy used to do this sort of thing with astonishing insouciance. Skinner rightly condemns his "mythology of doctrines" and his use of "language appropriate to the description of a growing organism" and is plainly skeptical of his "tracking a grand but elusive theme" through a "given period" or even "over many centuries."[12] Something like Lovejoy's "The Parallel of Deism and Classicism" is a dazzling (if very thinly documented) construction of a *mentalité* that turns out to exist mostly in his imagination. He plucks his examples from a wide array of writers from different countries across a period he never bothers to define but which seem to run the better part of two centuries.[13] Pocock and Skinner never do anything remotely like this. They are careful to avoid imputations of 'influence' in the bad old ways of two generations ago. Skinner points out that "Hobbes never explicitly discusses Machiavelli, and Locke never explicitly dis-

---

11. For Pocock's further thoughts on this book and replies to objections to it, see his "*The Machiavellian Moment* Revisited: A Study in History and Ideology," *Journal of Modern History* 53 (1981): 49–72.

12. Skinner, "Meaning and Understanding," pp. 83–84.

13. For a sharp critique of this long-cited essay, see Robert D. Hume, *Dryden's Criticism* (Ithaca: Cornell UP, 1970), pp. 158–62. Lovejoy's article was published in *Modern Philology* in 1932 and reprinted as ch. 6 of his *Essays in the History of Ideas* (Baltimore: Johns Hopkins UP, 1948).

cusses Hobbes."[14] We are certainly entitled to analyze their various uses of what appear to be similar concepts, but in many instances we cannot definitely identify a direct chain of transmission. A couple of centuries later we encounter this problem in the use of Freud: all sorts of people know about the id and the super ego, though they have not themselves read Freud.

Scholars often disagree, sometimes violently, about the views of a single author. Pocock's account of Aristotle's idea of 'republicanism,' for instance, has been sharply challenged.[15] Here at least we are dealing with particular texts and relatively limited contexts. If we must confront considerable change or inconsistency, even in a single author, things start to get trickier. If we ask—to use an example on which I have worked myself—what John Dryden thought of 'imagination,' we find both change and inconsistency, but the canon is unproblematical and the investigation is firmly focused by the centrality of Dryden. Disagreements are by no means impossible, but the grounds of disagreement are easy to demarcate. If, however, we ask how Dryden's views of 'literature' relate to those of his English and Continental forebears and contemporaries, we have an almost infinitely messier set of problems to confront. We have limited knowledge of whom he read and what he read. He had little to say about a lot of critical issues that were hot on the Continent, and we cannot be sure how stable the meaning of a critical term was when used in apparently similar senses in French, English, Italian, Spanish, Latin, or Greek. Major writers are sometimes astonishingly ignorant of major contemporaries or predecessors—and are sometimes much influenced by people now regarded as utterly insignificant. No one has yet discovered a way to determine how much of a predecessor's work has been taken on board by a successor or with what degree of accurate comprehension. We cannot do a core analysis that would inform us that Locke had read 68% of Hobbes, and that his understanding of Hobbes computes to a heady 94% or a depressing 55%.[16] I do not see, however, that quantification would really help us very much. If one is committed to narrative

---

14. Skinner, "Meaning and Understanding," p. 76.

15. See Christopher Nadon, "Aristotle and the Republican Paradigm: A reconsideration of Pocock's *Machiavellian Moment*," *Review of Politics* 58 (1996): 677–98.

16. Even where ideas are very definitely known and used, they may be misunderstood, adapted for purposes not imagined by the source-thinker, or just plain perverted—as I discovered many years ago when writing "Kant and Coleridge on Imagination," *Journal of Aesthetics and Art Criticism* 28 (1970): 485–96.

history of Great Ideas, then one is almost compelled to presume a kind of organic, pseudo-biological evolution, but this is no more than a deceptive and misleading metaphor. One of the greatest virtues of both Pocock and Skinner is that though they freely compare use of ideas across decades and centuries they have rigorously eschewed the falsifications of developmental narrative and broad context of the Lovejoy variety.

The characteristic form of a Pocock argument is a summary reading of a text in conjunction with an assessment of its genetic context and original reception. This has the great virtue of locating potential debate and disagreement in relatively explicit and accessible territory. One is not lost in clouds of conceptual vapor, but can construct arguments from particulars. I should make three points about the way in which Pocock conceives and presents his cases. First, he is wonderfully clear and explicit about signposting. He says things like "It has been the argument of this study so far that late medieval thought was limited by an epistemology of the particular event..." (*MM*, p. 114). You can agree or disagree, but you know where the man is going. Second, Pocock habitually writes chapters as proofs of a conclusion rather than as a formalized recreation of his investigation — a choice that tends to produce the ex-cathedra air that annoys some of his critics. Friendly readers have been quite aware of the degree to which the contextual reading method tends to generate multiple readings and alternative possibilities, but Pocock seems to have little patience for presenting and critiquing his own discarded readings (though he will sometimes perform the chore when assessing the work of predecessors). Third, a high proportion of Pocock's 'proofs' (especially in *Politics, Language, and Time* and to a lesser degree *The Machiavellian Moment*) consist of generalized footnotes to modern scholarly books. Given the breadth of his subjects, this is probably unavoidable, but it does leave the reader to wonder how many of his conclusions might now be undercut as the increasingly dated scholarly monographs he has relied on come under challenge themselves. In fairness, however, we should acknowledge both that the resuscitator of James Harrington cannot be said to have avoided obscure primary texts[17] and that Pocock's conclusions are anything but derivative from the predecessors he so freely and generously cites.

Pocock is famous for nuanced readings of the difficult texts and for matching those accounts against historicized readings that depend on a

---

17. See Pocock's massive edition of *The Political Works of James Harrington*. Pocock rescued Harrington from relative obscurity.

sympathetic but skeptical analysis of genetic origins and the circumstances of reception. Unlike Skinner, he has not been free with the word 'intention,' but his method presumes that effective analysis of authorial intention is possible. Since this has been a fiercely contested subject for nearly half a century, we need now to examine more closely the nature of his explicit and implicit claims and the objections that can be raised to them.

Intentionality

For a 'literary' scholar like myself, the decision *circa* 1970 to appeal to 'intention' as a basis for textual interpretation has to seem profoundly ironic. The publication of Wimsatt and Beardsley's essay on the 'intentional fallacy'[18] and the excesses of New Criticism led to a very odd craze in literary studies for outlawing any appeal to an author's intentions. Students were not actually whipped for using the word 'intention,' but if my undergraduate teachers had known how to wash a student's brain out with soap when encountering such a horror, they would certainly have done so, though the 'death of the author' movement was yet to come.

We may readily admit some practical problems. Authorial intention does not necessarily control the verbal meaning of the resultant text, let alone the ways in which different readers may construe that text. Information about intention may be unavailable, incomplete, or inaccurate. The fact remains that texts do not come into the world by some immaculate process of self-conception and delivery. They have authors, their authors affect them, and the scholar may legitimately investigate the circumstances and background of the author and hu illocutionary designs in the text. The idea that any such appeal is illegitimate and should be *verboten* is one of the odder twists in the tortuous history of methodology in literary studies during the twentieth century. It led, naturally enough, to the opposite extreme, to be found in E.D. Hirsch Jr.'s *Validity in Interpretation* (1967), which lays down the maxim that *only* a meaning designed by the author is legitimate. Barthes, Foucault, and Derrida tugging firmly in the opposite direction helped clarify the *difficulty* of establishing meaning and a limited context without really confronting the practical problems that needed to be addressed.

---

18. Monroe Beardsley and William K. Wimsatt's "The Intentional Fallacy" first appeared in 1946 in *The Sewanee Review*.

Pocock and Skinner differed radically in their response to chaos in the theory of textual interpretation. Pocock chose almost entirely to ignore the debate. One of his rare admissions of its existence comes in the first paragraph of text proper in *Barbarism and Religion*, when he says of Gibbon and the *Decline and Fall*, that "I take him to have been the author of that text, and believe the text to be intelligible as the product of his activity," adding snidely in a footnote, "A bibliography of the extensive literature by those who deny the reality of authors and the readability of texts will not be included in this book" (*BR 1*, p. 13). Skinner, in sharp contradistinction, was systematically engaging with French poststructuralist reading-theory critiques by 1970, and over the years he has patiently replied, entertained challenges, rebutted attacks, and modified his own positions without ever abandoning them. Anyone who compares chapters 4 and 5 of *Regarding Method* with their originals (1969 and 1972) must admit that Skinner has been admirably conscientious and responsible. Of necessity, anyone wanting a Cambridge School justification of appeal to intention has to rely almost entirely on Skinner. I think Pocock would basically agree with the theoretical foundations Skinner has constructed for intentionalism, though I suspect he has no patience at all for trying to reason with dogs barking up the wrong tree.

The position Pocock sketched in 1971 in "Languages and Their Implications" has held up remarkably well over the last thirty years. There are few crudities, but in most regards the essay is positively prescient. Pocock expressed his commitment to discovering "what the author meant to say" and emphasized the importance of the particularities of political *language* as a means of getting at ideas (*PLT*, pp. 9, 15). We may now wince at the assertion that languages "are simply there," but Pocock was at least a decade, and sometimes more, ahead of almost everyone else in understanding that human variation inevitably produces widely differing reader responses to the same text. Likewise his recognition of the multiple linguistic functions of the same utterance and his insistence on the multiplicity of levels and contexts is simply astonishing for 1971 (*PLT*, pp. 26, 29, 17, 18). The essay is more theoretical than methodological, but Pocock cites Skinner's "Meaning and Understanding" at key points, and I presume that he agrees (and continues to agree) with both the theory and suggested principles of application to be found there. The scholar is to consider what the author *could* have intended to communicate for the specific audience addressed; the appropriate focus is "essentially linguistic, and…concerned with the recovery of intentions."[19] *What the author "could" have intended* is the crux here. The interpreter must consider four factors:

what we know of the constructor of the text; the circumstances in which the text was written; the meanings of the relevant *langue(s)* at the time of dissemination; and the ideologies and outlooks of the apparent audience(s). Combining a judicious analysis of each, the interpreter arrives at a reading or a spectrum of plausible readings.[20] So far as 'proof' of anything goes, Skinner makes a key statement: "The social context figures as the ultimate framework for helping to decide what conventionally recognisable meanings it might in principle have been possible for someone to have intended to communicate... The context itself can thus be used as a sort of court of appeal for assessing the relative plausibility of incompatible ascriptions of intentionality." By this process one may proceed towards "grasping the necessary conditions for the understanding of utterances."[21]

Few theorists of textual interpretation would have predicted thirty years ago that this position would seem tenable at the beginning of the new millennium. Skinner's 2002 version of "Motives, Intentions and Interpretation" (orig. 1972) is remarkably difficult to fault. He soberly and carefully responds to Wimsatt and Beardsley, Barthes, Foucault, and Derrida. His distinction between 'meaning$_1$' (textual meaning) and meaning$_2$ (reader-response meanings, as I would call them), and meaning$_3$ (what the author meant in an illocutionary sense)—drawing on J.L. Austin—is a considerable help in practical disentanglement, as is the distinction between prolocutionary intention (what the writer hoped to achieve) and illocutionary intention (why the writer wrote what hu did). Skinner bluntly denies that finding the meaning intended by the author "must form the whole of the interpreter's task," saying "I see no impropriety in speaking of a work having a meaning which its author could not have intended." He also says flatly that we are not obliged to accept the word of the author as our final authority, despite the "obviously... privileged position" of the position" of the author.[22] In "Interpretation and the Understanding of Speech Acts" (orig. 1988) Skinner goes so far as to say that "theory does *not* tell us, nor do I believe, that the intentions of speakers and writers con-

19. Skinner, "Meaning and Understanding," p. 87.

20. Pocock's most explicit account of his method of reading is probably "The Reconstruction of Discourse: Towards the Historiography of Political Thought," *Modern Language Notes* 96 (1981): 959–80.

21. Skinner, "Meaning and Understanding," p. 87.

22. Skinner, "Motives, Intentions and Interpretation," in *Regarding Method*, pp. 90–102 at 101.

stitute the sole or even the best guide to understanding their texts or other utterances. He says outright that contextual interpretation does not always produce useful results and will sometimes produce useful resultsand will sometimes fail entirely. "Some utterances are completely lacking in the sorts of context from which we can hope to infer the intentions with which they were uttered...Derrida remains right to insist that we can never hope to know 'for sure' or by any 'infallible means' what may have been meant." 'Intention' does not control meaning, but is merely one of several important factors in construing it. The Cambridge School position seems to be that the duty of the scholar is faithfully to determine the meaning designed by the writer, but that in a sense the scholar can 'know better' than the author being studied. All admissions, modifications, qualifications, and graceful pirouettes aside, Skinner yields no essential ground: "It scarcely follows, however, that we can never hope to construct and corroborate plausible hypotheses about the intentions with which an utterance may have been issued."[23] So far as I can see, Pocock would endorse this position. To do otherwise, or at least to refuse to accept it as a working hypothesis, would be *de facto* to adopt the position that there is no point in anyone's writing about anything. Whatever potent objections may be raised against Cambridge School history of political discourse, its reliance on intentionalist principles would not seem to be among them.

Challenges to the Cambridge School

I shall not linger over the obvious place to begin, which is *Meaning and Context: Quentin Skinner and his Critics*.[24] This volume prints five of Skinner's classic essays, seven critiques of his work by diverse hands, and his 58-page "Reply to my Critics." The critics are, variously, uncomfortable about intentionalism, hostile to speech-act theory, committed to Gramsci or Lyotard, determined to brand Skinner a closet positivist, and dismissive of historical reconstruction. One can easily find similarly unsympathetic responses to the work of Pocock, though he has been less in the line of fire, no doubt because he is less inclined to proffer theoretical and methodological specifics.

---

23. Skinner, "Interpretation and the Understanding of Speech Acts," in *Regarding Method*, pp. 110, 121, 122.

24. *Meaning and Context: Quentin Skinner and his Critics*, ed. James Tully (Cambridge: Polity Press, 1988).

We need to consider an oddity that can be found in attacks on the work of both men. Critics sometimes suggest (in essence) that their writing of history is quite fine, but their method is rubbish.[25] This bifurcated verdict seems highly peculiar to me. In principle, I suppose a 'working historian' might attempt a very different sort of theoretical work and do it badly. But where the principles and procedures laid down in theory lead directly to the processes and conclusions of the practical history, I think one should be very slow to assume that the good history has been the result of dumb luck. Pocock and Skinner are not exactly idiot-*savants*, and the critics who like their work and dislike their theory probably need to reconsider their own theoretical and methodological biases. Such 'theory' as the Cambridge School people have propounded has, to be sure, been decidedly tame and pragmatic, intended merely to be helpful to practitioners. In this respect Pocock and Skinner are descended from an English empiricist episteme whose take on the theory/practice dichotomy is a red flag for intellectual historians from different philosophical backgrounds. Even those hostile to the empiricist bent, however, should grant that Cambridge School theory is not designed as an argumentative weapon. It is not profound, terrifyingly complex, or couched in jargon employed to intimidate the reader. One cannot charge either Pocock or Skinner with being the sort of hot-air theorist who spouts off about what 'should' be done without ever putting out actual historical scholarship and submitting it to the verdict of hu peers. Both have been massively productive 'working historians,' and anyone who wants to condemn their theory and methods needs to show either that the resulting work itself is bad or that it does not in fact represent the product of the theory and methods. I am content to leave evaluation of results to specialists, but as far as I can see most of the objections raised have to do more with the *kind* of work than with its quality. To say that they ought to do something else (basically, less historicist/contextual) is quite different from maintaining that what has been done was done badly (or even that it is useless).[26]

---

25. See, for example, Hampsher-Monk, "Political Languages," p. 105. For useful surveys of responses to the Cambridge School, see Peter L. Janssen, "Political Thought as Traditionary Action: The Critical Response to Skinner and Pocock," *History and Theory* 24 (1985): 115–46, and Eckhart Hellmuth and Christoph von Ehrenstein, "Intellectual History Made in Britain: Die *Cambridge School* und ihre Kritiker," *Geschichte und Gesellschaft* 27 (2001): 149–72.

26. See the conclusion of "Meaning and Understanding" for Skinner's elo-

I should like now to turn specifically to the reception of the first two volumes of Pocock's *Barbarism and Religion* (1999). In some respects any reviewer is at a terrible disadvantage in tackling two massive, erudite vol umes that are merely a first installment on a study whose future shape is not clear even to its author. Pocock does not arrive at the specifics of *Decline and Fall* until late in Volume III (2003). Almost all reviewers sa lute the author's reputation and acknowledge his doyen status; some con tent themselves with descriptive summary and respectful words—but quite a few are uncomfortable and say so with varying degrees of po liteness. Four criticisms recur, and they are worth pondering. (1) Pocock does not accept what Gibbon himself says about *Decline and Fall*. (2) *Barbarism and Religion* is "not a work of fundamental research" (meaning, it is based on known materials). (3) It is an "idiosyncratic" venture that does not meet "generic obligations" to predecessors by engaging closely with their particular arguments. (4) It is "oracular" and gives an "impression of the tablets being brought down from the mountain."[27] I find little merit in any of this sniping. Only a genuine slave of intentionalism would believe that we *must* believe what Gibbon says about his work. This would be an especially perverse thing to do, since Gibbon's commentary comes large ly in the multiple and somewhat contradictory versions of his much later *Autobiography.* To challenge things he said in 1774 would be quite a differ ent matter. As for "fundamental research," manuscript discoveries are not always to be had—and massive reading in obscure books in multiple lan guages across several centuries does not seem such a bad claim to orig inality. As for "idiosyncratic," yes, *Barbarism and Religion* is that, but it is supplied with a plenitude of footnotes and lengthy bibliographies. Some of the things whose omission has been objected have already turned up in Volume III. As for the oracular manner and the style, I suppose *chacum à son gout* is fair enough, but several of the reviewers seem singularly deaf

---

quent insistence that historical reconstruction helps us recognize and reject the "contingencies of our local history and social structure" and hence to reject the "unrecognised constraints" that our society places upon our imagination (p. 89).

27. These criticisms may be found in reviews by Peter Ghosh, *English Historical Review* (2002); Ralph Lerner, *Law and History Review* (2001); David P. Jordan, *History and Theory* (2001); P. N. Furbank, *New York Review of Books*, 30 No vember 2000; Michael C. Carhart, *Storia della Storiografia* 39 (2001): 123–39; John Robertson, the same *Storia*: 140–51.

to Pocock's pervasive irony, which here as always he regularly deploys against himself.[28]

To review an enterprise on this grand scale by a senior historian as though it were a monograph out of a recent thesis seems more than a bit wrongheaded. I can agree with David P. Jordan that "Were this not Pocock's work, we would be far less patient trying to understand his unconventional approach."[29] But this *is* Pocock's work, and the publisher having given him an extraordinary opportunity to work beyond the usual specialist monograph limits, perhaps we should be slow to condemn the results for not being standard stuff.

As best I can see in contemplating the first three volumes of *Barbarism and Religion*, Pocock is less trying to 'prove' anything than he is simply attempting to supply a series of perspectival takes on Gibbon and his history — providing us, as it were, with some of the contextual knowledge that an interpreter might want to draw on. If 'conclusions' are going to be drawn, they will probably emerge late in the series of books. Pocock is not giving us 'question/answer' history, or 'thesis/proof' history. Certainly he is not offering 'story/history.' What we have here is context/history' on a truly grand scale. In Volume I we get authorial background: Gibbon's family, early education, religious conversion, general reading, time in the Hampshire militia, his encounter with 'Erudition and Enlightenment' in Paris (1761–63), his early writing, residence in Lausanne, and experience in Rome. Volume II gives us a survey of history and historiography written by important predecessors and contemporaries, most notably Giannone, Voltaire, Hume, Robertson, Adam Smith, and Ferguson. Volume III presents a survey of the idea of Decline and Fall itself in 'the Tacitean narrative,' 'the Gracchan explanation,' Orosius, Augustine, Otto of Freising, Leonardo Bruni, Flavio Biondo, Machiavelli, and a host of other historians. As of the end of Volume III, 'conclusions' are not yet the point.

Some reviewers clearly feel that what results is self-indulgent antiquarianism. A more sympathetic way to view the first three volumes is to say that Pocock is sharing with us the fruits of a lifetime of arcane and wide-ranging reading. The results are not 'efficient.' Immediate pertinence to *Decline and Fall* is rarely the point. If you want to 'apply' the fruits of Gibbon

---

28. For an exasperated but admiring response to Pocock's earlier style in *The Machiavellian Moment* (and a rigorous but respectful critique of its method and arguments), see J.H. Hexter, *On Historians* (Cambridge, MA: Harvard UP, 1979), ch. 6.

29. Jordan, *History and Theory* (2001).

to the twenty-first century, then Pocock is not where you want to begin. If, however, you want to 'comprehend' what is attempted and said in *Decline and Fall*, and to seek a serious understanding of what it does and says, then you need to grapple with more than its text. A standard approach to genesis and context would dictate the construction of simple causative relationships between biography and text and between source-and-influence texts and Gibbon's (both of which Pocock eschews). Thus far Pocock is more concerned with surveying the multiple contexts that contributed to the shaping of a major historical/cultural vision. In sum, he is doing the groundwork towards establishing the setting in which his kind of precisely situated reading can be carried out. Shorter, tidier arguments can be made (and have been) about Gibbon, but this is not what Pocock is attempting to do. I shall return to the aims and methods of *Barbarism and Religion* in the final section, but I must conclude for present purposes that no very telling charges have yet been brought against it.

Looking more broadly at Pocock's work, two general issues seem worthy of consideration. In a generally sympathetic critique in the context of *Begriffsgeschichte*, Melvin Richter says that a "lacuna in the treatment of political thought by Pocock and Skinner, who prefer to deal with individual theorists, is their lack of interest in the way groups, movement, or parties perceive and evaluate structural changes." He praises Pocock's *Virtue, Commerce, and History* (1985) for providing "one such notable study, which deals with the conflicting ways in which English and Scottish theorists registered the advent of commercial society in the eighteenth century." He concludes, nonetheless, that "such analysis of the linguistic aspects of large-scale structural changes is for the most part lacking in his work, as in that of Skinner."[30] Most readers would probably agree with this view,[31] and the difficulty of applying the method to groups is unquestionably a limitation, but I would question the degree to which declining to engage in such "large-scale" analysis should be viewed as negative. One of the greatest virtues of Cambridge School scholarship lies in its specificity, its

---

30. Melvin Richter, *The History of Political and Social Concepts* (New York: Oxford UP, 1995), ch. 6 at 137.

31. But, for a more positive comparison of Skinner and *Begriffsgeschichte*, see Kari Palonen, "Quentin Skinner's Rhetoric of Conceptual Change," *History of the Human Sciences* 10 (1997): 61–80. For a broader perspective, see Jacques Guilhaumou, "De l'histoire des concepts à l'histoire linguistique des usages conceptuels," *Genèsis* 38 (2000): 105–18, who distinguishes between the "contexualisme" of Skinner and Pocock at 111.

concentration on the utterances of individuals and the reconstruction of their particular viewpoints and circumstances. The problems posed by 'groups' are very murky indeed. What constitutes a group? Does the individual have to be conscious of belonging? How is the scholar to arbitrate apparent disagreements between members? Are we entitled to create ex-post-facto groups (e.g., the 'English romantic poets,' who joined the club posthumously and willy-nilly)? Pocock and Skinner have been quite ready to compare the views of numerous contemporaries and to jump from century to century, but they have been wonderfully resistant to the temptation to fall into easy period generalizations. Whatever the virtues of *mentalité* scholarship, it is not Pocock's game.

A more interesting problem is raised by Richard Buel Jr., in his review article on *Politics, Language, and Time*.

For the purposes of argument, I concede to Pocock what many will dispute, that political language can be seen in terms of identifiable paradigm structures, and that in theory two historians looking at the same multivalent and ambiguous language could identify the same paradigm structures in it even though the speaker or writer himself might not be aware of them.[32]

The crux here is replicability of results. Language is slippery enough at best, and especially if we are dealing with something of which the speaker or writer is not aware, how confident can we be that what is perceived is not merely something in the eye of a prejudiced or befuddled historian? If historians B, C, and D with different backgrounds and training independently arrive at readings essentially conformable to those offered by A, then we have a powerful argument for the plausibility of the interpretation. If they do not, then we have a problem which may be resoluble by means of comparative analysis of plausibility-in-context. Essentially, however, the historian performs a reading whose satisfactoriness must ultimately be judged in a kind of comparative beauty contest with others.

Buel raises another important issue when he points out that "In drawing attention to what will usually be fragmented linearities, Pocock's method sheds little light on the relative roles played by the multiple paradigms which comprise the static structures all writers create. Perhaps it is not accidental that except for the essay on Hobbes there is little evi-

---

32. Buel, in *History and Theory*, p. 260.

dence that Pocock is interested in exploring such synchronic relationships."[33] This seems to me a legitimate criticism of *The Machiavellian Moment*, but when we get to *Barbarism and Religion* we will find Pocock devoting many hundreds of pages to exactly such matters.

Pocock on *Begriffsgeschichte*

As a means of obtaining a different perspective on Pocock's work, I want at this juncture to turn to a comparison with *Begriffsgeschichte*, and in particular with the practice embodied in the *Geschichtliche Grundbegriffe: Historiches Lexikon zur politische-sozialer Sprache in Deutschland* and the work of its principal architect, Reinhart Koselleck. During the last decade a number of commentators have called attention to common ground shared by this venture and the Cambridge School. The *GG*, as it is familiarly known, came into print in eight volumes between 1972 and 1997 and has generated ancillary multi-decade projects. My object is not to attempt to render judgment on the German enterprise, but rather to see what light it sheds on Cambridge School practice.

The *GG* has been championed by Melvin Richter in his *History of Political and Social Concepts*.[34] He devotes chapter 6 to "Pocock, Skinner, and *Begriffsgeschichte*," offering a variety of useful comparisons. The School is much less oriented towards *mentalités*.[35] The *GG* tends to assume a higher degree of uniformity in use of language than do Pocock and Skinner, so much of whose work has been devoted to very particular discourses: Richter reminds us that Pocock believes "that more than one discourse, vocabulary, or idiom may be found in a single text. For better or worse, Pocock's "conceptual apparatus" and ways of tracing "conceptual and semantic" change are by *GG* standards "relatively eclectic, unsystematic, and not always consistently applied."[36] To this I would rejoin that eclecticism can imply either deplorable inconsistency or admirable flexibility and sensitivity to what the text demands.

33. Buel, in *History and Theory*, p. 261.

34. Richter supplies alphabetical lists of the concepts covered in the then seven volumes of the *GG* and the then 11 volumes of the *Handbuch politische-sozialer Grundbegriffe in Frankreich, 1680–1820* (1985–).

35. Richter, *History of Political and Social Concepts*, p. 125.

36. Richter, *History of Political and Social Concepts*, pp. 128, 129.

In trying to chart the congruences and divergencies of the two methodologies, we are fortunate in having from Pocock a short but meaty "Comment on a Paper by Melvin Richter," a polite but distinctly skeptical set of observations and questions about the *GG*.[37] This little-known piece is even more quizzical and irony-laden than one expects from Pocock, but I commend it to interested readers as a relatively recent statement of his views of method and theory.

Pocock asks what are "the differences between a history of concepts and a history of discourses, languages, ideologies, or whatever you prefer to call them?" Quentin Skinner, he points out, has flatly asserted "that a history of concepts cannot in fact be written."[38] The key issue here, crudely stated, is whether concepts exist in themselves or only in particular exemplifications of them. Taking the two positions at their extremes, the *GG* folk believe that a kind of composite sense of a concept evolves over time as the result of many individual usages and appeals to it, whereas the Cambridge School people prefer to treat each usage as a unique phenomenon demanding separate analysis. Of course this statement exaggerates the distance between the two. The *GG* does attempt "to provide both the contexts of concepts and their uses in argument" in ways that the *Historisches Wörterbuch des Philosophie* does not,[39] while Pocock and Skinner have always been prepared to look at the positions of multiple authors within brief periods and to compare views widely separated in time. Whether the difference is a matter of degree or kind, however, I believe it is important. The *GG* is at bottom a text-centred enterprise whereas the Cambridge School is fundamentally committed to reconstructing the circumstances and outlook of the writers of texts as a means of interpreting what is written. Pocock's long-ago decision not to call himself a "historian of ideas" is a crucial indication of his position here. Do ideas exist in the abstract? Pocock's bedrock conviction seems to be that they exist only when put into language in particular circumstances.

Surveying the state of Anglophone political historiography as of 1996, Pocock comments in a very rich passage that "since languages or discourses are complex structures whose components exist concurrently

---

37. Pocock, "Concepts and Discourses: A Difference in Culture?," in *The Meaning of Historical Terms and Concepts: New Studies on Begriffsgeschichte*, ed. Hartmut Lehmann and Melvin Richter (Washington, D.C.: German Historical Institute, 1996), pp. 47–58.

38. Pocock, "Concepts and Discourses," p. 47.

39. Richter, *History of Political and Social Concepts*, p. 134.

in time, to study them is to set a premium upon the synchronic." However "heavily committed to the dynamic," historians are "better at establishing the character of innovations in the synchronic than at tracing the more long-term pattern of changes in the diachronic." He adds by way of explanation: "This is especially true because long-term patterns of change in language use are difficult to reduce to the performances of identifiable authors and lend themselves to description in terms of the implicit and the ideal — both of which are mistrusted." Though politely expressed, Pocock's skepticism is manifest in almost every paragraph. How can the *Begriff* historian pay enough attention to particular examples? Any history of concepts "must still be a selection" — both of the concepts themselves, and of exemplifications of them. The stability of word usage is a huge problem even within one national language. The *GG* tries to identify concepts "that have remained continuous and stable, those that have undergone archaisation, and those that have been the subject matter of neology." Pocock objects that he has often found "the same term, concept, or construct...undergoing all three at the same time," and hence that we cannot say that "every begriff must fall into one of three taxonomic categories...to the exclusion of the others. The history of discourse as I know it simply does not look like that."[40]

How does 'concept history' connect up with events? with periods? Pocock's queries in these realms are less developed than we might wish, but his teasing ruminations on the legitimacy of *Sattelzeit* (what we might call a 'bridge-period') are more skeptical than positive, though he had ventured to use the term in chapter 9 of *The Varieties of British Political Thought, 1500–1800* (1993) "as a device for bringing that period to an end." The problem, as Pocock bluntly formulates it, is

How far a begriffsgeschichte, especially one lexically and alphabetically constructed, lends itself to the formulation of historical generalizations and hypotheses — or how far these are introduced after having arisen elsewhere — in order that the begriffsgeschichte be a means of testing them.[41]

Does the concept history, in short, have an existence in its own right, or is it merely the reflection of something else? Should we be looking for exemplifications of a chosen *Begriff*, or a set of them? Or ought we to be

40. Pocock, "Concepts and Discourses," pp. 49, 51, 52, 53–54, 56.
41. Pocock, "Concepts and Discourses," p. 56.

analyzing the outlooks and utterances of individual writers in whatever terms they may choose to employ? Pocock is a particularist.

A perpetual problem in 'history of ideas' is transmission. When and how does B learn about the ideas of A? We might reasonably suppose that Pocock and Skinner would have been aware of a major development in German historiography that was occurring just about the time they were publishing their own foundational theory, and Skinner published his scathing analysis of Raymond Williams' *Keywords* as early as 1979,[42] but he says in an essay of 1999 that "It is no doubt deplorable, but it is nevertheless a fact" that he "had no knowledge of Koselleck's research programme" in the 1960s or 1970s and was made aware of its importance only by Richter's articles of the 1980s. Skinner comments that "my approach differs markedly from that of Koselleck and his associates, who have chiefly been preoccupied with the slower march of time and much less concerned than I have been with the pointillist study of sudden conceptual shifts." He seems, however, readier than Pocock to accept the idea of a connection to *Begriffsgeschichte*. He expresses himself "not unhappy" with "Palonen's recent suggestion" that Skinner's own research "might be regarded as a contribution to one aspect of the vastly more ambitious programme" pursued by Koselleck.[43] He concludes *Regarding Method* with the observation that Koselleck "is interested in nothing less than the entire process of conceptual change" whereas he (Skinner) is "chiefly interested in one of the techniques by which it takes place. But the two programmes do not strike me as incompatible."[44] I suspect that Pocock is more skeptical about concepts as the basis for a history of political thought.

Pocock's Practice of Contextual Historicism

Surveying Pocock's books from *The Ancient Constitution and the Feudal Law* (1957) to the third volume of *Barbarism and Religion* (2003), one finds enormous range in subject and technique but at bottom a high degree of con-

---

42. See esp. Skinner, "The Idea of a Cultural Lexicon," *Essays in Criticism* 29 (1979): 205–24; revised as ch. 9 of his *Regarding Method*.

43. Consult Kari Palonen, "Rhetorical and Temporal Perspectives on Conceptual Change," *Finnish Yearbook of Political Thought* 3 (1999): 56–57.

44. Skinner's "Rhetoric and Conceptual Change," first appeared in 1999 in *The Finnish Yearbook of Conceptual Thought*; I quote from the version republished in *Regarding Method*—pp. 177, 180, 186–87, 187 ("Retrospect").

ceptual and methodological consistency. Acute appreciation for particularity of outlook is everywhere to be found, from the delineation of Sir Edward Coke's failure to realize the nature of the radical break between the feudal period and his own times (*ACFL*) to the punctilious insistence on refusing to draw on Robertson's *History of America* (1778) because it did not appear until after Gibbon's first volume was published in 1776. Pocock can sweep across hundreds of years, but he never loses his grip on individuals, particular texts, and specific dates. Generalizations are carefully earned and meticulously qualified. Obviously they can be challenged (and have been), but exact precision of broad characterization is not feasible in the analysis of historical discourse, where one can more easily demonstrate error or implausibility than one can 'prove' correctness. The nature of Pocock's understanding of political and historical thought is definitely a constant. However dissimilar *Barbarism and Religion* and *The Machiavellian Moment* may be in focus, structure, and aims, their author's approach to concepts remains familiar. The sketch of Florentine political thought in *The Machiavellian Moment*, for example, is essentially similar to the 'backgrounds' now being supplied in *Barbarism and Religion*: the chronological and geographical limits are different, but Pocock is making sense of multi-person territory over long spans of time. The thematic connections are at times absolutely plain, as in the account of *libertas* and *virtus* in *Barbarism and Religion* (*BR 3*, p. 419).

If we wish to characterize the objectives of the leading exponents of the Cambridge School, we may usefully look to two recent statements. In his "General Preface" to *Visions of Politics*, Skinner says that

we need to situate the texts we study within such intellectual contexts and frameworks of discourse as enable us to recognise what their authors were *doing* in writing them. To speak more fashionably, I emphasise the performativity of texts and the need to treat them intertextually. My aspiration is not of course to perform the impossible task of getting inside the heads of long-dead thinkers; it is simply to use the ordinary techniques of historical enquiry to grasp their concepts, to follow their distinctions, to recover their beliefs and, so far as possible, to see things their way.[45]

I believe Pocock would endorse this statement of general objective. At the end of his introduction to *Barbarism and Religion*, he gives us a helpful hint towards understanding his more particular aims: "It has been put to me

---

45. Skinner, *Regarding Method*, p. 187 ("Retrospect").

that I am attempting an ecology rather than an etiology of the *Decline and Fall*; a study of the world in which it existed, not confined to its genesis in that world" (*BR 1*, p. 10). In other words, he is looking to put Gibbon and his book in their multitudinous and changing contexts, not merely to study the origins that helped make the book what it became.

The practical basis of Pocock's scholarship lies in his insistence upon exploring a plurality of relevant contexts and considering the multiplicity of readings that those contexts help generate. Flagrant self-confidence and oracular manner notwithstanding, Pocock steeps himself in the evidence. Geert van den Bossche seems to me absolutely correct when he praises Pocock and Skinner for their "insistence on detailed empirical work" and points out that their "methodology insists on the reconstruction of available *alternatives* in order to make sense of the option which was actually adopted."[46] Any context reconstructed by the historian for interpretive purposes is, obviously, *constructed*. It is a selection made by the investigator, not a guaranteed accurate and complete simulation of the original circumstances. We cannot be certain what our subject author knew or chose to conceal or misrepresent. Contexts change constantly, and the importance we lay upon our subject being 'exposed' to something may be quite wrong. Operating amidst these fogs and quicksands, Pocock is notable for his belief that valid interpretation is often possible; his commitment to multiplicity in explanation; and his considerable prudence in assigning causation. He could be more helpful in explaining the practical basis of his process of selection.

An obvious but useful example of Pocock's commitment to plurality is his flat denial of the concept of a unitary 'Enlightenment.'

> It is a premise of this book that we can no longer write satisfactorily of 'The Enlightenment' as a unified and universal intellectual movement...Gibbon and his book will be situated in contexts formed by a number of continuous patterns of discourse, humanist, philosophical, juridical, theological and controversial, which joined with the discourse of historiography proper to constitute the great personal discourse of the text and author of the *Decline and Fall of the Roman Empire*...offer...a series of contexts in which it can be interpreted. (*BR 1*, pp. 13–14)

Each country has a set of evolving Enlightenments: "continuous patterns of discourse" do not allow us to take refuge in tidy periodization

---

46. Geert van den Bossche, "Is there Nationalism after Ernest Gellner? An Exploration of Methodological Choices," *Nations and Nationalism* 9 (2003): 506, 500.

or to ignore changes that may occur within very brief timespans. By no means, however, is Pocock clinging to outmoded notions of national history. He recognized the artificiality of national boundaries and advocated a kind of 'Atlantic' history many years before that became fashionable.

If I were asked where in Pocock's practice I find myself most uneasy, I would have to admit that I sometimes find him too inclined to believe what his writers say. Political discourse is often calculated to appeal to parts of the audience, or to damage opponents. How much of what is said is cynical, hypocritical, or plain fabrication? If a writer directly admits influence, is the claim an appeal to authority? a tactical gesture?, an act of pietas? tongue-in-cheek? a smoke-screen? an act of political correctness? I have indulged in all of these manœuvres myself. Simple name-dropping is common in modern scholarship and was not unknown in the seventeenth and eighteenth centuries. A bit more attention to simple rhetorical tricks might not come amiss. When I read Burke, I never know how far to trust him.

Returning to the questions posed near the outset of this essay, let me address very explicitly the problem of identifying the underlying assumptions, the basic method, and the product that we have been analyzing. There are two fundamental *assumptions*. First, that verbal meaning can usually be established with fair assurance. Second, that such meanings can in many cases legitimately be compared across substantial gaps in time. The essence of the *method* is a highly localized kind of close reading carried out with particular concern for illocutionary intentions. Secondarily, the method involves analytic comparison, either within a relatively brief time-frame or across gaps in time and from country to country. The resulting *product* is a contextually oriented *explication de text* relying heavily on the skill and knowledge of the historian. This kind of reading presumes the feasibility of analysis and application of the circumstances, outlook, and motivations of both writer and audience(s), though more in the realm of ideas than personal biography. To say that the reader must be willing to accept the foundational assumptions is to state the obvious. Anyone unwilling to do so will have little or no use for the results.

Pocockian analysis of political discourse is not susceptible of 'proof' in strict logical ways, let alone quantitative ones. The product is not the result of a mechanical process; it depends on the skill, knowledge, and historical sympathy of the reader. It falls under the heading of what I would would call 'extrapolative analysis,' somewhere between essentially factual 'historical reconstruction' and the broad, speculative sweep of 'historical theorizing.'[47] The resulting characterization of the thought of individual writers is certainly open to challenge, but the kinds of connections made across time are even more a matter of hypothesis rather than demonstrable 'fact.' Such hypotheses remain subject to objection and contradiction. Corroborative evidence and argument can be supplied in their support, but rigorous proofs are not usually feasible.[48]

A key concept in Cambridge School scholarship is 'usefulness.' Utility, to be sure, lies in the eye of the scholar and depends almost entirely on hu notions of aim and feasibility. You find what you believe you can look for. Turn Freud, Joseph Campbell, and Deleuze/Guattari loose on the same text, and you will probably get more than one reading. Pondering Pocock and Skinner, one thinks in such terms as (in)determinacies or language in context, local performativities, and theory-dubious non-positivist empiricism (if there is such a thing). A reader seeking a background to this mindset could do worse than explore the middle and later Wittgenstein. At a number of points Skinner cites Wittgenstein on the recovery of meaning (and J.L. Austin's elaboration of his ideas), notes "the Wittgensteinian character" of his intellectual commitments, and grants his debts in philosophy of language to Wittgenstein's *Philosophical Investigations* and Austin's *How To Do Things With Words*.[49] For Pocock, the ties to the Cambridge / Wittgenstein tradition are less clear and explicit, but I would suppose that there is at least a generalized influence.

How well do Pocock's contextual methods stand up after nearly half a century of use? Astonishingly well. For me, the bottom line is that Pocock and Skinner have rightly insisted that political theory should not be abstracted from the persons and circumstances that produced it. The 'Great Texts' theory of interpretation works badly in the realm of literature and worse in political thought. Contextual discourse analysis of the sort Pocock practices is, of course, very much a text-oriented enterprise, and one that depends on having the right sort of texts to interpret. Several charges can be brought against 'circumstantial reading.' It is slow,

---

47. For these concepts, see Robert D. Hume, "The Aims and Limits of Historical Scholarship," *Review of English Studies*, n.s. 53 (2002): 399–422.

48. For an example of strenuous objections to Pocock's tracing of neo-Harringtonian ideas, see Michael P. Zuckert, *Natural Rights and the New Republicanism* (Princeton: Princeton UP, 1994), ch. 6.

49. Second editions of *Philosophical Investigations* and *How To Do Things With Words* appeared in 1958 and 1980, respectively. See Skinner on Wittgenstein and Austin: *Regarding Method*, pp. 82, 104, 120, 161 (n.).

messy and requires a great deal of erudition and preparatory labor. One can never be certain that one has accurately understood either the designs of the creator of the text or the verbal meaning of the text itself. One can be even less sure that one accurately grasps the complexity of responses and misreadings on the erudition, imagination, and judgment of the historical scholar/reader. The 'proofs' that can be offered in support of the scholar's conclusions are rarely of the kind that put matters beyond further question and dispute. The fact remains that we are crippling ourselves as readers (while perhaps simplifying our scholarly lives) if we deprive ourselves of authorial and reception context when we attempt the elucidation and interpretation of historical texts.

Part Two: Political Language

3. Civic Humanism and the Logic of Historical Interpretation

MICHAEL McKEON

At one end of J.G.A. Pocock's long and influential career stands *The Ancient Constitution and the Feudal Law* (1957), a remarkable study that set the highest of standards for the history and historiography of seventeenth-century political thought. At the other end is Pocock's massive study of Edward Gibbon, *Barbarism and Religion* (1999–2005). Mediating between these two celebrated projects is the body of work on the tradition of civic humanism or classical republicanism, for which Pocock probably is better known than for any other of his scholarly achievements.[1] The focus of the following essay is this middle range of Pocock's career, and my aim is to discuss my skepticism about not only the findings of, but also the method pursued in, this body of work. My skepticism has gestated over the years in which I've read and re-read Pocock's principle books on the subject of civic humanism, and it's fueled by my high expectations of the author of *The Ancient Constitution*, by my appreciation of Pocock's attention to theoretical issues of historical method, and by the surprising degree of uncritical reception (or so it seems) the work on civic humanism has enjoyed. I'll begin with a brief look at the second of these considerations.

---

1. Given the several names associated with this body of thought — civic humanism, classical republicanism, Machiavellism, country ideology — I'll confine my usage for the most part to the first.

Theory

Pocock's ambition to disclose the historicity of political thought is most succinctly expressed by his long-standing methodological commitment to the literal and the metaphorical language of "language." On the one hand, we gain access to political thought in and as language, and its intelligibility therefore depends on our ability to construe its meaning, as we do that of all language, by placing linguistic texts (whether individual words, phrases, or sentences) within the linguistic contexts that make them intelligible. On the other hand, Pocock uses the metaphors of "language" and of the grammatical "paradigm" to express the idea that political thought is like a set of languages that are united in their concern with the subject of politics but distinct from each other in the ways they engage and express that concern. As literal languages cohere through systematic rules of grammar and syntax, so figurative "'languages" can be seen to cohere in the words and ideas they employ and in the way these elements typically come together in historical usage. For Pocock, the work of the historian of political thought entails the close reading of language in the literal sense of the term in order to identify languages and paradigms in the metaphorical sense of the term.

Although he uses the linguistic metaphor to clarify the proper method for determining the meaning of political thought, however, Pocock doesn't minimize the difficulty of making that determination. When a political language becomes "paradigmatic," he writes, it has something like the systematic and normative modelling force of a grammatical paradigm. "It invokes values, it summarizes information, it suppresses the inconvenient,... prescribing an authority-structure in the act of performing an intellectual (or linguistic) function."[2] The coherence of such a paradigm is therefore independent of authorial intent. "Once history is seen in linguistic depth..., the paradigms with which the author operates take precedence over questions of his 'intention'..." The task of the historian "is to identify the 'language' or 'vocabulary' with and within which the author operated, and to show how it functioned paradigmatically to prescribe what he might say and how he might say it" (*PLT*, p. 25).

But the coherence of such a paradigm, Pocock realizes, is also far less determinant than that of its literally linguistic counterpart. This is partly

---

2. Pocock, "Languages and Their Implications: The Transformation of the Study of Political Thought," in *PLT*, p. 18; hereafter cited parenthetically.

because the notion that political thought is unified in its subject matter is acknowledged to be something of an illusion. "Political speech does not refer alone to the structure of political activities, institutions and values conceptualized as the subject matter of political theory, and conceivable as theoretically constant in a wide range of political societies" (*PLT*, p. 21). Indeed, "any formalized language is a political phenomenon in the sense that it serves to constitute an authority structure …" (*PLT*, p. 15). If in its performative capacity language is inherently "political," then the stability of the category "political subject matter" becomes problematic. And in any case, the difficulty of establishing the identity and persistence of a political paradigm is equally a matter of the sheer "richness of texture" evident in "the history of political thought. That history might be defined as a history of change in the employment of paradigms, the exploration of paradigms and the employment of paradigms for the exploration of paradigms" (*PLT*, p. 23). The political paradigm itself, moreover, is possessed of a rich texture: "diversity of function and diversity of origin both operate to ensure that its employment remains multivalent and ambiguous," and political paradigms exist "in many contexts and on many levels simultaneously" (*PLT*, pp. 23, 18). A "multivalent paradigm, simultaneously performing diverse functions in diverse contexts, must simultaneously designate and prescribe diverse definitions and distributions of authority…" (*PLT*, p. 18). To complicate things still further, "paradigms migrate from contexts in which they have been specialized to discharge certain functions to others in which they are expected to perform differently. If the philosopher is concerned to keep statements of different orders distinct from one another, the historian is concerned with whether or not they were kept distinct, and with what happened as a result of either" (*PLT*, p. 21). But since a solution to "the philosopher's" problem of distinguishing paradigms from each other must be presupposed to some degree in "the historian's" task of tracking their relationship over time, the labor of the historian of political thought could hardly appear more daunting than it does in Pocock's model.

Practice

Four years after this essay was published there appeared *The Machiavellian Moment*, Pocock's major statement on the political language of civic humanism and its paradigmatic authority. Ten years later, the publication of *Virtue, Commerce, and History* made collectively available a number

of more recent essays that refine or elaborate the argument of *The Machiavellian Moment.*[3] The claims made by these writings for the coherence and
determinant force of civic humanism are breathtaking. In the early eighteenth century, the "Country ideology" was "in sole possession of a theory of virtue...," and the stress laid upon "virtue" in the debates of that
period "is so great that we have to recognize that the first chapter in the
history of political economy is also a further chapter in the continuing
history of civic humanism..." (*MM*, pp. 488, 426). "The dominant paradigm for the individual inhabiting the world of value was that of civic
[humanist] man," Pocock writes, and the "ideal of the social and political personality epitomised by the term 'virtue'..." The emergence of a real
alternative to it—what Pocock calls "commercial ideology"—was forced
by the civic humanist response to the "sudden and traumatic discovery of
capital in the form of government stock" in the wake of the financial revolution of the 1690s (*MM*, p. 466; *VCH*, pp. 108–9). In this crisis, according to Pocock, "[i]t may very well have been the Augustan debaters who
discovered, if they did not invent, the 'Protestant ethic'..." Indeed, in "what
scholars have called a 'Protestant ethic' of frugality, self-denial, and rein-
vestment, trading society" was "permitted its own version of that classical virtue which consisted in placing the common good (in this case the
circulation of trade) above one's personal profit" (*MM*, pp. 446, 464). In fact
it was only in the 1690s that, under the auspices of war and the financial
revolution needed to fund it, "an entity known as Trade entered the language of politics..." (*MM*, p. 425). Some important political terms—"corruption," "patriotism," "mixed government"—are in Pocock's view components of a specifically civic humanist vocabulary (*MM*, pp. 408, 409, 370).
Other usages owe their currency (like "trade") to the influence of the civic humanist paradigm: blaming the king's ministers; the language of
"manners," "refinement," and "politeness"; the debate over the relations
between reason, virtue, and passion; even, by implication "[t]he social
thought of the eighteenth century" (*MM*, p. 507; *VCH*, pp. 48–49, 115,
66–67, 69). Indeed Pocock argues that civic humanism furnished "the appropriate paradigmatic context for the growth of ideas about the significance of" the feudal past "in explaining English political change," and

---

3. Pocock: *The Machiavellian Moment: Florentine Political Thought and the Atlantic Republican Tradition*, and *Virtue, Commerce, and History: Essays on Political Thought
and History, Chiefly in the Eighteenth Century*; hereafter both works cited parenthetically.

"[t]he emergence of the problem of history" in the early eighteenth century "enjoins a Machiavellian analysis..." (*MM*, pp. 357, 437).

What's surprising about these claims is not the significance of the transformations Pocock locates in the late seventeenth and early eighteenth centuries. Secularization, the emergence of capitalist ideology and social analysis, and the rise of a historical understanding of political change are too broad to be easily situated in any single period, but many historians would agree that the claims of 1688–1720 are as good as any. What's surprising is Pocock's discovery of the paradigm of civic humanism at the very center of these developments. For although his methodological essay stresses the linguistic paradigm's complex "diversity," an overview of civic humanism in Pocock's analysis shows it to be a remarkably singular discourse, coherent in its identity and monolithic in its primacy, agency, and determinant force. As Pocock makes clear, this is a revisionist reaction to what he deems the implausible force of the liberal and Locke-based paradigm. How does he more plausibly represent both paradigms in their reciprocally-delimiting relationship?

Oddly, the procedure of *MM* precludes an answer to this question. Because Locke's "greatness and authority have been wildly distorted by a habit of taking them unhistorically for granted,... [t]he historical context must be reconstructed without him before he can be fitted back into it" (*MM*, p. 424). In his essay on method, we recall, Pocock had written that political paradigms exist "on many levels simultaneously," and in *MM* he observes that "the causes of epistemological change in this era were numerous and complex, but we are going to find that the language of republican humanism played an important part in the process..." (*PLT*, p. 18; *MM*, p. 402). But if the operation of a single paradigm is "multivalent and ambiguous," how can contemporaneous paradigms that are parts of the whole of epistemological transformation be studied in isolation from each other without distorting them, along with the historical context that's under reconstruction (*PLT*, p. 23)? How can we understand the force of a conceptual language like civic humanism without also knowing the force of other languages — Locke's, or for that matter the tradition of natural law theory in which he wrote — with which it might be said to be in competition for paradigmatic dominance? If the aim is to counter the reductiveness of the Whig interpretation of history, isn't the more promising strategy not a reductively anti-Whig interpretation but one that does justice to the partial truth of each?

But although Locke is thus set aside in *MM*, Pocock does engage there the question of interlinguistic competition in the course of his inquiry into how the tradition of civic humanism came to be so successfully "domiciled," as he understands it to have been, in seventeenth- and eighteenth-century England (p. 334). The first two parts of *MM* are devoted to a discussion of the conceptual background of civic humanism and to its full elaboration in Renaissance Florence. In the third part of the study Pocock undertakes to solve the problem of how civic humanism was accommodated to the very different context of seventeenth- and eighteenth-century England and North America. In this accommodation, Pocock writes, civic humanism had to "compete" with other "modes of civic consciousness," that is, with other ways "the Englishman could develop... an awareness of himself as a political actor in a public realm." However civic humanism's competition — "earlier political languages" characterized by "monarchical, legal, and theological" rather than republican assumptions — was crucially defective (pp. 334, 335). For the older languages lacked an essential element of civic consciousness that only civic humanism was able to express, a conception of "civic activity" and its "vulnerability to fortune" (p. 349). This dynamic vision was of course central to Machiavelli's republicanism. But monarchy, the common law, and Protestant Christianity were enthralled, on the contrary, to "the hierarchy of degree, the community of custom, [and] the national structure of election," all three of which "presumed that the individual acted in a stable scheme of moral authority...." (p. 350).

So when John Pym argues that the parts of a state are best ordered as a "mutual relation" that must be adjusted periodically to repair the effects of time, his language, Pocock writes, "blends hierarchy with republic" (p. 358). By implication, the outbreak of civil war — the destabilization of static hierarchy in church and state — is coextensive with the outbreak of civic humanism. Hierarchy and stability define the comparative immobility of the older modes; only republican thought, categorically antithetical to hierarchy, can challenge its stasis. The chapter from which I've been quoting is the linch-pin of *MM*, and the problem with Pocock's argument here is disarmingly intimated by his willingness to refer to the other modes of civic consciousness that are embodied in monarchy, the common law, and Protestantism as "the different versions of civic humanism" (p. 340). Because the other modes of civic consciousness are other modes of civic humanism, they are by definition inferior to it, and the apparently open-nended search for major competitors has really had the tautology of a demonstration that the only adequate mode of civic humanism is civic humanism.

In the collection of essays that was published a decade after *MM*, Pocock once again tries to do justice to his theoretical model of how political paradigms coexist in complex interrelationship by situating civic human-ism in the broadest possible intellectual context. By this overarching ac-count, there are two fundamental paradigms of Western political discourse, the philosophical-juristic and the civic humanist (*VCH*, p. 39). And un-like the earlier comparison of civic humanism with its defective rivals, here the competition is one between equals. The philosophical-juristic and the civic humanist, the socioeconomic and the political, the "liberal" or "populist" and the "republican," the "rights"-based and the "virtue"-based: both categories are historically-embedded, conceptually-expansive, and "personality"-enabling enough to cover the field of reference and to con-stitute structurally equal alternatives to one another (*VCH*, pp. 44, 46, 47, 48, 104). Pocock's basic division of political language at the most abstract-ed level of analysis therefore would seem to prepare us for a concrete study of the interaction between the two languages at the crucial historical mo-ment of concern. And yet this never happens.[4] Instead, Pocock leaves his account of the competition between the two great political languages at the level of abstraction. Here paradigms can be described as autonomous systems of thought rather than treated as parts of a concrete histori-cal context in which actual speakers avail themselves of the "richness of texture" characteristic of political thought in its historical practice (*PLT*, p. 23). In fact, Pocock's method programmatically avoids encountering the rich texture of political thought. Handsomely acknowledging the co-herence and influence of a rights-based reading of the political history of property in the late seventeenth and early eighteenth centuries, Pocock nonetheless proposes to "put forward an alternative thesis…[I]f one em-ploys the paradigm of classical politics, rather than that of natural jurispru-dence in interpreting this great revolution in the concept of property…

---

4. Pocock's acknowledgment in *VCH* that the philosophical-juristic para-digm has a crucial historical importance before the eighteenth century no doubt improves upon the broad viewpoint of *MM*. It seems to me nonetheless that this account of the history of political thought as an enduring competition be-tween two great paradigms is fundamentally flawed. The eighteenth-century advent of modernity entails not, I think, the defeat of one paradigm by another —of the civic by the juristic, of virtue by rights, of politics by economy—but the disentanglement and autonomization of categories that traditionally had been conceived as distinguishable but inseparable from one another. Although I will not pursue this line of argument directly in the following pages, its im-plication will be evident in much that I have to say about Pocock's historical method.

one is not discounting the importance of ideas about property derived from natural jurisprudence... We shall have to return to them, but for the present it will be contended that the story can be better understood by operating with the idea of classical politics" (*VCH*, pp. 105–6).

It's hard to know how to construe the implications of Pocock's promise to "return to" the jurisprudential model of property, but not "for the present." It's not simply that no such return is made. Pocock explicitly excludes the rights-based model from historical analysis because "the story can be better understood" if reduced to a shapely and monocausal narrative. Pocock the historian gives way to Pocock the advocate. It's as though the concept of the paradigm now works not as a heuristic device to illuminate how political ideas are deployed in and by communities of speakers, but as an argumentative topos to be extracted from that community and used by the historian to make a case to hu readers by telling a story in a way that's more persuasive for being more simple and partial.

The problem with Pocock's procedure concerns the way he deploys conceptual wholes and parts, and it can be felt not only at the general level of the broad relationship between paradigms but also at the local level of the paragraph and the sentence. The attentive reader of his work characteristically experiences a slippage between discourse that seems to address the overall conditions of political thought in a given period and discourse that describes the nature of civic humanist thought in particular. And the result of this slippage, in either direction, is that civic humanism appears to have a representative status and an explanatory force far greater than it can bear. To say that Pym's language "blends hierarchy with republic," for example, by taking "republic" to be synonymous with "civic humanist," is not only to conceive civic humanism as non- or anti-hierarchical, but also to imply that it's the only alternative to a hierarchical model available to Pym. This may be a plausible description of the ancient, ideal type of Aristotelian civic humanism, where the hierarchical exclusion of women and slaves is an assumption so basic as to be nearly tacit, but surely not of (say) Bolingbroke's version, whose support of social hierarchy is clearly visible in his scornful opposition to social mobility. Pocock places the difficult problem of how civic humanism was translated to English political culture at the center of his argument; but he formulates and reformulates the problem in such a way as to prefigure its solution. Why should we understand as specifically civic humanist Pym's incipient insight that the king is one part of a greater whole? Where's the evidence of civic humanist vocabulary in his formulation —

or is the insight itself civic humanist by virtue of being republican in the fundamental sense of advocating the rule of more than one? Are all republican ideas, in this basic sense of the term, also civic humanist ideas? The most important classical forebear of Anglo-American civic humanism is Aristotle. Is the authority of civic humanism coextensive with the authority of Aristotle, who is the source not only of republican thought but of Western political thought as such?

The Secularization of Personality

The argumentative slippage I'm trying to describe can be seen with some clarity in the issue of secularization, which in Pocock's treatment turns out to be a function of civic humanism. What about the secularizing tendencies internal to Protestantism itself? At one point in *MM* (pp. 462–63) Pocock addresses this question through a line of argument that has the following, loosely enthymemic, form. "The story" thus far, that of the development of civic humanism, has been concerned with the encounter between its Athenian ideal of political man and the Christian ideal of religious man. The development of Protestant and especially Puritan thought involved a "secularization of personality." For Montesquieu the secularization of personality was relatively easy to conceive: he "could reiterate Machiavelli's acknowledgement that civic virtue was self-contained and secular…" For English Puritans the task was more demanding: "as the citizen became less like the saint, his civic personality required a *virtù* less like his soul's capacity for redemption and more like the autonomy of Aristotle's megalopsychic man…[,] and this morality required a foundation less spiritual and more social and even material. We have seen how this foundation was supplied, first by arms and then by property.…Land and inheritance remained essential to virtue…" Ergo, the Puritan secularization of personality was founded in civic humanism and its distinctive regard for the right to bear arms and for the virtue of freehold real estate.

What's the logic of this passage? Pocock begins with the ongoing story of Aristotelian-Machiavellian civic humanism. How does this come to incorporate, and to explain, the story of Protestant secularization? One important crux is the reference to Montesquieu, since Pocock's unstated but implicit argument here is a (persuasively imperfect) proportional analogy: as Montesquieu's vision of a secularized virtue was readily derived from Machiavelli, so that of the Puritans was more problematically derived from the same source. It's important to see that no empirical ev-

idence is advanced for either part of this analogy. Rather, in the following sentences Pocock makes one story stand for another: he makes a particular species of secularity—that of civic humanism—stand for the entire genus. And he achieves this rhetorical effect by using the specialized language of civic humanism, first, as a metonymy for the general
phenomenon of secular virtue (thus Machiavellian "*virtù*" names the general condition of civic secularity needed by Puritan thought), and then as
a metaphor for that general phenomenon of secular virtue (thus what was
needed by Puritanism—which has just been reconceived in specifically
Machiavellian terminology—is like nothing so much as "the autonomy
of Aristotle's megalopsychic man").

Although specious as logical argument, the metonymy might appear
somehow empirically justified by the immediately preceding example
of Montesquieu, whose "reiteration" of Machiavelli sounds explicitly and
solidly citational, and therefore prepares us to see the case of Puritanism
in the same light. But if we actually turn to the passage in *Esprit des Lois*
on which Pocock bases his reading we find no evidence that Montesquieu's
broadly secularist affirmation takes Machiavellism (rather than, say, the
natural religion of deism) as its privileged source or model (p. 491n78).
Again, Pocock's metaphor might seem empirically justified simply by the
fact that a broad similarity can indeed be found between the autonomy
of the individual in secularized Protestantism and in Aristotle; but their
resemblance is no greater than that of the former and the autonomy of
the individual exemplified by, say, Hobbes's natural man. In other words,
the civic humanist credentials of Puritanism (and Montesquieu) are established by nothing more than an associational rhetoric. If Pocock's story is
the relatively focused one of civic humanist secularity, no connection is
demonstrated between this and the story of Puritan secularization. If his
story is the quite general one of secularity and secularization as such, the
connection between civic humanism and Puritanism is no more intimate
than that of any two species within an encompassing genus.

Pocock's interest in Protesant secularization—in the way "religious
man" learned to become "political man"—stems from his view of Protestantism itself as one of the incomplete modes of civic consciousness
that were inherited by seventeenth-century England. But Pocock's premise that the completion of this process was achieved as it were from without, through the encounter of Protestantism with civic humanism, sets a
limit on this interest. He is most attentive to that aspect of Puritan thought
that entailed national apocalyptic expectation, which held the promise
of militant action that was secular in both the worldly and the temporal

senses of that term: "Radical or conservative, God's Englishmen might inadvertently secularize their thought either in asserting or in resisting a revolutionary impulse which we may now see as antinomian..." (*MM*, p. 347). Moreover Pocock sees national apocalyptic expectation as reinforced by the doctrines of labor discipline and the vocation: "The sense of a calling peculiar to the Puritan saint had operated to give these soldiers [of the New Model Army] a sense of the irreducible personality — the 'talent' or 'nature' — inherent in each one of them... [T]he calling, as an act of grace, must be thought of as operating upon the individual in time, and... time conceived in such terms must be conceived prophetically or apocalyptically." Furthermore, so far from being "alienated from his inherited laws and liberties," the English saint was "involved in them to the point where his calling did not liberate him from them, but liberated him to transform them... We can see how the individual's conviction of a radically free natural capacity within himself intensified his ability to engage in radical action based upon radical criticism of his laws and liberties in their inherited form... [However] we are not yet at a Machiavellian moment in English thought..." (*MM*, pp. 374–75).

Our previous discussion may encourage us to read this particular evocation of the "Machiavellian moment" as meaning "secularization" — that is, the moment at which the secularizing tendencies of Protestant thought became capable of subsistence without benefit of religious content. For Pocock, the secularity of civic consciousness is manifested, as here, by evidence of an impulse toward tangible and "public" political action. The point is well taken — and yet the exclusivity of this emphasis consigns other sorts of evidence to obscurity. A case in point is the odd fate of the "Protestant ethic," which we might have expected to play a much larger role in Pocock's argument about seventeenth-century Protestant secularization. When the term does arise, however, Pocock is more inclined to treat it as an epiphenomenon of later debate and as stimulated (as we now know to anticipate) by the civic humanist ideal itself (*MM*, pp. 446, 464). Indeed, he appears to see "the so-called Protestant ethic" as better-called a "morality for the trading man," an already secular conception by which "the trader" and "the financier" vainly strove to meet the standard of "civic virtue" already set by civic humanism (*MM*, pp. 445, 431). "Bourgeois ideology," "a civic morality for market man" and "a paradigm for capitalist man as zōon politikon," seems in Pocock's view to be the fulfillment of the "morality for the trading man," at long last a mode of civic consciousness of comparable force to that of civic humanism and a direct product of the civic humanist challenge that, if anything, "hampered" the development of bourgeois ideology because it virtually defined rentier and entrepreneur as corrupt..." (*MM*, pp. 432, 460–61).

Pocock's skepticism about the Protestant ethic suggests that despite his professed interest in Protestant secularization, his eye is on secularity not secularization, the product not the process—and therefore on change as impingement from without rather than as internal development. The subtext here is of course a repudiation of Max Weber's celebrated thesis that subtly adduces a psychological connection between the "Protestant ethic" and the "spirit of capitalism"—although Pocock calls Marxist rather than Weberian the notion that "an intensely religious consciousness of individuality was secularized into bourgeois rationalism overnight, since it had never been more than the ideology of an emergent class..." (*MM*, p. 338). Here and elsewhere in his writings Marxist thought is Pocock's default antagonist, and the substitution of Marx for Weber may aim to justify the treatment of a thesis that here, in the form to which it's been contemptuously reduced ("overnight," "had never been more than"), could never command anyone's credence.

Now, Weber's argument turns on the Puritan doctrines of labor discipline and the vocation, which Pocock understands (as we've seen) to have a relevance to matters of secularization and civic consciousness only in so far as they conduce to manifestly "public" political activity. Weber's interest lies rather in the evident relationship between, on the one hand, the psychology of capitalist individualism and its ethic of enterprise and industry, and, on the other hand, the radically individualized and subjectivized standard of salvation that's entailed in the Calvinist doctrine of justification by faith. You don't have to be a Weberian or a Marxist to want to take rather more seriously than Pocock does the suggestive interaction between the "religious" language of vocational discipline and the "secular" language of industry and improvement that animates an emergent capitalist ideology. John Bunyan, for one, expressed his disapproval of the way the former can stealthily devolve into the latter in the figure of Mr. Mony-love, who propounds the following case of conscience:

Suppose a minister, a worthy man, possessed but of a very small benefice, and has in his eye a greater, more fat, and plump by far; he has also now an opportunity of getting at it; yet so as by being more studious, by preaching more frequently, and zealously, and because the temper of the people requires it, by altering some of his principles, for my part I see no reason but a man may do this (provided he has a call)... [A] minister that changes a small for a great, should not for so doing, be judged as covetous, but rather, since he is improved in his parts and industry thereby, be counted as one that pursues his call, and the opportunity put into his hand to do good.[5]

Here the connection between the Protestant ethic and the spirit of capitalism seems, if nuanced, also undeniable. That is, Mr. Mony-love's casuistry of discipline in the calling clearly both exploits the slippery circularity of the doctrine of election and moralizes the "capitalist" impulse toward unlimited acquisition. And we're further reminded by Bunyan's ironic portrait that although Pocock's language implies that what delayed the emergence of bourgeois ideology was nothing but the civic humanist stricture against corruption, centuries of religious writings consistently condemned the economic and financial practices we associate with capitalism with a vehemence whose force, longevity, and pertinence to the issues at hand are far greater than those of civic humanism.[6] Pocock purports to defend his own version of the "rapid secularization of consciousness," but his unwillingness to countenance the idea that Protestantism may have preceded civic humanism in bringing a "civic personality" to England obliges him to propound a crudely mechanical view of secularization as a collision in which "religious" belief—specifically, the Puritan apocalyptic mode—bumps up against "secular" belief (here, civic humanism) (*MM*, p. 338). Whatever difficulties there may be with the Weber thesis, it gets much closer than this to describing secularization as a historical process in which change is both an intrusion from without and an immanent development, generated from within ongoing conceptual structures. Indeed, the essential continuity and determinant force of civic humanism in Pocock's argument actively militate against a subtler view of historical process because its role in seventeenth-century English political thought is to provide external solutions to internal stalemates, to stimulate change from without.

In Bunyan's depiction, the relationship between vocational discipline and industrious activity is of course negative and hypocritical; but we needn't seek far for a more positive picture. In his most famous sonnet ("When I consider how my light is spent" [1652?]) John Milton, no orthodox Calvinist, employs the venerable figure of labor service and payment to express the otherwise ineffable state of passive readiness to do God's

---

5. Bunyan, *The Pilgrim's Progress*, Pt. 1 (1678), ed. N. H. Keeble (Oxford: Oxford UP, 1984), pp. 84–85.

6. For the classic study, see R.H. Tawney, *Religion and the Rise of Capitalism* (London: John Murray, 1926).

work in terms of a calling that programmatically blurs the line between the religious and the secular, the private and the public. Elsewhere Milton asserts the crucial importance of discipline in terms that do evoke the contest between *virtù* and fortune by the historian but that are pointedly non-Machiavellian in their religious provenance and language:

[T]here is not that thing in the world of more grave and urgent importance throughout the whole life of man, then is discipline…He that hath read with judgement, of Nations and Common-wealths, of Cities and Camps of peace and warre, sea and land, will readily agree that the flourishing and decaying of all civill societies, all the moments and turnings of humane occasions are mov'd to and fro upon the axle of discipline. So that whatsoever power or sway in mortall things weaker men have attributed to fortune, I durst with more confidence (the honour of divine providence ever sav'd) ascribe either to the vigor, or the slacknesse of discipline…And certainly discipline is not only the removall of disorder, but if any visible shape can be given to divine things, the very visible shape and image of vertue, whereby she is not only seene in the regular gestures and motions of her heavenly paces as she walkes, but also makes the harmony in her voice audible to mortall eares… [H]ow…can we believe that God would leave his fraile and feeble…Church here below to the perpetuall stumble of conjecture and disturbance in this our darke voyage without the card and compasse of Discipline. Which is so hard to be of mans making, that we may see even in the guidance of a civill state to worldly happinesse, it is not for every learned, or every wise man, though many of them consult in common, to invent or frame a discipline, but if it be at all the worke of man, it must be of such a one as is a true knower of himselfe…[7]

Milton's tract of 1642 exemplifies how confidently, and how early in the century, the Puritan idea of discipline could underwrite, without limiting itself to, the call to political action. And in the richness of its reference to classical, Renaissance, and Reformation culture it reminds us of what Pocock's method too often encourages us to forget. The history of ideas is a dense texture of disparate and overlapping threads of thought that stubbornly resists the unraveling of a single favored tradition which all others subserve. Only to one who conceives the theological and the secular, the religious and the political, to be mutually exclusive realms of

---

7. John Milton, *The Reason of Church Government Urged against Prelaty* (1642), ed. Don M. Wolfe in *The Complete Prose Works of John Milton*, ed. Don M. Wolfe and others, 8 vols. (New Haven: Yale UP, 1953–82), 1:751–52, 753.

thought in 1642 (which Pocock clearly does not) might the claim seem plausible that Milton's notion of discipline fails to qualify as a notion of "civic consciousness"—in Pocock's paraphrase, as "an awareness of himself as a political actor in a public realm" (*MM*, p. 335). The only alternative way to save the appearances would be to claim (perhaps through the elasticity of the term "republican") that the very overlap between Milton's and Machiavelli's ideas shows Milton to be a civic humanist. But this implicit incorporation of Puritanism within civic humanism would contradict Pocock's own differentiation of them and invite us to see civic humanism as more or less coextensive with early modern thought as such.

Parts and Wholes, Texts and Contexts

To be persuasive, Pocock's thesis that civic humanism is an identifiable political "language" that becomes "paradigmatic" in England toward the end of the seventeenth century requires adducing evidence that there exists a recognizably coherent body of thought and vocabulary that, although it may adapt over time to changes in context, nonetheless persists in being intelligible as itself. The slippage that's characteristic of Pocock's method and that makes his thesis unpersuasive owes to the fact that in his usage, civic humanism lacks such integrity. To coin a maxim of intellectual historiography, the number of terms that are required to name a discourse is inversely proportional to its conceptual coherence.[8] Not that Pocock ignores, or fails to justify, basic adaptations entailed in the passage from the Florentine to the English context—for example, the shift from arms to real estate as the foundation of civic virtue, and from fortune to corruption as its great nemesis. The problem is rather that at many stages in his argument, Pocock writes as though the integrity of civic humanism, potential in the most concentrated, Machiavellian articulation of that discourse, is actualized by the English use of one or two of the verbal parts of which the whole of the discourse is composed. Indeed, he's prepared to discover civic humanism even when only "some" or "certain elements" or "fragments" or "overtones" of it—or when arguments "which may well recall" it—are audible or evident (*MM*, pp. 351, 354–55, 365, 380, 382, 437). Of course, it's in the nature of intellectual history—not to mention the figuration of thought as a language—that the

---

8. See above, n1.

demonstration of coherence and continuity be subject to standards of probability a good deal less rigorous than, say, those appropriate to natural history. The most persuasive discrimination of one discourse from all others is likely to hinge not on its use of language or ideas to which it can lay unique claim, but on its assemblage and coordination of several shared terms or concepts to form a discourse that's distinctive and unshared. To address the case at hand, civic humanism is a coherent, recognizable, and influential ideology, we might say, as it assembles and coordinates some if not all of these eighteenth-century commonplaces in a distinctive fashion: a conviction that the land is a fundamental source of value, a conception of virtue and personality as grounded in material autonomy, a commitment to limited suffrage, a humanist disposition to secularize Christian authority, a sensitivity to the contingencies of fortune, and a spirited opposition to governmental authority, professional politicians and soldiers, financial exchange, luxury, and corruption. But these commonplaces also have roots in diverse traditions of thought and experience that share little else with civic humanism.

If textual meaning is determined by context, both the signification and the significance of key words must be altered by their abstraction from the context of one political language and applied in another context. An example is provided by Pocock's reading of Andrew Marvell. In *MM* Pocock finds that Marvell's *Account of the Growth of Popery and Arbitrary Government* (1677) "belongs to the same intellectual stream" as neo-Harringtonian argument. The evidence lies in Marvell's indictment of the corruption entailed both in the Court's patronage of members of the House of Commons and in the absence of annual or even triennial parliamentary elections. "The key term is 'corruption,'" writes Pocock, "which marks a further stage in the assimilation of English constitutional theory to the categories and vocabulary of civic republicanism" (*MM*, pp. 406, 408). Pocock is right to note Marvell's indignation at Court corruption, but his demonstration that this makes him a neo-Harringtonian defies logic. He begins his reading of Marvell by asserting that nascent "Country ideology" criticized parliamentary corruption as "the substitution of private for public authority, of dependence for independence," and that it demanded frequent parliamentary elections, which were "consciously seen as a Machiavellian *ridurre ai principii*..." But no citation, from either Marvell or elsewhere, confirms the latter claim; we're only reminded that Machiavelli himself affirmed the value of elections (*MM*, pp. 407–8). As for the former, Marvell points out that any honorable member of parliament will feel compromised by Court patronage "lest his gratitude to his master, with his self-

interest, should tempt him beyond his obligation there to the publick."[9]
By extending the case into the realm of private ethics, Marvell's following words—"[t]he same excludes him that may next inherit from being
guardian to an infant"—alone suggests that his concern here is the general one of a conflict of interests rather than the specific one that virtuous public service requires an independent income.[10] Despite this, Pocock claims that from Marvell's attack on corruption "it followed that
virtue was represented only by the Country members,...and that corruption could be avoided only by those willing both to enjoy no source
of income but their estates, and to eschew either the possession or the
pursuit of executive power. And it further followed that...parliament...
could not but be visualized as a mechanism for the corruption of property, independence, and virtue" (*MM*, p. 409). But in the remainder of
this digression on parliamentary corruption Marvell says nothing of the
kind; he doesn't even single out "the Country members" for commendation. Pocock's assimilation of Marvell to the language of civic humanism has no basis in the language of Marvell's text. It seems to depend on
the assumption ("it followed") that the criticism of court corruption is
ipso facto country ideology and therefore a civic humanist criticism: that
is, that it must be supported by the sorts of argument that animate civic
humanists.[11] But even if Pocock were correct in this assumption, his reading appears to affirm that to borrow one principle from civic humanism
is to "belong" to that "stream"; and Marvell's incendiary tract, despite the
diversity of its aims and achievements, therefore becomes a document
of civic humanism. It seems to me more fruitful—more illuminating of
the principles that guide a tract whose animus is, after all, against the twin
targets of popery and arbitrary government—to assimilate Marvell's di-
gressive critique of parliamentary corruption not to civic humanism but
to his opening critique of corruption in the Roman Catholic Church.[12]

---

9. [Andrew Marvell], *An Account of the Growth of Popery and Arbitrary Government in England...*(1677), in *The Complete Works in Verse and Prose of Andrew Marvell*, ed.
Alexander B. Grosart, 4 vols. (London: Robson and Sons, 1875–75), 4:324.

10. Marvell, *Account of the Growth of Popery*, p. 324.

11. Compare Pocock's claim here that "patriotism" is "a term which had carried 'Country' and 'commonwealth' connotations since the seventeenth century"
(*MM*, p. 409). For a more accurate account of the variability with which the term
was applied, see Ronald Knowles, "The 'All-Attoning Name': The Word *Patriot*
in Seventeenth-Century England," *Modern Language Review* 96 (2001): 624–43.

12. See Marvell, *Account of the Growth of Popery*, pp. 251–53.

Three Revolutions: Financial, Commercial, Capitalist

The case is both more complicated and more consequential with the word
"trade," which, as we saw, Pocock believes entered the language of English politics only in the 1690s (*MM*, p. 425). That trade—its growth and
decay, its freedom and protection, its supposed affinity with industrious
dissenters—was a major player in political language far earlier than the
last decade of the century is so evident[13] that the reader may suspect hu's
misunderstood Pocock's meaning. And this is no doubt true—although
what Pocock really means to be arguing on this score must be sought in
the absence of clear direction from him.[14] The financial revolution of the
1690s is able to assume the proportions of an epochal watershed for Pocock because he conflates it with the commercial and the capitalist revolutions. The benefit of this conflation is that it gives civic humanism
the crucial role in the formation of liberal and capitalist ideology. But because it can't really explain the complex social and ideological history of
the period, the conflation appears and disappears according to the argumentative demands of the moment.

Characteristically Pocock subsumes the capitalist under the commercial in pre-eighteenth-century discourse—thus his reference to "[t]he
commercial" as what "Marxists call the bourgeois order." Through this
subsumption, the conflict between the "landed interest" and the "monied
interest" that erupted in the 1690s is a local manifestation of "an enduring conflict" between "agrarian" and "commercial" ideals. Civic humanism
had long sponsored a conception of civic personality associated with the
agrarian; its injection into English debate in these years therefore precipitated (by this way of thinking) the formulation of a counter-conception
of civic personality which Pocock calls "commercial ideology" (*VCH*, pp.
107, 109). Yet as I've suggested, the evidence that seventeenth-century
England already possessed a commercial ideology—a view of commerce
or trade as the foundation of a public personality—isn't hard to find. An
unusually rich account is provided by Thomas Deloney in *Jack of Newberie*

---

13. For example, in debates that arose during the prosecution of the three
Anglo-Dutch trade wars. See also J. A. W. Gunn, *Politics and the Public Interest in the
Seventeenth Century* (London: Routledge, 1969), ch. 5.

14. For an earlier effort at this, see McKeon, *The Origins of the English Novel,
1600–1740* (Baltimore: Johns Hopkins UP, 2002 [1987]), pp. 159–69, which reads
Pocock in the context of the rise of the gentry controversy.

(1597), a narrative set in pre-Reformation England in which the epony-
mous hero is an upwardly-mobile clothier who leads his fellows in principled opposition to the protectionist policies of corrupt courtiers at whose
head is the Lord Chancellor, Cardinal Wolsey. In the present context the
narrative is instructive on a number of fronts, since Wolsey's corruption
is an amalgam of political and religious interest. That is, Deloney's story
makes clear how the critique of corruption, so far from being the trademark of civic humanism, was more famously associated with the politico-
religious attack on the Roman Catholic Church. In contrast to Pocock's mechanical model of secularization, Deloney depicts an intimate coexistence
of religious and secular motives. In a tract whose attention to religious matters is, after all, decidedly secondary, Wolsey's charge that the industrious
labor organizer Jack is "infected with *Luthers* spirit" exemplifies the subtle coimplication of Protestant and "capitalist" modes of thought on which
Weber's thesis is based. Moreover Jack's virtue is ostentatiously public: at
one point he takes to the field of battle in support of his king at the head
of a personal army of 150 retainers.[15] But as Lewes Roberts made clear several decades later, the public personality of the trader didn't require that
he be associated with overt political action like military service. A thriving nation is blessed with merchants whose "care of their own profit, is
so necessarily interwoven with the care of the commonwealth's and its
good, that to themselves and to their country, their labours…do bring in
thus mutually, not only a commodity, but also an honour." Edward Misselden's rhetorical questions pushed the claim further: "[I]t is not lawful for merchants to seek their privatum commodum in the exercise of
their calling?…Is not the public involved in the private, and the private
in the public? What else makes a commonwealth but private wealth…of
the members in the exercise of commerce amongst themselves and with
foreign nations?"[16]

---

15. Thomas Deloney, *The pleasant Historie of Iohn Winchcomb, In his yonguer yeares
called Iack of Newbery, The famous and worthy Clothier of England…*(1597), in *Shorter
Novels: Elizabethan,* ed. Philip Henderson (London: Everyman, 1972), p. 53; see
also p. 27 on Jack's army of retainers. For a brief reading of *Jack of Newberie,* see
McKeon, *Origins of the English Novel,* pp. 223–25. Needless to say, Deloney's story
qualifies as political language in the broad terms Pocock applies to that category
(see above, nn2–3).

16. Lewes Roberts, *The Merchant's Mappe of Commerce* (1638), p. 21, and Edward
Misselden, *The Circle of Commerce* (1623), p. 17; both quoted in Gunn, *Politics and
the Public Interest,* pp. 211, 232

The ready availability of evidence like this suggests that when Pocock speaks of "commercial" ideology and personality he really means something that's much less available in the early seventeenth century, 'bourgeois' or capitalist ideology and personality. And this might seem to be confirmed by his emphasis on the terms of the conflict between the landed and the monied interests in the 1690s: "This was a momentous intellectual event: there had been a sudden and traumatic discovery of capital in the form of government stock and a sudden and traumatic discovery of historical transformation as something brought about by the advent of public credit" (*VCH*, p. 108).[17] Now, the debate over public credit and the other virtual forms of value, like paper money, with which it sometimes was associated is undeniably one of the most arresting controversies of this period. Whether it entailed the sudden discovery either of capital or of historical transformation is another matter. In the debates over the insubstantiality of credit Pocock discovers an apprehension of capitalism as "speculation" rather than "calculation," as "fantasy" rather than "cold rationality" (*VCH*, pp. 69, 113). This is no doubt true: but it doesn't tell, as Pocock assumes it does, in favor of the notion either that capitalist ideology was a historical function of civic humanist apprehensions or that the first critiques—and defenses—of capitalist speculation and fantasy come in the 1690s.

In 1622, Thomas Scott attacked all "Improuers of our Land" who "study to doe such acts, and invent such projects, as may vndo the publique for their priuate and inordinate desires," who "liue in this world as *in a market, [and] imagine there is nothing else for them to do, but to buy and sell, and that the only end of their creation and being was to gather riches, by all meanes pos-*

---

17. In fact, the proximity of this passage to the one in *VCH*, p. 109 quoted above suggests that Pocock here regards capitalism as a sub-category of commercialism. This conflation would be more useful and less confusing were it not that the conflict between the "landed" and the "monied" interests in the 1690s depended entirely for its significance on the distinction between the innovative monied interest, which the landed interest reviled, and the traditional practice of trade, of which the landed interest was understood for the most part to approve: see W.A. Speck, "Social Status in Late Stuart England," *Past & Present* 34 (1966): 127–29, and his "Conflict in Society," in *Britain After the Glorious Revolution*, ed. Geoffrey Holmes (London: Macmillan, 1969), p. 145. Pocock rightly avoids the confusion of trade with the monied interest in *MM* (pp. 447–48). The hypothesis that he means to distinguish trade from commerce as old vs. new (i.e., financial or monied) ways of gaining wealth is belied by the apparently interchangeable usage of *MM* (pp. 424–25).

sible." Scott's prescient language captures "the market" in its infancy, before the explicit argument of simile has been transmuted into the virtual
reality that the market has come to possess in the modern world.[18] In 1642,
John Denham, also troubled by the imaginative creation of imaginary
desires, looks down from Coopers Hill on the City of London, wrapped

> in a thicker cloud
> Of businesse, then of smoake, where men like Ants
> Toyle to prevent imaginarie wants;
> Yet all in vaine, increasing with their store,
> Their vast desires, but make their wants the more.
> As food to unsound bodies, though it please
> The Appetite, feeds onely the disease...

And about ten years after Denham's poem was published, Marvell attacked the Dutch by wittily associating their proclivities toward liberty
of conscience and liberty of trade as a single and singular indulgence of
credulity:

> Hence Amsterdam, Turk-Christian-Pagan Jew,
> Staple of sects and mint of schism grew,
> That bank of conscience, where not one so strange
> Opinion but finds credit, and exchange.[19]

These passages suggest that when Pocock takes civic humanism to be
the opening critique, and the constitutive cause, of capitalist ideology in
the 1690s, he mistakes as an origin the culmination of a process that began a good deal earlier and that betrays no special debt to the language
of civic humanism (unless we take Scott, Denham, and Marvell to be ipso
facto civic humanists). But the virtuality of exchange value was also being

---

18. On which, see Jean-Christophe Agnew, *Worlds Apart: The Market and the
Theater in Anglo-American Thought, 1550–1750* (Cambridge: Cambridge UP, 1986,
ch. 1, esp. sec. 3.

19. Thomas Scott, *The Belgick Pismire...*(1622), pp. 32, 34; John Denham, *Coopers
Hill* (1643), in *Expans'd Hieroglyphicks: A Critical Edition of John Denham's "Cooper's
Hill,"* ed. Brendan O'Hehir (Berkeley and Los Angeles: U of CA P, 1969), pp. 111–12
(ll. 28–34); Andrew Marvell, *The Character of Holland* (1672), in *Andrew Marvell: The
Complete Poems*, ed. Elizabeth S. Donno (Harmondsworth: Penguin, 1978), p. 113
(ll. 71–74).

theorized at mid-century in the dispassionate terms of a proto-political economy. Anthony Ascham didn't need the institution of the stock market to observe, in 1649, that "money is an invention onely for the more expedite permutation of things." Such "things" are items of private property, whether land or labor. Some, like Scott, feared that commercial exchange threatened to sacrifice the public good to private interests. But Ascham for one toyed with the notion that commerce was, on the contrary, no more than a new (admittedly more privatized) method of attaining the old end of the common good: "Instead of Community therefore we now have commerce, which *Commercium* is nothing else but *Communio mercium*," the public sharing of merchandise and the foundation of an authentic civic personality. Locke was soon to make explicit the connection between "own" and "owner," propriety and property: "[E]very Man has a *Property* in his own *Person*... The *Labour* of his Body, and the *Work* of his Hands, we may say, are properly his." "A mans Labour also," Hobbes wrote, "is a commodity exchangeable for benefit, as well as any other thing..." William Petty thought the most important consideration in political economy was "how to make a Par and Equation between Lands and Labour, so as to express the Value of any thing by either alone." By such equations, land undergoes an "expedite permutation" into something else: first, into a monetary medium of exchange, and then (for example) into labor.[20]

Interlinguistic Entanglement: Civic Humanism, Protestantism, Aristocracy, Capitalism

Marvell's critique of speculation, in particular, may remind us that both language and conceptualization are far more complicated than Pocock's account of civic humanism as a "language" would suggest. As we've seen before, although religious and secular thought may be distinguished from

---

20. Anthony Ascham, *Of the Confusions and Revolutions of Governments*... (1649), pp. 27, 30; John Locke, *An Essay Concerning the True Original, Extent, and End of Civil Government* ("*The Second Treatise of Government*") (1690), ch. 5, sec. 27, in *Two Treatises of Government*, ed. Peter Laslett, 2nd ed. (Cambridge: Cambridge UP, 1967), pp. 305–6; Thomas Hobbes, *Leviathan, or the Matter, Forme, & Power of a Common-wealth Ecclesiastical and Civil* (1651), ch. 24, p. 127; William Petty, *Political Anatomy of Ireland* (1691), pp. 63–64, quoted in Joyce O. Appleby, *Economic Thought and Ideology in Seventeenth-Century England* (Princeton: Princeton UP, 1978), p. 84.

one another at this time, their confident separation, on which Pocock's championing of civic humanism depends, is hard to credit when confronted with the actual usage of contemporaries. Speculation conjoined "capitalist" and low-church Protestant behavior not only because many thought mercantile success was a specialty of dissenters, but also because ungrounded speculation seemed to many the amoral hallmark of exchange value and of Calvinist justification. Indeed, Bunyan felt it necessary to defend against the latter charge by creating characters like Ignorance for Christian to refute: "For what matter how we live," says Ignorance, "if we may be Justified by Christs personal righteousness from all, when we believe it?" Hence we may well understand the attack on "Whiggish Phanatical Credit" made in the title of an essay published decades later, during the debates on public credit, to imply that the link between Whigs and dissenters is based in part on the link between the virtuality and incredibility of political fantasy on the one hand and of religious fanaticism on the other: "The False Fits of Whiggish Credit Discovered; or, An Account of the Turns and Returns, Comings and Goings, Visits and Departings of that Subtle Pharisaical Lady call'd Whiggish Phanatical Credit." The critique of financial speculation is thus tightly entangled with that of soteriological speculation.[21]

Other linguistic entanglements are equally evident. After quoting a long passage from Defoe's *Review* on the allegorical figure Lady Credit, Pocock writes: "The student of Renaissance humanism has no hesitation whatever in identifying the rhetoric of this passage...[as] the idiom employed by Machiavelli to describe *fortuna* and *occasione*..." (*MM*, p. 453). We may welcome the Renaissance student's attentiveness without being inclined to agree that this is "*the* rhetoric" of Defoe's essay. Defoe first

---

21. Bunyan, *Pilgrim's Progress*, p. 121; *The Moderator*, 25 August 1710, quoted in *The Spectator*, ed. Donald F. Bond, 5 vols. (Oxford: Clarendon Press, 1965), 1:15 (n1); hereafter I cite the Bond edition of the *Spectator* parenthetically. A discursive form like Bunyan's allegory attests, in an entirely implicit but deeply persuasive way, to the contemporary understanding that the problem of religious salvation was intimately analogous to the problem of sovereignty in the early modern state. This is because Bunyan uses, as the allegorical figure that signifies the journey of the Christian soul toward heaven, the late-medieval story of an impoverished commoner whose upward mobility takes him from cruel exploitation at the hands of a local lord to the feudal protection of a competitor whose authority is established by his status as the emergent lord of lords, the national monarch. For a full reading, see McKeon, *Origins of the English Novel*, pp. 302–11.

names his allegorical subject in the following sentence: "Her Name in our Language is call'd CREDIT, in some Countries Honour, and in others, I know not what" (*MM*, p. 452). Lady Credit is the very model of inconstancy and insubstantiality. What if we pursue Defoe's richly allusive account of her not only in the direction of "fortune" (a word Defoe doesn't use in this passage) but also in the direction of "honour"? Charles Davenant, one of Pocock's civic humanists, compares financial credit not to fortune but to "that fame and reputation which men obtain by wisdom in governing state affairs." However "fantastical" it may appear to be, good repute is the reward we give to those who deserve it. So although the statesman may temporarily lose his reputation, it "will be regained, where there is shining worth, and a real stock of merit. In the same manner, Credit, though it may be for a while obscured, and labour under some difficulties, yet it may, in some measure, recover, where there is a safe and good foundation at the bottom."[22] Davenant's emphasis on the "real stock of merit" that underlies good reputation suggests that his discursive context is, at least in part, the seventeenth-century critique of aristocratic honor and its axiom that birth equals worth.[23]

Like Davenant, Defoe insists on the separability of worth from birth:

> For if our Virtues must in Lines descend,
> The Merit with the Families would end:
>
> ....
>
> For Fame of Families is all a Cheat,
> 'Tis Personal Virtue only makes us great.[24]

Is this, too, as Pocock might argue, the language of civic humanism? From one perspective, the critique of aristocratic ideology as such is so broad a phenomenon in the seventeenth century that it needs to be recognized

---

22. Charles Davenant, "Discourses on the Public Revenues" (1698), in *The Political and Commercial Works of…Charles D'Avenant…*, ed. Charles Whitworth, 5 vols. (London: R. Horsfield and others, 1771), 1:151.

23. On this critique, see McKeon, *Origins of the English Novel*, ch. 4. "Merit" and "virtue" were frequent synonyms for worth, signifying that normative criterion of personality which is only arbitrarily assumed (according to the critique) to be coextensive with elevated birth.

24. Defoe, *The True-Born Englishman* (1700), in "Vol. 6: 1697–1704", ed. Frank Ellis, of *Poems on Affairs of State: Augustan Satirical Verse, 1660–1714*, gen. ed. George deForest Lord and others, 7 vols (New Haven: Yale UP, 1963–75), 6:308, 309 (ll. 1195–96, 1215–16).

as a rhetorical commonplace that might be used to support a number of different ideologies (e.g., the Puritan ideology that would substitute for it an aristocracy of grace). From another perspective, the critique of aristocratic ideology is, relatively speaking, a negligible string in the bow of civic humanist ideology, which, as Pocock teaches us, is far more interested in the critique of royal patronage and corruption, and is a species of elitism — the rule of the few — that's not easily dissociated from that of aristocratic ideology itself. Of course, the corruption of royal patronage on occasion was explicitly tied to the critique of aristocratic ideology (more often that critique avoided potential implications regarding royalty). In a celebrated analysis, Lawrence Stone once argued that under James I and Charles I the royal sale of honors increased to such a degree that contemporaries experienced it as an "inflation of honors."[25] Thomas Scott thought that "to purchase honour without some worthy action foregoing" was to be possessed of nothing but "*Parchment* honour."[26] The impeachment of the Duke of Buckingham in 1626 was in part justified, according to an enemy, by his instigation of "the trade and commerce of honor...He was the first that defiled this virgin of honor so publickly."[27]

Now, it might be argued that so far from documenting the non-civic humanist provenance of Defoe's Lady Credit, these attacks on corrupted honor as insubstantial parchment, these characterizations of true honor as a defiled virgin actually confirm the civic humanist source of all of this early-Stuart language. But we're in the presence here of language that's shot through with ideological vectors that defy the discovery of any single ideological genealogy. My point, in other words, is not that Defoe's essays on public credit entail the rhetoric of early Stuart anti-absolutism rather than that of Italian Renaissance civic humanism, but that as students of political language we're well-advised to avoid having to choose between rhetorics, and between contexts of signification,

---

25. See Lawrence Stone, *The Crisis of the Aristocracy, 1558–1641* (Oxford: Clarendon Press, 1965), p. 65.26. Scott, *Belgick Pismire*, p. 30. For Defoe's association of credit with the willingness to credit paper money and bills drawn on the Exchequer, see his *Review*, 14 June 1709.

27. John Rushworth, *Historical Collections*, 2 vols. (1721–22), 1:334, 336, quoted in Stone, *Crisis of the Aristocracy*, pp. 113–14. For Defoe's identification of Credit as a "Beautiful Virgin Lady," see his *Review*, 16 June 1709. Pocock dismisses the notion that by "honor" Defoe might have meant something more historically concrete than "other-directed intersubjectivity" (*MM*, p. 465). For the argument that Defoe's language of "honor," here and elsewhere, needs to be read more inclusively, see McKeon, *Origins of the English Novel*, pp. 205–6.

which can only result in the hypostatizing of a "language" too pure and monochromatic to be historical.

Intralinguistic Entanglement: Commonplace and Ideology

In the end, Pocock's reading of Defoe is so closely attuned to linguistic echoes of civic humanist language alone that Defoe himself, using the "rhetoric" and "categories" of civic humanism, can be assimilated comfortably into "the civic humanist succession..." But then in Pocock's view, so can all the writers on land, trade, and credit from 1690 to 1727. The serviceable malleability of civic humanist language, moreover, helps explain the bad odor of political inconstancy and opportunism that sometimes emanates from these writers: "Swift, Davenant, Defoe — to go no further — were found in differing company at different times of their lives; and... these changes of front are best explained not by attempting to assess questions of commitment and consistency, venality and ambition, but by recognizing that they were employing a highly ambivalent rhetoric... [T]here were no pure dogmas or simple antitheses, and few assumptions that were not shared, and employed to differing purposes, by the writers on either side" (*MM*, p. 446). Indeed, this would seem to exemplify Pocock's theoretical point about the diversity of a paradigm — that "its employment remains multivalent and ambiguous" because its scope is broad and plurisignificant (*PLT*, p. 22). Understood in this way, the paradigm of civic humanism is a relatively neutral rhetorical commonplace, a language in which to formulate questions rather than one that dictates ideologically-specific answers. The problem is that Pocock also would make the opposite point about paradigms: that they're only relatively neutral, "prescribing an authority-structure in the act of performing an intellectual (or linguistic) function" (*PLT*, p. 18). Understood in this way, the paradigm of civic humanism isn't multivalent or plurisignificant, because for an author to employ or for a historian to ascribe it is to radically specify the political significance of an utterance. By this way of thinking, civic humanism is not a neutral rhetorical commonplace but on the contrary an ideologically-specific doctrine (as the term "Country ideology" makes clear[28]).

My aim in teasing out these two, seemingly antithetical, dimensions of the linguistic paradigm as Pocock describes it is not to lay at his door

---

28. For a summary description of this ideology, see *MM*, p. 486.

the charge of logical contradiction. Rather it seems to me that the acknowledgement of two distinct but simultaneous levels of discourse is justified and fruitful. To generalize: On the one hand, the discourse of civic humanism is composed of commonplaces that are familiar to contemporaries from a range of usage that includes but exceeds those exemplary of civic humanist discourse. These commonplaces are aids to thought and expression that communicate values so fundamental to the common culture as to be intelligible across a very broad semantic range of applications. On the other hand, there's a dimension of such discourse that depends on, yet lies as it were "beneath," the familiarity of commonplace usage, gaining access to understanding by virtue of that usage but entailing a specificity of application that implicates the generality of commonplace in the particularity of doctrinal or ideological argument. My distinction between commonplace and ideology in discourse aims to be schematic and heuristic, not definitive. We might speak of three, four, or more levels of discourse so long as the crucial dialectic between discursive generality and particularity is appreciated — that is, so long as not only the relation, but also the difference, between them is acknowledged.[29]

The problem I'm getting at in Pocock's deployment of the paradigm model is therefore not that he relies upon this distinction between two levels of language use but that he doesn't make the distinction methodologically explicit. The result is that the category of civic humanism, rather than being subjected at each stage of its application to the careful sort of analysis that would distinguish between levels of commonplace and ideology and would make clear which level is being emphasized at that stage, floats between these two poles of signification in a way that encourages a perpetual slippage of meaning between them. When he welcomes Defoe into the civic humanist succession Pocock points out that he shares political commonplaces with Swift and Davenant. But by calling this succession "civic humanist" he seems to claim for Defoe what Defoe manifestly doesn't share with those others, a civic humanist ideology. In fact Pocock often ascribes a civic humanist provenance to commonplace categories and concerns — virtue, inconstancy, credit, insubstantial fantasy — that he hasn't shown deserve to be so labelled. And because the difference between commonplace and ideology isn't addressed in Pocock's

---

29. For a fuller account of this method of reading, see Michael McKeon, *Politics and Poetry in Restoration England: The Case of Dryden's "Annus Mirabilis"* (Cambridge, MA: Harvard UP, 1975), pp. 33–35.

reading of Defoe, the ideological semantics of civic humanism bleed into its role as a bearer of commonplace meanings. The confusion is double. On the one hand, the specifically ideological usage of civic humanism is confused with a more broadly commonplace generality, as when a commonplace regarding credit is taken to be specifically civic humanist ideology. On the other hand, confusion is encouraged by the assumption that any ideological critique of credit is civic humanist in its tendency — that is, that civic humanist ideology is a commonplace of the age.

The Mobility of Property or Absolute Private Property?

One of the chief principles of English civic humanism, according to Pocock, is that civic virtue must be independent of government power, and that it sustains its independence through its property in real estate. And the thesis that civic humanist argument precipitated capitalist ideology turns on the role of the financial revolution in raising the mobility of property to political consciousness. Central to the debates of the 1690s, Pocock writes, is the fear that the new system of public credit, by making property mobile on a large-scale basis, would create "a new and enlarged mode of dependence upon government patronage[,]…not property in exchangeable commodities…but property in government office, government stock, and government expectations to which the National Debt had mortgaged futurity…" (*VCH*, pp. 68–69). These fears, Pocock claims, provoked the recognition that "major changes had occurred in the character of property itself, and consequently in the structure, the morality, and even the psychology of politics" (*VCH*, p. 67).

It seems to me that there are two important difficulties with this analysis. First, even if we accept Pocock's contention that capitalist ideology originally emerged as a response to the critique of public credit in the 1690s, he fails to show that this critique was demonstrably civic humanist in character. That is, although most of the public sentiment about the new financial instruments was negative, there's no evidence that the fear of increased dependence on the government was its central concern. Pocock cites nothing to support such a thesis; as we've seen, his major emphasis is on the new system's speculative insubstantiality, not on any purported consequence of that insubstantiality in increased government control. P.G.M. Dickson, the historian of the financial revolution, documents a range of opinions about the dangers of the new financial instruments, at one point characterizing that range in terms that situate

Pocock's theme of government patronage as one part of a larger whole. Having quoted Bolingbroke on how the great funding companies have become "the real masters of every administration," and how their directors, "born to serve and obey, have been bred to command even government itself," Dickson remarks: "It was possible to argue in this way that the development of the National Debt had led to a shift in the centre of gravity of government toward the private sector, but it was also possible to argue that the growth of taxation accompanying the rise of public borrowing had greatly increased the power of the state."[30] If, as Pocock has taught us, the independence of the moral rulers of the countryside from the corrupting power of the state was a defining imperative of civic humanist ideology, his thesis that specifically and identifiably civic humanist complaint was at the heart of the uproar over the financial revolution isn't supported by the evidence.

The second difficulty with Pocock's analysis has to do with his idea that it was the mobility of property, made dramatically clear by the seeming magic of financial exchange value, that, in defensive response to the civic humanist critique, "rapidly and abruptly" fomented the emergence of capitalist ideology in the 1690s (*VCH*, p. 69). Once again, I think, Pocock mistakes a culmination for an origin — in this case, the mobility of property for the consolidation of absolute private property. Indeed, for all his interest in changes in the "character of property" during the seventeenth century, Pocock overlooks the most important change of all, the emergence and conventionalization of absolute private property, without which the financial revolution would have been impossible. Pocock's version of the change in the character of property "began with spectacular abruptness, to be discussed in the middle 1690s..." (*VCH*, p. 67). But monumental changes that are said to occur with spectacular abruptness are best entertained with circumspection. True, there exists a spectacularly abrupt phase in the consolidation of absolute private property in England: namely, the parliamentary abolition of feudal tenures and the Court of Wards in 1646. Thanks to the abolition of feudal tenures, Defoe wrote, "the English gentry hold and inherit their lands *in capite*, absolutely and by entail...All the knight's service and vassalage is abolish'd, they are as ab-

---

30. P.G.M. Dickson, *The Financial Revolution in England: A Study in the Development of Public Credit, 1688–1756* (Aldershot, Hampshire: Gregg Revivals, 1993 [1967]), p. 20, quoting Henry St John, Viscount Bolingbroke, *Some Reflections on the Present State of the Nation* (1749), in *The Works of the late Right Honorable Henry St. John, Lord Viscount Bolingbroke*, ed. David Mallet, 5 vols. (London, 1754), 3:151.

solutely posssess'd of their mannours and freehold as a prince is of his crown." It's in this spirit that Robinson Crusoe models his claimed ownership of the island on the absolute monarch: "How like a King I look'd. First of all, the whole Country was my own meer [i.e., complete, absolute] Property; so that I had an undoubted Right of Dominion. *2dly*, My People were perfectly subjected: I was absolute Lord and Law-giver..." John Lilly believed that "an absolute proprietor hath an absolute Power to dispose of his Estate as he pleases, subject only to the Laws of the Land." In his visit to the Royal Exchange, Mr. Spectator was struck "to see so many private Men, who in [past] Time would have been the Vassals of some powerful Baron, Negotiating like Princes for greater Sums of Mony than were formerly to be met with in the Royal Treasury!" To Addison these men exemplify a distinctive personality of civic virtue: they're "a Body of Men thriving in their own private Fortunes, and at the same time promoting the Publick stock..."[31]

In strictly legal terms, absolute proprietorship of the land had been possible for centuries.[32] The parliamentary abolition of feudal tenures was an official acknowledgement—reaffirmed by the Convention Parliament of 1661 (12 Car. II. c. 24)—of changes in economic and social practice that had been under way for the past hundred years.[33] According to

---

31. Daniel Defoe, *The Compleat English Gentleman* (written 1728–29), ed. Karl D. Bülbring (London: David Nutt, 1890), pp. 62–63; Defoe, *Robinson Crusoe* (1719), ed. J. Donald Crowley (Oxford: Oxford UP, 1981), p. 241; John Lilly, *The Practical Register* (1719), quoted in G. E. Aylmer, "The Meaning and Definition of 'Property' in Seventeenth-Century England," *Past & Present* 86 (1980), 95; Joseph Addison, *Spectator*, 19 May 1711 (Bond edn, 1:296, 294).

32. See Alan Macfarlane, *The Origins of English Individualism: The Family, Property, and Social Transition* (Oxford: Blackwell, 1978).

33. Of most importance in the present context, of course, is not socioeconomic but conceptual practice. In his first book Pocock did as much as anyone to show how "feudalism" was "discovered" in the seventeenth century as a way of life against which the present might define itself. The discovery and distantiation of feudalism is a sign of contemporaries' readiness to periodize the recent past, to separate it out from the present as a time characterized by a dependence of baronage on monarchy that was now being definitively replaced by the separation out—the independence—of the one from the other. It seems to me that Pocock's insistence on the significance of contemporaries' discovery of "civic humanism" in the middle of the seventeenth century is a weak version of that earlier argument that lacks the evidence supporting the thesis of a contemporaneous discovery of feudalism and which only obscures the clarity of Pocock's initial insight.

Pocock, "[w]e no longer see the essential shifts in either the structure or the ideology of English property as taking place" before the Glorious Revolution (*VCH*, p. 67); but this curt summation of 'our' beliefs is understandably silent on just whom is included. Certainly many contemporaries saw it differently, as the vast anti-enclosure literature of the earlier period suggests. This is because they understood the importance of the shift in the ideology of property of which the enclosure movement of the seventeenth century was only the most conspicuous sign.[34] As Defoe's words suggest, the independence of the English landholder was not just a civic humanist aphorism but a tangible development of the period, and unlike the language of civic humanism, the language of absolute private property was rooted in contemporary experience and in "rights-based" rather than "virtue-based" modes of civic consciousness. Over time, the ideology of absolute property replaced a more traditional way of conceiving a customary sort of independence. Although English common law conceived all property to be held in fee from one's lord—which early on meant, ultimately, from the king—the property of commoners was seen customarily as a use-right that might under different circumstances be both inclusive and exclusive, both shared with others and conditionally "privatized" to some or one.[35] The quintessential mark of absolute private property is unconditional alienability. To own something is to be able to disown it, a capacity that allowed seventeenth-century landowners to assert their independence of the king even as it prohibited their own tenants from enjoying the traditional independence of use-right. Pocock sees the discourse of the 1690s as not only "a further chapter in the continuing history of civic humanism" but also "the first chapter in the history of political economy" (*MM*, p. 426). But the evidence is far more persuasive that the 1690s debates were an early chapter in the history of political economy because they were a further chapter in the continuing history of the unconditional alienability and exchangeability of private property.

---

34. According to J.R. Wordie, 71% of England was already under enclosure by 1699: "The Chronology of English Enclosure, 1500–1914," *Economic History Review*, 2nd ser., 4 (1983): 502.

35. See C.B. Macpherson, "The Meaning of Property," in *Property: Mainstream and Critical Positions*, ed. C.B. Macpherson (Toronto: U of Toronto P, 1978), pp. 1–13, and his "Capitalism and the Changing Concept of Property," in *Feudalism, Capitalism and Beyond*, ed. Eugene Kamenka and R.S. Neale (London: Edward Arnold, 1975), pp. 104–24.

The Language of the Imagination

The debates of the 1690s take on a more plausibly hybrid character once we listen to them with an ear open not just for civic humanism but for other languages as well. One of these languages is the discourse that was beginning to coalesce around the category of 'the imagination.' As Pocock shows, Defoe at one point in the *Review* epitomizes the mysteries of financial exchange with "this Ejaculation—Great is the Power of Imagination!" Pocock would have us see Defoe's ambivalence about credit's dependence on the insubstantial volatility of the imagination as "evocative of [Machiavelli's] most innovative ways of thinking," whereby *fortuna* and *virtù*, the cause and the cure of the problem, bafflingly intermix with each other (*MM*, p. 454). But Defoe is more obviously exemplifying the ambivalence of contemporary English people about the power of the imagination and its increasingly evident role in human affairs. Jonathan Swift may be counted a civic humanist in his support for the Property Qualifications Act of 1711 because he thought it would ensure that "our Properties lie no more at Mercy of those who have none themselves, or at least only what is transient or imaginary." But Swift, impatient with the modern "Contempt for *Birth, Family*, and *ancient Nobility*," nonetheless also grants that "ancient and honorable Birth" may be, if socially useful, yet of "imaginary Value."[36] The heart of the problem for Defoe and Swift is how something that has neither essential nor material reality can, if credited, have real value.

Clearly this problem extends beyond the fictions of aristocratic honor and public credit. John Dryden, mindful that the rules of poetry may be needed to restrain our "otherwise lawless imagination," also refuted the need for rules like the dramatic unities of time and place by arguing that the pleasure and value we find in the art of drama depends entirely on the power of our imagination: "And indeed, the indecency of [staged] tumults is all which can be objected against fighting. For why may not our imagination as well suffer itself to be deluded with the probability of it as with any other thing in the play? For my part, I can with as great ease persuade myself that the blows that are struck are given in good earnest, as I can that they who strike them are kings or princes, or those persons

---

36. Jonathan Swift, *Examiner*, 29 March 1711 and 10 May 1711, in *The Prose Works of Jonathan Swift*, ed. John Herbert Davis, 14 vols. (Oxford: Blackwell, 1940), 3:119, 150–51.

which they represent."[37] The language in which our modern notion of the aesthetic was being theorized at this time — the idea that we may credit what we know has no empirical existence (the "willing suspension of disbelief," as Coleridge later put it) — penetrates the language that Defoe and Swift use to comprehend the virtuality of the market and society. Indeed, the problem of the mobility and evanescence of real property can be "solved," after a fashion, by recourse to the pleasures of the imagination, which have the power to mitigate the suspect workings of exchange value by recasting them as a species of aesthetic value.

In Addison's words, "[a] Man of a Polite Imagination, is let into a great many Pleasures that the Vulgar are not capable of receiving. He can converse with a Picture, and find an agreeable Companion in a Statue. He meets with a secret Refreshment in a Description, and often feels a greater Satisfaction in the Prospect of Fields and Meadows, than another does in the Possession. It gives him, indeed a kind of Property in every thing he sees, and makes the most rude uncultivated Parts of Nature administer to his Pleasures..."[38] George Berkeley's formulation carries the virtualization of real property even further. He has "a natural Property in every Object that administers Pleasure to me. When I am in the Country, all the fine Seats near the Place of my Residence, and to which I have Access, I regard as *mine*... By these Principles I am possessed of half a dozen of the finest Seats in *England*, which in the Eye of the Law belong to certain of my Acquaintance, who, being Men of Business, chuse to live near the Court." Of such people Berkeley wittily affirms that "I have a real, and they only an imaginary Pleasure" in their estate.[39] The mobility of property transports it, in other words, not just into 'the market' but finally into the mind. My point, once again, is not that the developing discourse of the aesthetic provides the true key to the significance of the debates that surround and succeed the financial revolution, but that if we pursue the intellectual genealogy of Defoe and Swift's observations on the "imaginary" value of "credit" in this direction we find ourselves in the presence of language whose contemporary pertinence both to those obser-

---

37. John Dryden, *Of Dramatic Poesy: An Essay* (1668), in Dryden, *Of Dramatic Poesy and Other Critical Essays*, ed. George Watson, 2 vols. (London: Everyman's Library, 1962), 1:104–75. Although it's not material to my point, I take the accustomed liberty of reading Dryden's character Neander as his spokesperson.

38. Addison, *Spectator*, 21 June 1712 (Bond edn., 2:538).

39. Berkeley, *Guardian*, 2 May 1713, in *The Guardian*, ed. John C. Stephens (Lexington: U of Kentucky P, 1982), pp. 193–94.

vations and to the emergent discourse of capitalist ideology is a good deal more compelling than are Machiavelli's *fortuna* and *virtù*.

The Mobility of Property or Mobility as Such?

So on the one hand, the mobility of property was debated by Swift and Defoe's contemporaries in a number of overlapping languages, some of which have only a marginal relevance to civic humanism. On the other hand, as the financial revolution is only one part of the encompassing capitalist revolution, so concern at the mobility of property in the 1690s is only one manifestation of a greater, and precedent, concern at mobility as such. I've already anticipated much of this argument. Because Pocock's great ambition is to explain vast intellectual transformations by reference to a relatively specific and circumscribed factor—the revival of civic humanist language—his argument is bound to be vulnerable to the charge of tendentious selectivity. And the fact that Pocock explicitly acknowledges his selectivity—e.g., his bracketing of the philosophical-juristic paradigm—doesn't vindicate his procedure since the magnitude of his claims about civic humanism depends largely on his having bracketed its competitors. In fact, Pocock's historical method bears an uncanny resemblance to his description of the ideological work of a historical paradigm: "It invokes values, it summarizes information, it suppresses the inconvenient...prescribing an authority-structure in the act of performing an intellectual (or linguistic) function" (*PLT*, p. 18). If we're to evaluate the force of the factors Pocock deems so crucial, we need to place them within the contexts whose significance they themselves strive to suppress. Few would quarrel with the notion that Machiavelli's thought provides an extraordinarily powerful and profoundly influential model for conceiving the world in its contingency, as a realm not of static hierarchy but of dynamic mobility. What Pocock's method suppresses is all the other languages that in their own terms record the emergent condition of dynamic mobility that we associate, in the broadest sense, with the experience of entering the modern world: natural law theory, the complaint at status inconsistency, Protestant reform and secularization, print-culture and the dialectic of publication and privatization, and the like.[40]

---

40. Pocock takes it for granted that the language of normative "agrarian values of independence and virtue," and of a negative "corruption," is that of civic

One consequence of this suppression is Pocock's claim that only "a Machiavellian analysis" was able to do justice, at the turn of the century, to the "emergence of the problem of history"—by which he means "the difficulties of constructing a fully legitimized history out of the movement from" land to trade, gentleman to merchant (*MM*, pp. 436–37). The aforementioned tautology may be in operation here—the only "fully legitimized history" is by definition a civic humanist history—but it's worth observing that the movement from land to trade that Pocock speaks of was not so difficult to historicize as he maintains. The key to it was social mobility, and in a system of primogenitural inheritance like England's the figure of the younger son was often made to stand for the virtuous commoner at large. Many of these problem-solving histories, moreover, envision a civic personality fueled by the Protestant ideology of discipline in one's calling and by its own condemnation of a "corruption" that's both secular and Roman Catholic. An early tract advised gentlemen that apprenticeship was "a vocation simply honest, and may proue a stay to posteritie, and give credit to their names, when licentious and corrupted eldest sonnes haue sold their birth-rights away… [P]ut your children to be Apprentises, that so as God may blesse their iust, true, and virtuous industrie, they may found a new family, and both raise themselues and theirs to the precious and glittering title of Gentlemen."[41] Another author detected a pattern in which younger sons of "ancient Gentry" become wealthy "Citizens"; these "New Men" retain a gentility of behavior and are successful enough to eventually establish new "Gentile Families."[42]

---

humanism. But this is also the province of pastoral, a language more ancient, and far more omnipresent in the discourse of this period, than civic humanism. The interpenetration of pastoral and civic humanist language is a phenomenon that Pocock's selectivity prohibits us from appreciating. On the transformation of pastoral in seventeenth- and eighteenth-century England, see McKeon: "The Pastoral Revolution," in *Refiguring Revolutions: Aesthetics and Politics from the English Revolution to the Romantic Revolution*, ed. Kevin Sharpe and Steven N. Zwicker (Berkeley and Los Angeles: U of CA P, 1998), pp. 267–89, and "Surveying the Frontier of Culture: Pastoralism in Eighteenth-Century England," *Studies in Eighteenth-Century Culture* 26 (ed. Syndy M. Conger and Julie C. Hayes) (1998): 7–28.

41. Edmund Bolton, *The Cities Advocate, in this case or question of Honor and Armes; whether Apprenticeship extinguisheth Gentry?…* (1629), pp. 51, 52.

42. John Corbet, *A Discourse of the Religion of England…* (1667?), p. 47. The substance of the following paragraph is drawn from McKeon, *Origins of the English Novel*, pp. 219–23.

As Defoe succinctly expressed this circular plot, "thus Tradesmen become Gentlemen, by Gentlemen becoming Tradesmen." One method of becoming a gentleman was to consult "the Herald's office, to search for the Coats of Arms of their ancestors..." But this step was also expendable. "In this search we find them often qualified to raise new families," Defoe remarks, "if they do not descend from old; as was said of a certain tradesman of *London*, that if he could not find the antient race of Gentlemen, from which he came, he would begin a new race, who should be as good Gentlemen as any that went before them." Granted, it might take more than one generation to establish a new personality, but the heirs of the founder "in a succession or two are receiv'd as effectually, and are as essentially gentlemen, as any of the antient houses were before them," "and are accepted among gentlemen as effectually as if the blood of twenty generations was running in their veins." But in Defoe's eyes, what was problematic about the movement from land to trade had nothing to do with the uncertainty of the merchant's civic virtue, which was evident in his industrious discipline and confirmed by his worldly success. The question concerned the merchant's outward breeding and his acceptance by others, both of which could be ensured nonetheless by adequate socialization. However outward breeding was not the most important possession, and assimilation was not the only model of upward mobility. The more important possession for both gentleman and merchant was virtue: temperance, frugality, honesty, prudence, "the practise of all morall virtues." When these are wanting, "or degenerated or corrupted in a Gentleman, he sinks out of the Rank, [and] ceases to be any more a Gentleman." Nor need the rise of the virtuous merchant be accompanied by his assimilative acquisition of gentility or nobility. "Many of our trading gentlemen," Defoe writes, "refuse to be Ennobled, scorn being knighted, and content themselves with being known to be rated among the richest Commoners in the nation."[43]

These techniques of historicizing the movement from land to trade were grounded in a less ostensible but more fundamental innovation in the way English people conceived the existence of virtue over time. By this I mean the long-term shift from a status-based to a class-based conception of social relations, in which public virtue can be seen to be a function not of landed or social status but of private virtue. This is the

---

43. Daniel Defoe, *The Complete English Tradesman, in Familiar Letters...*, 2nd edn., 2 vols. (1727), 1:310–311, 308; Defoe, *Compleat English Gentleman*, Bülbring (ed.), pp. 262, 275, 177.

tradition of thought that generates pronouncements like the following: "Let the People of England... get their Livings by Industry, and never exceed the limits of their private Fortunes, and all complaints of venality and Corruption will fall to the Ground... There is no sure Method, therefore, of preventing Corruption, but by preventing Necessity... Let them secure private Virtue and they will see all public Virtue rise out of it."[44] Needless to say, there's no basis for attributing this vision of civic personality to the influence of civic humanism.

Unified Versus Undifferentiated Personality

Reminding ourselves of this vision sheds light on some of the problems of interpretive logic that mar Pocock's method. The reason the civic humanist view of "social and political personality" seems to him the only game in town is because within that category he secretes a special criterion that, although logically unwarranted by the category itself, ensures that only civic humanism (or related modes like aristocratic ideology) will qualify. This is the requirement not only that the personality of the subject bespeak one morally qualified for political and social action, but also that it be "unified." According to Pocock, civic humanism represented "the unity of human personality," the "unity" and the "ideal of the undifferentiated personality" (*VCH*, pp. 122, 111, 118). The understanding of personality enunciated by Defoe and others in the passages I've just quoted may fairly be said to involve, on the contrary, a "differentiation," even a separation: the "private" virtue of the merchant is what grounds hu "public" capacity as a civic actor. As in the aristocratic assumption that worth is entailed in birth, the relationship between the private and the public in civic humanist idelogy is conceptually seamless: the private virtue of the independent landowner is presumed as a function of hu capacity for public virtue in political community with others of similar capacities. Over the course of the seventeenth century this fiction lost its broad credibility. However the consolidation of absolute private property, and the discourse that accompanies and justifies it, mark not a threat to the theory of human personality but the emergence of a radically new

---

44. James Pitt, *Daily Gazeteer*, 15 November 1735 and 13 March 1936, quoted in Shelley Burtt, *Virtue Transformed: Political Arguments in England, 1688–1740* (Cambridge: Cambridge UP, 1992), p. 124. On the transition from status to class, see McKeon, *Origins of the English Novel*, pp. 162–67.

version of it. In fact, it's only from the perspective of civic humanism itself that the differentiation of the undifferentiated personality might amount to an attack on personality as such (the partiality of such a judgment becomes clear if we suppose, in an analogous vein, that the movement from status to contract amounted to an attack on the theory of political and social obligation).

At one point Pocock refers to the unified and the differentiated personality as "two modes of individualism," a usage that glosses over this fundamental difference because it applies to both a term — "individualism" — that common usage would reserve for the differentiated or "separated-out" model alone (*VCH*, p. 107). In the modern notion of the "individual" we refer to a subject whose independence and autonomy are a function of hu freedom from the state, whose potential as external constraint is the dialectical precondition for the liberty of the civil subject. This is the model of "negative liberty," in contrast to which historians have posited the more traditional model of "positive liberty," in which the condition of the freedom of the subject is predicated not negatively, in separation from others, but positively, in community and social connectedness.[45] Of course Pocock knows these heuristic categories, and he associates civic humanism with the model of positive liberty in accord with his understanding that it posits a unified or undifferentiated personality (*MM*, p. 232; *VCH*, p. 40).[46] As he observes, the difference between the two models can be seen as a difference between the two stories they tell about how the "private" subject becomes a "public" or political subject. James Harrington's "individuals never occupy a state of nature; they are naturally political, having been created by God in His image as capable of intelligent self-rule" (*VCH*, p. 106); and their public and private capacities are therefore "unified" because they can be distinguished but not separated from each other. The story of how civil society is established through the decision of individuals to vacate the state of nature by creating a political state to which some freedoms — including the freedom of self-rule — are sacrificed in order to ensure the preservation of others is a story of negative liberty, in which liberty is defined

45. Although most commonly advanced in strictly theoretical terms, the difference between notions of positive and negative liberty conceived in chronological terms is encouraged by Pocock's view of civic humanism as an ancient doctrine crucially instrumental in stimulating modern ones.

46. Characteristically he also seems to regard civic humanism as the original, overarching, and only mode of positive liberty and undifferentiated personality.

over against the political state that both makes freedom possible and threatens its existence. One hallmark of negative liberty is the separability of individual from community, of private from public. Another is the conviction that as the state of nature necessarily precedes the political state, so individual is prior to community.

Pocock's confusing reference to civic humanism as a mode of individualism stems, I think, from a confusion between the autonomy entailed in the "independence" of the landowner and the autonomy entailed in the status of the modern "individual." The independence of the landowner in the classic conception of civic humanism looks like a negative liberty because it appears to posit a power on which the landowner otherwise would be dependent. But this is a hypothetical and notional dependence—the possibility of "tyranny"—negatively posited by the logic of positive liberty as an immanent condition, rather than by the apprehension of an actual external power—the reality of the state—that threatens and thereby defines the liberty of the landowner. Hence the analogy with divine self-rule: if the civic humanist subject is dependent on God, he is also like God in his self-subsistent independence. In so far as actual dependence on human entity is a factor in the model of positive liberty, it defines the freedom of the natural elite not negatively but positively, as that which binds individuals together in the mutual interdependence of the members of a collectivity. For this reason the independence of the civic humanist subject is better understood as an interdependence than as an individualism, as an embeddedness within collectivity rather than an abstraction from it.[47]

It's in this sense that "classical republicanism" means the commitment of public people to res publica or public things, rather than the opposition of private people to the public rule of monarch or tyrant. The continuity Pocock would find between the Aristotelian theory of the republican rule of the few and the republican opposition to Charles I and, then, to George III is very much worth pursuing, but the discontinuities are greater than he's willing to acknowledge. In its conviction that politics

---

47. The history of the word "individual" itself records the history of the change from a positive to a negative model of liberty. As Peter Stallybrass has used the *OED* to document, in the early modern period the meaning of "individual" shifts from "indivisible" to "singular": see "Shakespeare, the Individual, and the Text," in *Cultural Studies*, ed. Lawrence Grossberg, Cary Nelson, and Paula Treichler (London: Routledge, 1992), pp. 593–95. Pocock's interest in "language" has little to do with this sort of attention to the historicity of semantics.

and economics are coextensive authorities, the classical republicanism of the civil war years looks less like a break with royal absolutism than like an anti-royalist version of absolutism. Some familiar articles of American revolutionary ideology, like the opposition to a standing army and the championing of militias peopled by yeomen farmers, are clearly continuous with the classical republicanism of the late seventeenth and early eighteenth centuries. More fundamental principles are not: for example, the disarticulation of the right to rule from land ownership, or the ethical belief that the relationship between property and virtue is empirically demonstrated rather than assumed as a given. The difficulty of Pocock's exercise in tracing continuity lies in the fact that even by 1642 let alone by 1776, the normative understanding of the political personality of the citizen is well advanced in its long-term transition from the dominance of a positive to that of a negative model of liberty. Another way of saying this is that by the middle of the seventeenth century, a "rights-based" is being separated out from a "virtue-based" conception of politics sufficiently to lay claim, in coming years, to offering the only true foundation for public virtue. Not that the republicanism of the civil war and the interregnum is therefore "modern" rather than "traditional." The challenge is instead to understand how the two models interpenetrate each other on the level of historical contingency, where the heuristic purity of categories like civic humanism yields to the rich messiness of actual language use and meaning, for which it offers no more than a useful guide. By the time of Swift and Bolingbroke, civic humanism's principled rule of the few—the inseparability of government from an elite of governors—had ineluctably devolved into an ideal of service to a state that's fundamentally separate from, and that stands over against, its citizen-statesmen. Even the protest against government corruption in the early decades of the eighteenth century resembles no more the classic civic humanist model of interdependence than it does the interregnum protest against feudal tenures.

The most important change in political thought during the seventeenth century is marked not by the financial revolution but by one of its enabling conditions, the separation out of civil society from the state, whose corollary is a separation out of the economy from the polity that is formally ratified by the English republic's abolition of feudal tenures. Identifying civic humanism with the belief in "political man," Pocock refutes the contention that "somewhere in the eighteenth century or the nineteenth must be found the moment when political man died and economic man reigned in his stead"; on the contrary, he writes, the two persist in "bitter, conscious, and ambivalent dialogue" (*VCH*, p. 70, 71). But this refutation of crude antinomy is itself too crude an account of historical change. What happens to the relationship between the political and the economic in the modern world is not (even) a radical rebalancing but a growing conviction of their separability. From imposing "public," protectionist policies on "private," economic activity the early modern state learned the wisdom of a laissez-faire policy, which represents a further stage in the separation of polity from economy. But separation inevitably entails transformation: in the very process of disentanglement not only the realm of the economic, but also the realm of the political, is reconceived to such a degree that the modern persistence of "polity" on which Pocock rightly insists nonetheless says nothing at all about the putative persistence of civic humanism. If civic humanism "dies" in the modern world, it does so not because "political man," but because the belief in the inseparability of political man and economic man, dies in the modern world. But if this is so, then the perdurability of "political man" in Pocock's civic humanist sense of the term — that is, the ideal of the undifferentiated personality — is a contradiction in terms. True, to suggest this is already to solicit dissent. The re-conflation of economy and polity, of individual and collective personality, is an ambition shared by a range of modern social and political movements, whose projects are more or less utopian according to the degree to which they envision the return of a Golden Age of undifferentiated personality and sociopolity. For the most sagacious of civic humanists — I'm thinking of Swift's talking horses and his Lord Munodi — this ideal was representable only as parabolic and by definition unrealizable fiction.[48] To conceive how the ideal might be accommodated to reality we need to look to those movements that acknowledge not only what has been lost but also what has been gained in the advent of modernity — not civic humanism, that is, but some form of socialist humanism.[49]

---

48. See Jonathan Swift, *Gulliver's Travels* (1726), ed. Herbert Davis (rev. 1959 [1941]) in *The Prose Works of Jonathan Swift*, ed. Herbert Davis and others, 16 vols. (Oxford: Blackwell, 1939–74), 11: pt. 4; pt. 3, ch. 4.

49. E.g., see *Socialist Humanism: An International Symposium*, ed. Erich Fromm (Garden City, NY: Anchor, 1966).

4. Republican Virtue Reconsidered, or a Sop to Cerberus

J.A.W. GUNN

To presume to consider John Pocock's *Machiavellian Moment* a book that removed the adjective 'magisterial' from general circulation and confined its application — is to confront a threefold challenge. There is the account of a form of political discourse as it may have existed in the centuries that bridge Machiavelli's time and the American founding. In addition, there may be — though at best elusively in the Pocockilly canon and much more obtrusively in the other literature that it has inspired — a vision of the good polity for our own time. This is normative political philosophy, sometimes at least purporting to follow from prior historical investigation. Finally, and informing the historical narrative — if that is indeed what it is — there has been a body of advice emanating from a group of scholars with links to Cambridge. This tells us how to mend our ways so that our labours on the past of political thought yield a more truly historical understanding. Here I am then offering a triptych. But I can better underline the threeness of my concern by characterizing the three heads for discussion of republican substance presented historically, of a moral to be drawn and of a method for doing the history — as not entirely dissimilar from that great creature from Greek mythology that welcomed newcomers to its territory and ensured that their stay would not be a brief one. The last generation or so of students of what used to be called the history of ideas has both been enticed by these three heads and then confined by the profundity of their import. Not for a moment have I been

ambitious to supply the heads of Cerberus with faces. Rather I am doing
much as did John Pocock when, in responding to critics, he depicted himself as placed between those fabled British brutes Gog and Magog. The
place into which one is cast by my three sources of puzzlement bears
some similarity to that guarded by the original Cerberus if only because,
along with the enticement to visit and the difficulty of departing, it is extensive and has not, to my knowledge, been definitively mapped.

The paper proceeds in that spirit of "cordial disagreement" by which
John once described his inability to make common cause with the late
C.B. Macpherson, one of my mentors and another great figure from whom
I learned a lot by pondering why it was that I could not endorse either
his conclusions or his way of reaching them. My own views remain too
tentative to go much beyond my striving to be precise about the basis for
my various puzzlements. Even when I was working on British thought
of the eighteenth century—an activity that ceased more than twenty years
ago—I was quite content to toil happily in the documents of the past with
only a rare glance at what my contemporaries were saying. A reviewer
of my book of essays of 1983 expressed consternation that I had so neglected the subject of Pocock. For some commentators on political ideas,
this silence would surely have masked an intent to communicate an
esoteric insight. Alas, the truth is far less intriguing, for I was aware only
that I wanted to say different things and in a form that required no judgement about that other agenda. One reader who did understand was Pocock himself.[1] Only rarely since then have I entered the thickets of debate about method and my only previous notice of the present subject was
to express my high regard for the generous ecumenism in which Pocock
said whatever he was saying. I was even quite circumspect about alluding to my often being in the dark as to what exactly that was. In that capacity I may still not be entirely without company and I must, this time,
pursue the issue more vigorously.

In Search of the Republican Tradition

It seems strange that the subject of *The Machiavellian Moment* should have
generated such a body of scholarly polemic. Here, after all, were thoughts
of a scholar, already hugely accomplished, and possessing powers of anal-

---

1. Pocock, review of *Beyond Liberty and Property*, in *Eighteenth-Century Studies*
18 (1984): 112–15.

ysis and a fund of allusion beyond the ordinary even for learned people. One might expect the outcome to be a landmark of authoritative pronouncement. The tale to be told was, to be sure, ambitious and entailed tracing the tradition through three different places and at least that many times. Ample scope then for trenching on the turf hitherto commanded by others and we all now know how important both land and arms have been in the Atlantic tradition. Naturally then, sturdy yeomen and active citizens of all sorts streamed forth to protect their own; they have been so engaged now for a quarter of a century. But surely, it was more than that tendency, well developed amongst historians, to rise up against intruders that accounts for the remarkable measure of controversy that has attended this study.

The book is, of course, a challenging one, powerfully enigmatic in several dimensions. For one thing, despite a wealth of articles detailing what he was up to, Pocock left some at least of his readers unclear as to what sort of enterprise the book was about, for there seemed to be no positive assertion that corresponded in its force to his announcement in the second paragraph that this was not a history of political thought "whatever that might be." So what was it and what legitimate expectations might one entertain? My complaint may well be unsubtle and artless but I should have been enlightened so much sooner had the work itself contained some sentence as informative as that offered by a reviewer, both perceptive and admiring, who wrote that the republican tradition "asserts human choice as the ground of virtue against necessity, chance, nature or God."[2] Nor do these words lack that rhetorical grandeur that was so marked in the original. Furthermore, there was the disconcerting presence of a good many props that seemed not to relate in any obvious fashion to the subject announced on the title page. No simple inventory of the resources of republican language seemed to necessitate such close attention to the relative poverty of modes of historical explanation available to the medieval mind. I asked myself too why the place accorded to realism and a focus upon universals seem altogether too great and the recognition of the brilliant nominalism of an Ockham or an Autrecourt has dwindled to nothing. What one thought that one knew has vanished from the account and what is left seems, in places, difficult to accept and this reader was left dazzled by the light yet not sufficiently enlightened. So there are both presences and absences that left me uneasy. Finally, and most conspicuously, when with preliminaries over and done with we meet both

---

2. Nathan Tarcov, review in *Political Science Quarterly* 91 (1976): 382.

Florentine political thought and the Atlantic republicans, the emphasis often seems to invite debate rather than awed acceptance. The upshot of this is that, in a work where it was notoriously difficult to hold all the themes together, subsequent controversy was focussed largely on specific Machiavellian moments. These, we now know, may occur when political arrangements were confronted with an awareness of their own finitude and the struggle of virtue against corruption, or against time itself, could be seen. It has been a debate conducted on many fronts, not all of them having to do with instances of the republican tradition, as my own difficulties with Pocock's account of the medieval background attest. What I wish to emphasize here are those various engagements where the issue has been whether a given text or author or school of thought has been classically republican or civic humanist in the fashion suggested by the *Machiavellian Moment*.

Amongst those claims that seem to deserve attention, pride of place must belong to the one that argued that Machiavelli's own participation in the Florentine experience was not unambiguously such as to qualify him for a leading role in the drama of his own moment. Whereas Giannoti and Guicciardini may appear to have said the right things, there is at least some doubt as to whether Machiavelli's own position did sound the genuine Aristotelian note. This is not, assuredly, to recycle age-old concerns about how to reconcile the Machiavelli who wrote *The Prince* with that of the *Discourses*; rather, it has to do with those texts that were offered to document the position. Pocock tells us, early in his account of certain themes in *Il Principe*, that he will not deal with "certain aspects" of that book. This disarming admission leads already to the suspicion that evidence may not all point in the same direction and that the criteria that serve to certify membership in the republican tradition may be open to contestation. Specifically, the devotion to the public good and public service — notions having some currency in all forms of government — may contain a degree of self-interest in the Machiavellian version that militates against their serving as the true heirs of the classical tradition. Machiavelli's comments upon liberty may be similarly at odds with views held to be his.[3] Let it not be assumed that the foregoing constitutes a stern rebuke to Pocock's scholarship; rather it raises the possibility that the tale here told with such learning is subject to the objection that the pieces

---

3. Vickie B. Sullivan, "Machiavelli's Momentary 'Machiavellian Moment': A Reconsideration of Pocock's Treatment of the *Discourses*," *Political Theory* 20 (1992): 309–18.

of evidence needed careful selection to ensure the proper degree of continuity from one thinker or language to the next. The connections may just be too loose and require too imaginative a leap to save the phenomenon. A case in point is Pocock's statement, in the course of treating Machiaavelli's *Arte della Guerra* where he writes of the republic itself as the common good, the cause to which the citizen dedicated his life. A commentator, perhaps seeking too literal a meaning, insists that the thought is not one in keeping with Machiavelli's own expectations for citizens.[4] But the sentiment, as it appeared, is attached to no single figure, although its very presence in the discussion of Machiavelli invites the reader to assume a relevance that is suggested rather than argued. Were Machiavelli's credentials imperfect in terms of those demanded by the creator of this account, then we might expect to encounter difficulties in separating the genuine republican strain from other forms of discourse. It is a concern that deepens when attention shifts to England and other examples of republican speech and action. In the meantime, let it be said that if Giannotti were really a better exemplar of the right stuff, that does proffer a response to the hypothesis that Professor Hexter had offered in the form that Gionnotti's prominence was proportioned, not to his historical rank, but to our previous unfamiliarity with him.[5] That had always seemed less than convincing. However, if Giannotti earns his place through service, then the mystery is dissolved. Still, it would have been difficult to call the whole affair the Giannottian moment and understandably Princeton University Press would have been reluctant. Commerce, we may wish to murmur, has always been the enemy of virtue.

The English site chosen for the second major encounter with the tradition was, of course, the work of Harrington. Here republicanism takes its leave of the city state and enters, not entirely comfortably, into the world of representative government. Were one anxious to maximize the presence of republicanism in England, the choice of Harrington places the landfall much later than need be, for we know of a current of republican sentiment from deep in the previous century. Even though Harrington's editor decreed that republicanism in England was a language and not a programme — a thought that seems to get refracted in some

---

4. Pocock, *MM*. Ronald J. Tercheck, *Republican Paradoxes and Liberal Anxieties: Retrieving Neglected Fragments of Political Theory* (Lanham: 1997), pp. 64–65, 88.

5. J.H. Hexter, "Republic, Virtue, Liberty and the Political Universe of J.G.A. Pocock" in *On Historians* (Cambridge, MA: Harvard UP, 1979), pp. 255–303.

accounts of the issue[6]—there were reasons for the emphasis on Harrington, for it is he who serves to sweep the story forward into the next century. Just within the seventeenth-century context, however, one encounters again the possibility that the language that tells us that we were still in republican company appears not to be as distinguishable from other vocabularies as the ambition to identify a discrete tradition seemed to require. Here the impurity takes the form of Harrington's evident commitment to the language of "interest," the age's panacea for purging the body politic of all manner of ills. The consequence, as argued by Kathleen Toth, has been that Harrington's reliance on the trinity of virtue, fortune and corruption is much diminished. Indeed, she draws the conclusion that reliance on this concept allowed Harrington to argue for constituting a public realm based on private interest rather than virtue and the pursuit of the common good. Since she supports the claim with reference to my work on the seventeenth century,[7] I find myself recruited, after the fact, to support the criticism of a thesis of which I had been ignorant when I wrote. No prescience about the viability of the *Machiavellian Moment* can be claimed for thoughts that I committed first to paper in 1963 (and to print in 1968), but I had been conscious of the fact that Harrington's language had contained both an Aristotelian strain in relation to the public interest as well as another and more prominent emphasis upon the efficacy of self-interest as directed by orders judiciously arranged.

A yet more confident version of the concern comes in a monograph dedicated to the thought of that republican martyr Algernon Sydney, for there Harrington's reliance upon institutions is held to have banished entirely that moral concern that some, at least, find in Machiavelli. Later Jonathan Scott focussed directly on Harrington and offered a convincing denial of his republican credentials.[8] It speaks volumes for the

---

6. Pocock, *PWJH*, p. 15. For a different emphasis, see David Norbrook, *Writing the English Republic: Poetry, Rhetoric and Politics, 1627–1660* (Cambridge: Cambridge UP, 1999), p. 5.

7. Kathleen Toth, "Interpretation in Political Theory: The Case of Harrington," *Review of Politics* 37 (1975): 333–34. In the same vein, see Andrew Lockyer, "Pocock's Harrington," *Political Studies* 28 (1980): 462. See too J.A.W. Gunn, *Politics and the Public Interest in the Seventeenth Century* (London: Routledge, 1968), pp. 130–38.

8. Jonathan Scott, *Algernon Sidney and the English Republic, 1623–1677* (Cambridge: Cambridge UP, 1988), pp. 15n–16n. See too his "The Rapture of Motion," in *Political Discourse in Early Modern Britain*, ed. Nicholas Phillipson and Quentin Skinner (Cambridge: Cambridge UP, 1993), pp. 139–63.

hazards associated with tacking together an intellectual tradition that Scott's effort to drum Harrington out of the ranks of classical republicans, the better to make room for the different notes sounded by Sidney, should itself become subject to criticism on grounds not unlike those used against Harrington. A later work on the thought of Sidney returns to the charge that the language of the seventeenth century fits ill with the paradigm that Pocock calls civic humanism. Stated in the most extreme form, this amounts to saying that almost all of the allegedly republican principles ostensibly found in Sidney are quite compatible with that Lockean liberalism that it had been John Pocock's business to distance from the republican tradition. Talk of a state of nature, consent and the "collection of every man's private Right into a public Stock" were the thoughts and expressions that had been conspicuously missing in the language of the *Machiavellian Moment.* The absence of a classical theory of corruption or any apparent intention to follow Machiavelli in the ambition to return government to its first principles here support the contention that Sidney was more individualistic than paradigmatically republican. As in the earlier skirmishes over the meaning of Harrington, I again find my innocent formulations of long ago brought forward to endorse proposed revisions. Indeed, given the whole Canadian forests felled in the cause of arguing the differences between republicanism and liberalism, it is with some unease that I re-read my own serene opinion that "liberal or republican thought" tended to say the right things about that relation between individual and public good that it had been my intention to explain.[9] Some of us have been critics of the famous thesis only *avant la lettre* and while serving other causes.

This account has dwelt to date on the seventeenth century largely because it is here, and not in relation to the next century, that my writings have been drawn into the struggle. Already a general pattern should be clear: a particular language served to identify the tradition under examination, though seemingly not in the sense of supplying a fixed set of defining characteristics without which the tradition itself would disappear. The result then has been that what made Harrington a classical republican shows only partial continuity with the criteria that so identified Machiavelli and Sidney, in turn, showed significant differences in emphasis from those features so prominent in his predecessor. Arguments have

---

9. Alan Craig Houston, *Algernon Sidney and the Republican Heritage in England and America* (Princeton, Princeton UP: 1991), where my comments on Sidney are cited at pp. 121, 168n, 200. *Cf.* Gunn, *Politics and the Public Interest,* p. 300.

then been adduced in the case of each of the three figures that serve to challenge the presumption of his truly belonging to the school, though it might be retorted that there remains that sort of ineffable family resemblance that may be sensed rather than demonstrated in analytical terms. Whether it is a particular understanding of liberty or corruption, of sacrifice to the public good, of virtue or of defeating time, the language held to supply the ligaments that held together this mode of thought and action seem to be less an unvarying pattern than a number of elements any one or two of which might be missing in some version. Nor should this surprise us, since any attempt to trace continuities in thought must concede that thinkers worthy of our acquaintance will have an agenda that is peculiarly their own. Otherwise, their messages would be prayers or incantations that find their meaning in uncritical repetition. Continuity there must be, but only in a certain measure. A tradition is not altogether dissimilar from a rope where no strand may run the entire length but in which strands of varying length secure the identity of the whole.

If the argument of the *Machiavellian Moment* has found its critics, it may be that Pocock's elegant formulations of classical republicanism have not sufficiently prepared them for the inevitable discovery of divergences in emphasis, discontinuities and even self-descriptions, as with Harrington, that seem belied by that argument. The pattern just described is rehearsed, over and over, by the scholars seeking to explain and label those intellectual influences that bridged the late seventeenth century and the era of the American Revolution. Already, however, in the language of Harrington is visible those concerns that seem at odds with the civic-humanist tradition. When later figures then diverge from Harrington and his quest for an immortal commonwealth, the question posed is whether their bent was to reaffirm a republican tradition or further to dilute its influence. The very name of neo-Harringtonians is presumably no older than Pocock's essay of 1965, but he has never succeeded in creating a consensus as to what their ideology was. Adopting a rather more ample understanding of the scope of neo-Harringtonian thought, Jesse Goodale has argued that Pocock, in his retrospective fashioning of the school, got their views wrong. The claim that best resonates with those already recorded is that Pocock's treatment had neglected the language that spoke to the tension "between private and general interest," the vocabulary, that is, of individualism. John Pocock's gracious and accommodating response sticks on conceding anything on that point, though apparently ready to consider the merits of other claims. His reason was that, in the absence of textual citations, there was no convincing substitute for his own categories.[10] Nor, indeed, were texts cited on the exact point at issue, though there was mention of that famous passage from John Trenchard's *Short History of Standing Armies* (1698) where he contemplated a very Harringtonian arrangement of institutions where mechanical principles would do the work otherwise left to virtuous struggle. Sentiments that sought to reconcile "every man's true interest" and the "general interest" are not, however, difficult to locate in *Cato's Letters*, thus sustaining the original contention that the citizen's self-abnegation in the travail of virtue against corruption may just have been becoming unfashionable, if ever it did hold a place in Harringtonian thought. Other passages affirm the necessity of self-love or self-interest and present a very modest degree of public spirit.[11] I would not, incidentally, hold that such statements represented, by any means, individualism incarnate, for it might be perfectly compatible even with the scholastic maxim that *bonum communis eo melius*. The point is that talk of interests and the limits of public spirit does mark a departure from the vocabulary that was meant to distinguish republican language from others. It is in this sense that Harrington may well have bequeathed to his later admirers a poisoned chalice. The sources examined thus far are not the only ones to suggest that the transmission of classical republicanism raises problems as to what exactly was transmitted and what was lost in the process. J. C. Davis has made a case for the possibility that a supposed neo-Harringtonian such as Henry Neville rejected more than he absorbed from the teaching of his republican friend.[12]

The lingering impurities of Harrington's position are not, however, the only issue, for a greater measure of attention has always been directed towards John Locke's political language and its possible role in complicating the picture — one with Locke conveniently absent — offered in the *Machiavellian Moment*. We probably all are aware that Pocock's pos-

---

10. Jesse R. Goodale, "J.G.A. Pocock's Neo-Harringtonianism: A Reconsideration," *History of Political Thought* 1 (1980): 329; Pocock, "A Reconsideration Impartially Considered": 545.

11. Trenchard & Cato, *Cato's Letters*, ed. and annotated by Ronald Hamowy (Indianapolis: 1995), #89 (11 Aug. 1722) at 2:638–42. Shelley Burtt quotes the same passage for the same purpose, employing the earlier edition of the *Letters*. See *Virtue Transformed: Political Argument in England, 1688–1740* (Cambridge: CUP, 1992), pp. 77–78. For the other letters, see #31 (27 May 1721); #117 (23 Feb. 1722), and #35 (July 1721), in *Cato's Letters*, Hamowy (ed.), 1:222, 2:815, 1:250–54.

12. J.C. Davis, "Pocock's Harrington: Grace, Nature and Art in the Classical Republicanism of James Harrington," *Historical Journal* 24 (1981): 685.

ition on this major figure was to distance him from the tradition while showing slight enthusiasm for ceding him to those other major renderings of the period associated with the names of Strauss and Macpherson. The necessary conclusion to be drawn was that, on some issues at least, Locke's star set very soon after it had risen, a view supported by the research of John Dunn. Now not even Locke's American interpreters, one of whom favoured a portrait of him as a very advanced political radical, sought to make him a republican. Only some High-Church extremists have offered that view. Rather, Locke's relevance to the story is that Lockean categories seem to join with the different languages derived from Harrington to undermine any effort to offer a clear line of development that carries an unsullied tradition of classical republicanism into the eighteenth century, and perhaps even beyond. Whether the talk of rights and that of interests constitute but one language is not my business to pursue here, but undoubtedly both vocabularies figure in the thought of those classical republicans Trenchard and Gordon. The editor of 'Cato' insists on the presence there of Lockean themes and has also usefully emphasized the need to make Pocock's original paradigm something more robust and distinctive than a mere endorsement of being public spirited.[13] Although I would contend that virtue, corruption and time focus most happily on the question of how the welfare of the community is prescribed, it also seems true that to make the shibboleth of republicanism too easy on the tongue will turn everyone into an adherent and so render the whole exercise otiose.

As Oxford philosophy papers of the 1960s used to say, an item is best understood in a universe of items that differ from it. The work of Trenchard and Gordon may well have attracted more scholarly attention than their intellectual quality warrants, but this is because their 'Cato' stands as the major republican redoubt in early eighteenth-century Britain, since the uncontested republicanism of Andrew Fletcher of Saltoun did not equally secure passage to the new world. It has been the intent animating a considerable mass of scholarship to carry the redoubt of 'Cato' and so to stem Pocock's tradition even before it could gain a firm presence in America. The efforts appear, at least, to have diluted Cato's republican identity by adding a significant dose of Lockean natural

---

13. Ronald Hamowy, "*Cato's Letters*, John Locke, and the Republican Paradigm," in *John Locke's "Two Treatises of Government: New Interpretations,* ed. Edward J. Harpham (Lawrence: UP of Kansas, 1992), p. 169; and review of Jerome Huyler, *Locke in America,* in *William and Mary Quarterly,* ser. 3, 53 (1996): 403–5.

right[14] For those who delight in keeping track of the jarring sects that contend amidst the texts, one notes that in the forces assembled to relieve the English eighteenth century from a civic-humanist understanding were adherents both of the Marxish interpretation favoured by Macpherson and the Straussite persuasion—the two contending schools against which Pocock has taken so firm a stand.[15] Various accounts of the scholarly debate suggest that there has emerged, largely from the competition over the ideological character of 'Cato,' a new readiness to contemplate the possibility that the borders of a political language may not be coterminous with the space that divides one thinker or one text from another but may, inconveniently, run through an entity that had once been tidily consigned to one camp or to another. This is a conclusion of some importance, and I shall return to it presently.

For the time being, there are other connections along the route traced out by the tradition under scrutiny and these must be tested to see if they can safely bear their burden. In particular, the momentum of the republican influence had to be sustained through the middle decades of the eighteenth century. Here the torch must be carried, for part of the way, by that moral leper Bolingbroke and the going gets, at times, heavy. True, he railed against corruption, but more and more it seemed to entail learning displayed without conviction. As Professor Burtt has wisely observed, Bolingbroke's criterion of virtue lay in maintaining the supposed balance of the constitution and the sign of corruption was voting for the administration.[16] It may be of some significance that several of the *Machiavellian Moment*'s most complex sentences are to be found here as the argument confidently forges through the moral vacuum of English party politics. I find too my own work on eighteenth-century parties pressed into service, though only in a neutral way that makes no assumptions about its specfiic claims. My work, in fact, would not concur with Pocock's

---

14. See, for example, Jerome Huyler, *Locke in America: The Moral Philosophy of the Founding Era* (Lawrence: UP of Kansas, 1995), pp. 39, 210ff.

15. Isaac Kramnick, *Republicanism and Bourgeois Radicalism: Political Ideology in Late Eighteenth-Century England and America* (Ithaca: Cornell UP, 1990), pp. 36–40, and Thomas Pangle, *The Spirit of Modern Republicanism: The Moral Vision of the American Founders and the Philosophy of Locke* (Chicago: Chicago UP, 1988), pp. 30–33. Only Pangle deals spsecifically with Cato, since Kramnick's objections to claims about civic humanism are confined to the latter part of the century. Kramnick does, at his 167, take out of context Pocock's dismissal—in *PLT*—of Locke's influence and so exaggerates the position in a misleading way.

16. Burtt, *Virtue Transformed*, pp. 93, 99.

assumption that the age was incapable of generating a "satisfactory theory of party." I have long deemed Pocock's account of the Augustans to be a set of connections that convinces less than it should, though I can only applaud the generosity and insight of his tribute to those underrated Treasury journalists whose task it was to display the poverty of Bolingbroke's Country rhetoric.[17] My original thoughts on the classical conceits of Country journalism were dismissive—perhaps, I now think, excessively so—but they still seem to support the feeling of unease that others have experienced in coping with this portion of the argument.[18]

More important for his possible connection to the tradition is Hume and Pocock's evident desire to associate that name with civic humanism, consistent with our recognizing those aspects of Hume's thought that might lie beyond the pale or even be diametrically opposed to republicanism. The essay that best serves to draw in this great historian and social scientist is that on "Public Credit" which was the occasion for some oddly alarmist sentiments on the dangers posed by the national debt. Published initially in the same year that Henry Pelham finished the process of reorganizing the debt and succeeded in lowering the rate of interest to be paid to the state's creditors, the essay painted a grim picture of a nation subservient to a new race of stockjobbers. Though the observation that this group would, in effect, own all property "since the value of every object would now be the extent of its indebtedness" is an inference drawn by Pocock and is not quite as Hume put it, the tone of foreboding is faithful to Hume's own. Thus the meeting of virtue and corruption, ingeniously presented as visible in ever-changing forms, is again at centre stage.[19] Pocock has been a close student of the growth of credit and the burgeoning of public debt and, in one of his essays he recognized, as did Hume himself, the way in which the new financial instruments tied investors to the maintenance of the Revolution Settlement.[20] A particularly gaudy chapter in a long story of the tension between the commerce and the public good, Pocock's interpretation of the cause of Hume's very real anguish seems forced. A more recent version, written

---

17. Pocock, *MM*, pp. 485–86, 483n60, 480.

18. See Paul A. Rahe, *Republics Ancient and Modern: Classical Republicanism and the American Revolution* (Chapel Hill: North Carolina UP, 1992), p. 998n136.

19. Pocock, *MM*, pp. 496–97.

20. Pocock, "Early Modern Capitalism—the Augustan Perspective," in ed. E. Kamenka and R. S. Neale, *Feudalism, Capitalism and Beyond* (Canberra: Australian National UP, 1975), p. 71.

still under the spell of Pocock, substitutes international conflict and its costs for the supposed animus against commercial society and its tendency to generate debt[21] and thus brings the essay close to views that are readily attributable to Hume. But commerce as the nemesis of virtue is the secular equivalent of *fortuna* and so plays an important role in eliding the problems and language of one era with another. The obvious cost of the revision—by a scholar seemingly ill at ease in disagreeing with Pocock—is that a point of view consonant with civic humanism, is, in the same proportion, accorded less purchase on the middle decades of the century. In this campaign, Pocock's allies, like the mercenaries of old, sometimes seem on the point of desertion.

Duncan Forbes's review of the *Machiavellian Moment* offered the judgment that Hume had been miscast and that his presence was unconvincing unless it were but to serve as a "symbol for a mode of consciousness." The coolness of specialists on Hume has even extended to understanding Hume's experimental science as expressly intended as a challenge to classical republicanism.[22] When another scholar carefully identifies Hume as marking the limits of the tradition, dissents from Pocock's firm distinction between an agrarian ideal and commerce as alternative positions and even notes the relative lack of "canonical coherence" in the civic tradition,[23] one seems to be in the presence of a very faint commitment to the cause. Is it possible, one wonders, that the problems and the language of the eighteenth century resist presentation as classical republicanism?[24] Political economy and the legacy of Machiavelli were not, to all appearances, made for each other and this despite Pocock's attractive portrait of Charles Davenant as a neo-Machiavellian political economist. If Hume's admirers have, in good measure, liberated that name from the ranks of classical republicans or their fellow travelers, a yet stronger re-

---

21. Istvan Hont, "The Rhapsody of Public Debt: David Hume and Voluntary State Bankruptcy," in *Discourse in Early Modern Britain*, Phillipson and Skinner (ed.), pp. 321–22.

22. Duncan Forbes, *Historical Journal* 19 (1976): 553–55; James Moore, "Hume's Political Science and the Classical Republican Tradition," *Canadian Journal of Political Science* 10 (1977): 820, 839.

23. John Robertson, "The Scottish Enlightenment and the Limits of the Civic Tradition" in *Wealth and Virtue: The Shaping of Political Economy in the Scottish Enlightenment*, ed. Istvan Hont and Michael Ignatieff (Cambridge: Cambridge UP 1983), pp. 141, 159n139.

24. As argued in Felix Gilbert's review of *MM*, "Corruption and Renewal," *Times Literary Supplement* (19 March 1976): 306–8.

buff lay in store for those who sought to recruit Adam Smith. Harpham's answer to the work of Donald Winch—that Smith stands outside the tradition on important matters such as corruption and public mindedness—seems to be convincing. Still, there have been others who are partial to ceding Smith to the republican forces, or at least partitioning him.[25]

Of the final chapter that takes the republican tradition to the new world, I have little to say, because of the acrimony of the great debate and the distance of the texts from anything that I have studied. Long ago Pocock declared himself tired of this controversy[26] and I found myself with a surfeit of it even in the modest capacity of a reader of some of the manuscripts to which it gave birth. I could only account for being so employed because my silence on these issues must have left me one of the few students of relevant matters not already committed to the fray. One thing established is that Locke was not such a cipher either in Britain or in America as we had been led to think, for the efforts to apportion British texts between Lockean and republican influences naturally carried the struggle from Cato and James Burgh to the colonial thinkers who cited them. The debate opened up other questions of importance but these are best discussed under my two remaining heads.

A Morality Play?

When scholars contend for the relative importance of different points of view—say, republicanism and liberalism, as the protagonists have come, in some quarters, to be known—it seems natural that their attachment to the salience of one view or the other takes the form of a claim for the superiority of the position deemed to be the more important. Yet this need not be so at all, for it is quite conceivable that we may be committed to the presumed fact of the matter in terms of historical evidence and be neutral about the intrinsic qualities of the supposedly dominant factor. Although the normative status of our specimen need not be at issue, it

---

25. Edward J. Harpham, "Liberalism, Civic Humanism, and the Case of Adam Smith," *American Political Science Review* 78 (1984): 764–74 at 770. *Cf.* Jeffrey C. Isaac, "Republicanism versus Liberalism? A Recommendation," *History of Political Thought* 9 (1988): 369–70.

26. Pocock, "States, Republics, and Empires: The American Founding in Early Modern Perspective," in *Conceptual Change and the Constitution*, ed. Terence Ball and J.G.A. Pocock (Lawrence: UP of KS, 1988), p. 65.

seems true, nevertheless, that the very existence of disagreement about the relative influence of various vocabularies easily leads to the assumption that some excellence other than bare existence must attend our favoured view. Thus we find in Steven Dworetz's account of the republican interpretation—and especially its initial success against the traditional leaning towards emphasizing Locke's importance—the makings of a moral tale in which the forces of virtue triumph over liberalism and commerce. Citing Pocock's claim of Locke's apparent "indifference" to virtue, Dworetz allows himself to suggest that the champions of civic humanism attach some "normative superiority" to that view. He is sufficiently uncertain of the claim, however, to pose it as a question. The apparent reason for even conjecturing about a moral dimension lies in the vehemence with which the combatants, and some of the earlier scholarship on which they drew, tended to pursue a strategy of what Dworetz calls "all or nothing."[27] In this context, it meant that no school of thought was deemed content to have its chosen position share attention with a different strain and so followed Machiavelli's advice for dealing with the previous religion. I know of an island (Bermuda) where the presence in one part of large toads is paralleled by the predominance in the other part of giant cockroaches. One must assume that those conditions that caused one of these creatures to flourish were anathema to its disagreeable alternative. As the example shows, there remains room for a purely ecological enquiry, without characterizing the specimens in moral terms. However, when scholars vie with each other to nominate one set of ideas or another as the animator of great events, it seems at least possible that they may look with favour on the subject of their own hypothesis for reasons that go beyond its simply being theirs.

In the case of John Pocock's espousing the project of tracing the place in the world of civic humanism, does he emerge as its champion or just

---

27. Steven M. Dworetz, *The Unvarnished Doctrine: Locke, Liberalism and the American Revolution* (Durham: Duke UP, 1990), pp. 97–99, 122, 103, 104. Dworetz's assumption that Pocock argued for one paradigm's total extinction of the other is a misreading of p. 509 of *MM*, where the reference is to an interpretation by Hartz and others being replaced by that of Bailyn and Wood. Others who had earlier sought to rehabilitate Locke's American influence include James T. Kloppenberg, "The Virtues of Liberalism, Christianity, Republicanism, and Ethics in Early American Discourse," *Journal of American History* 74 (1987): 11. As it happens, this article deals fairly with the evidence but, owing to a faulty referent, leaves it ambiguous as to what Pocock's position was. See p. 26n23.

its patient chronicler? I know of nothing in the *Machiavellian Moment* that speaks unambiguously to this question. That book is the result of choosing to explore a particular language of politics but I find there no evidence that this one language is the home of valuable insight or moral standing. Thus, despite the fact that one tradition seems to have had a lock on a technical sense of virtue — and, moreover, to base itself in its very name upon the public good — the possibility of a portrait, warts and all, cannot be ruled out. It was the view of one careful and generally fair commentator on his republicanism that Pocock is an expositor of this paradigm and that he does not appear as its advocate. Nevertheless, the same author adds that Pocock describes his chosen focus "in unduly favorable terms."[28] Despite the disclaimer, the very title of this article refers to Pocock's republicanism, and this shows just how difficult it is to avoid crediting the expositor with an affinity for the ideas, languages or whatever it is that hu expounds. This lapse is especially hard to avoid if the historian in question has argued with some vehemence for the place of hu chosen language.

Additional support, though again not conclusive, might seem to be available from the claim, as seen in Dworetz and others, that there might be but one paradigm regnant, sovereign-like, at any one time and place.[29] It is revealing, however, that Pocock seems to have been ill served by at least two of the claimants for his "all or nothing" view. He seems, in fact, never to have held it. It is then the more remarkable that he has been quite courtly both in applauding Appleby's command of language and calling for collaboration with a critic who seems to have got him wrong.[30] Having, in good faith, attributed the "all-or-nothing" position to Pocock, people have assumed that, if we depict a language as especially domi-

---

28. Ian Shapiro, "J. G. A. Pocock's Republicanism and Political Theory: A Critique and Reinterpretation," *Critical Review* 4 (1990): 448. For similar signs of uncertainty, see Daniel T. Rodgers, "Republicanism: The Career of a Concept," *Journal of American History* 79 (1992): 19.

29. Joyce Appleby, *Liberalism and Republicanism in the Historical Imagination* (Cambridge, MA: Harvard UP, 1992), p. 334n, where she avers that an article of 1972 both disavows any such claim and then makes it. This seems unfair, however, for only the disavowal is unambiguous.

30. Pocock, "An Appeal from the New to the Old Whigs? A Note on Joyce Appleby's 'Ideology and the History of Political Thought,'" *Intellectual History Group Newsletter* (Spring, 1981): 47. Appleby's original appeared first in 1980 and is reprinted in *Liberalism and Republicanism* at pp. 124–39.

nating an age, it must possess some excellence that is in tune with that age, so to commend it. Again, I can find no explicit statement on the part of Pocock to this effect; so it must be an inference from the historical account in *The Machiavellian Moment* and certain of Pocock's articles that surrounded it, along with subsequent defense of the positions taken there. Indeed, it would be an odd position for such an erudite historian to proclaim, for he would have to know that it was false. The specific circumstances of the battle about republican as opposed to Lockeian influences and the assumption—by no means limited to Pocock—that Locke had been of little account, must explain this perception. Here is an issue where people talked past each other and it may both be correct to say that, in general, Pocock allowed for the coexistence of different and even competing paradigms and that, in the case of Locke's political influence in the eighteenth century, he argued long and hard for Locke's relative insignificance. Understandably, then, the particular issue overshadows a general openness to the prospect of competing languages. James Tully may well insist that Pocock never denied Locke's part in the American business,[31] but this overlooks the fact that the thesis of Locke's marginality had been argued by John Dunn and before him Caroline Robbins, Bernard Bailyn and Gordon Wood, and that Pocock often cited the conclusion, seemed to endorse it and never repudiated it. Also accounting for some arguments at cross-purposes was the quite different issue as to whether a given figure or text might belong simultaneously to more than one tradition. This is a matter that I shall take up again in the third section of the paper.

Adding in no small way to the uncertainty has been our central figure's readiness to tease his public as to his inclinations. The *locus classicus* here must be the article of 1981 where Pocock took stock of the book and its reception in order to express his reaction to the various ways in which he had been taken up. Here he complained, not for the last time, of being misunderstood from more than one vantage point. Specifically, he depicted British critics as assuming that he was defending the cause of civic humanism, whereas American tormentors were apparently more inclined to take him to be offering, in peculiarly devious form, a defence of the liberal ethos. This latter position must surely owe something to Pocock's own notion that the primacy of liberalism has been the conten-

---

31. James Tully, "Placing the 'Two Treatises,'" in *Discourse in Early Modern Britain*, Phillipson and Skinner (ed.), pp. 253–80 at 273n62.

tion of scholars who, whether from Straussite or Marxist assumptions, were emphatic about the prominence of an ideology the better to be provided with a whipping boy. By a tortuous form of logic—in which the victim seems complicitous—that would mean that Pocock's undisguised impatience with these schools must suggest a covert sympathy for their liberal opponents. The tone is not very different from that in which he proclaimed his liberalism in support of his independence.[32] This espousal of the comforts of liberal freedom follows the controversial book, so it can tell us nothing about the loyalties that inform the book itself. Thus far, then, one sees a resolve to confine discussion to the historical evidence without attributing to the author any political leaning in those historical patterns that he chose to examine. What, however, is the reader to make of several passages in the memorable retrospect of 1981 on the *Machiavellian Moment*? There is, for one thing, the passage where he states, almost primly, that the concern of the work was to deal with the perceptions about change on the part of past thinkers, not to endorse those perceptions. Yet the concluding sentences assert the fact that the book "forms part of the vision it aims to describe," an apparent admission of an attachment to the pattern of thought over which he had laboured so long. Not without the studied ambiguity apparent in other of his pronouncements, this does still seem to offer a degree of satisfaction. The comment comes in a paragraph in which Pocock also appears to have admitted a preference for seeing his period of British history in Whiggish rather than Jacobin terms, although neither expression had much figured in the battle to define eighteenth-century paradigms. Always jealous of enquiry about his own beliefs as opposed to his historical conclusions, he impishly adds the aside "if it matters." A commentator has read the paragraph as confessing a point of view but prudently added that it was done "elusively."[33]

But this apparent admission of some attachment to the tradition has not, as it happens, stilled all discussion of Pocock's ideological inclination. A very perceptive critic, noting Pocock's ready admission that the neo-Harringtonians were the home of a reactionary doctrine and one

---

32. Pocock, "*The Machiavellian Moment* Revisited: A Study in History and Ideology," *Journal of Modern History* 53 (1981): 69–71, and his "The Myth of John Locke and the Obsession with Liberalism," in *John Locke*, ed. Richard Ashcraft and Pocock (Los Angeles: Clark Library Publications, 1980), pp. 18–19.

33. Pocock, "*The Machiavellian Moment* Revisited," pp. 61, 72, and Don Herzog, "Some Questions for Republicans," *Political Theory* 14 (1986): 475.

that was "barren" in terms of its truculent mistrust of power, has concluded that the author of these words was "no partisan" of that republican tradition that he had done so much to unearth.[34] Yet the evidence is more mixed than this suggests. True, we are not all such Hegelians as to embrace those forces that command reality and there is every reason for the expositor of a position to admit its inadequacies, perhaps even to regret them. It is difficult to view Pocock as an apologist for republican institutions when he so readily cites Josiah Tucker's jibe that not only were slaveholders generally republicans but that the converse was true as well.[35] Never hesitant about making judgments, Pocock offers no objection to the charge. I have long thought that the elevated language and the rhetorical flights that abound in the *Machiavellian Moment* serve well to tell a story that is essentially tragic. Born of the noblest commitment to the public good, republics are historico-degradeable, to borrow a phrase from Kenneth Minogue. Virtue flies in the face of worldly greatness clad in diverse forms of corruption and, not surprisingly, given the uneven quality of the human materials with which it must work, it succumbs to the might represented by the prince, the standing army, the sinking fund and the civil list, places and pensions, commerce and luxury, the very development of 'culture' and, perhaps, just to sustain the high tone, we may add fortune and time itself to the ranks of the victors. Only in the debased arts does the hero triumph; the writers of high tragedy know better.

Not that Pocock has ever, to my knowledge, sought to lead the charge of those scholars who now offer us republican virtue as the latest variant on a long series of ways of tarting up the tired old language of liberal democracy and social conscience. It thus takes its place as the flavour that succeeds civil society and social capital, participant, public spirited and bowling, no doubt, by the legion. To this fashion Quentin Skinner has lent a name long associated with meticulous scholarship on the development of civic humanism and Philip Pettit has done the same in the furtherance of a normative enquiry that largely dispenses with an historical foundation. When confronted with the realities of the world, Skinner's

---

34. Zuckert, p. 170. Significantly, Appleby concluded just the opposite, but cautiously. See *Liberalism and Republicanism*, p. 133.

35. Pocock, *VCH*, p. 163, and Pocock, "Part II: Empire, Revolution and the End of Early Modernity," in *The Varieties of British Political Thought, 1500–1800*, ed. Pocock (Cambridge: Cambridge UP, 1993), p. 291.

undoubted sophistication can offer no more than the injunction to prefer the common good to our own selfish concerns, supported by the reminder that a society that does not prefer civic duty to individual rights
will doubtless find the rights themselves undermined.[36] Pettit's enthusiasm has been invested in the effort to sustain a firm distinction between
liberal views about liberty and those of what he takes to a republican
tradition.[37] If the debates sparked by Pocock's book establish anything, it
is surely the great difficulty of drawing firm distinctions between the
aims and the language of these two schools of modern applications. When,
moreover, we contemplate the sorts of objections that rise when the pro-
phet armed comes to solve the problems of our time, we doubtless gain
some intimation of why Pocock's account seemed so austerely confined
to ideology as it had functioned in the past. Amidst all of the dissent that
his history has endured, he has readily escaped the two major sorts of objection that a modern and morally committed republicanism readily
attracts.

One of these is a theme, not absent from the *Machiavellian Moment*,
that a civic humanism that proclaims the benefit of individual poverty
and rejects much of the ethos of a commercial society has turned its back
on the defining features of the modern world. Add to this the scope for
hypocrisy and rampant insincerity in a Country fixation on the common
good and a set of institutional imperatives that seems inconsistent with
the presence of competing political parties[38] — arguably, even in their
decline, the greatest invention of modern politics — and we are faced
with irrelevance in seemingly reactionary form. The skeptical heirs to liberal capitalism may even turn their attention to the equivalent of that
militia beloved of Machiavelli and the neo-Harringtonians. But it lacks
a rationale that is meaningful, save on the part of those who strive, un-
convincingly, to connect an armed citizenry with liberty. If the inspiration derived from earlier times seems to a critic such as Alan Ryan as ill
suited to our age, the second critique depicts it as literally dangerous, with

---

36. Skinner, "On Justice, the Common Good and the Priority of Liberty,"
in *Dimensions of Radical Democracy: Pluralism, Citizenship, Community*, ed. Chantal
Mouffe (London: Verso, 1992), p. 223.

37. Philip Pettit, *The Common Mind* (New York, 1993), pp. 318–19.

38. Alan Ryan, "Capitalism, Civic Virtue and Democracy," in *Virtue, Corruption
and Self-Interest in the Eighteenth Century: Political Values in the Eighteenth Century*, ed.
Richard K. Matthews (Bethlehem, PA: Lehigh UP, 1994), p. 152.

its communitarian emphasis on consensus and unity and its apparent un-interest in mechanisms for dealing with conflict.[39]

In proclaiming the importance of republican doctrine at a critical junc-ture of American history, Pocock did not incur a very friendly reception from many of the historians who were specialists on the newly independ-ent republic. That may seem counter-intuitive, but we must of course recall that it is rather a selective version of the republic that is presented in the *Machiavellian Moment.* Still less likely to be enthused with the theme are those of us who belong to parliamentary monarchies—with no tra-dition of rhetoric about republican virtue and no constitutional expe-rience sanctioning a musket (much less a flame-thrower) over the hearth. For us, the current fashion for applauding republican virtue must seem distinctly odd. Whether Pocock's ancestors were redcoats is for him to say; mine certainly were. Civic humanism smacks, for most of us, of the *quattrocento.* Of the connotations of the term republic, there is a little story about a meeting, in 1933, of the Rotary club of a town east of Montreal. The lunchtime speaker was a politician who talked up republican mores against the cronyism that Latins sometimes call *caciquismo.* Spying an Anglo-Saxon and retired military man, obviously glowering at mention of the republic, the speaker hastily assured this defender of king and coun-try that he meant only to endorse the goodness of the Latins' *res publica.*[40] Only in that guise can many of us, whose society was founded in some considerable measure in flight from republican institutions, embrace the relevant language. Whatever Pocock's reasons for being less than explic-it about his commitments, there is a very respectable case to be made for separating one's ideological preferences from that curiosity that moves us to try and find out, in historical terms, the fact of the matter. I still re-call my own impatience with the assumption that, in trying to explain individualistic vocabulary of the seventeenth century, I was in Macpher-son's camp, or that the intellectual challenge of making sense of Disraeli's correspondence signalled a quite different political disposition. I suspect that keeping history and moral ratification in different boxes may have been especially important for an historian who had set out to unscram-ble the different activities of the historian and the philosopher. On that note, let me turn my attention to the third head of Cerberus, that of meth-od. It has been a particularly growly one.

---

39. Hertzog, "Some Questions for Republicans," pp. 486–87.

40. Telesphore D. Bouchard, *Republicanisme contre caciquisme* (St. Hyacinthe, 1933), pp. 3–4.

Genuinely Historical Principles?

It seems reasonable to contend that some difficulties that reside in Pocock's reconstruction of political thought rest, in considerable measure,
on the effort to instantiate a particular method of doing the task. It seems
to be the case that a number of gifted scholars, most with some connection to Cambridge, decided that political thought had too often been badly done and that it would be their business to do it right for the flourishing of truth and the edification of us all. I cannot see that they have, in
the main, succeeded in teaching us a new skill and where the history that
has emerged is successful—as often it is and more—that is not attributable to any dramatically new mode of writing about ideas in time. So it
failed to save practitioners from misadventure and cannot, it seems,
take credit for their undeniable successes.

An effort to understand and improve scholarly attention to political
ideas was evident early in the second half of the twentieth century. John
Pocock's most substantial contribution of these years was an article that
regretted the tendency, by privileging abstract formulations, to turn the
writing of the relevant sort of history into philosophy. Characteristically
open to the many possibilities of inspiration, he showed himself ready to
welcome efforts to write about the philosophy of some past thinker, but
only when the language being used and its level of generality had been
sorted out. In a later, and less accommodating piece, Pocock cited the
confusion that had beset one Richard Aaron when he used philosophical analysis, bereft of sufficient knowledge of the historical circumstances,
to misunderstand what Locke had been about. Between these two statements about method, Quentin Skinner had offered his pronunciamento
on the subject and had already served up the same unhappy Aaron for
ritual sacrifice. Although Skinner's document was noteworthy for its sustained dispraise of his elders, Pocock's struck a more positive note but,
puzzlingly, cited some scholars whose work had made us aware of the
different languages in which political discourse had been conducted.[41]

---

41. Pocock, "The History of Political Thought: A Methodological Enquiry,"
in *Philosophy, Politics and Society*, ed. Peter Laslett and W. G. Runcimann, 2nd ser.
(Oxford: Oxford UP, 1962), pp. 187, 201–2; Skinner, "Meaning and Understanding
in the History of Ideas," *History and Theory* 8 (1969): 14; and Pocock, "Languages
and their Implications: The Transformation of the Study of Political Thought,"
in *PLT*, pp. 26–27.

There was no evidence, however, that most of these, save perhaps for his mentor Butterfield, had been devotees of his or Skinner's methods. An apparent difficulty in accepting how anyone could get it right from other than Cambridge premises has long been apparent and noted by others.[42] That sort of relation between substance and method is a continuing theme in my understanding of the Cambridge school.

By the time of these further thoughts on the state of the art, Pocock had appropriated Kuhn's notion of paradigm for purposes of handling the materials of political thought; it served as the container that separated them from extraneous languages. Alternatives that would have been possible, prior to the new methodological self-awareness, had become the marks of the unsophisticated. Neither the "history of ideas," which suggested the toil of A.O. Lovejoy, nor a preoccupation with texts—guilty of slighting linguistic context—could easily pass muster and even the ambition to write insouciantly of the thought of some figure might betray the presence of suspect tendencies. New princes of scholarship, aflame with the ambition to make everything new, can be a little tedious. Happily, it is scarcely in the nature of things for them to be able to realize their designs. In the case of Quentin Skinner, his stern teaching gave way to some excellent intellectual history, relatively free of those counsels of perfection that would have had us pursue the intention behind individual locutions or statements and would have barred us from trying to trace the morphology of an intellectual pattern over time.[43] His own intellectual history was released from the inhibitions directed at others, though he did tend to focus upon schools of thought and offered more by way of social context than had earlier students who had presented philosophical systems.

There is a dilemma that must often confront scholars who presume to tell others how to conduct their common business. They may, as did Skinner, retreat gracefully from the exposed position and replace precept by example. Such a manoeuvre may, of course, attract the not-always-

---

42. See H. Höpfl, "John Pocock's New History of Political Thought," *European Studies Review* 5 (1975): 205; John E. Toews, "Intellectual History after the Linguistic Turn: The Autonomy of Meaning and the Irreducibility of Experience," *American Historical Review* (1987): 893; and Peter Berkowitz, *Virtue and the Making of Liberalism* (Princeton: Princeton UP, 1999), p. 200n15.

43. See Gunn, "After Sabine, After Lovejoy: the Languages of Political Thought," in "Intellectual History: New Perspectives," *Journal of History and Politics*, special issue, 6 (1988–89): 30–31.

charitable observation that one fails to practise what one preached, or at least, not much. More likely to dwell in the public eye is the alternative of, perhaps, undertaking to deliver on one's programme but the resulting attention may also be malign. Pocock's original advice on method had been gentler, far less abrasive, than that of the younger scholar and his great book far more controversial in its substance than were Skinner's acclaimed volumes of 1978. It is not easy to say what relation the *Machiavellian Moment* bore to the earlier teaching, though in no obvious sense could it be said to have set it aside. Reviews of the book were often quite critical of its argument and sensed there an undeclared structuralism, but said little of the rules of the game as set out in previous publications. Whereas Skinner followed up the famous article with a flurry of refinements, spanning the next five years or so, Pocock produced his complex argument on republicanism and then subsequently took to fiddling with his understanding of method. The process was continuing, in lively fashion, as late as 1987, though it is less evident since that time. What the fiddling amounted to was to express concern about the aptness of certain notions that Pocock had allowed to govern his historical reconstruction. Most prominent here was the fashionable concept of the paradigm, useful perhaps for the history of science but the impact that Kuhn's term had on the world of scholarship, along with the mocking tribute in one British publication—"brother, can you paradigm?" It took some time for Pocock's enthusiasm for paradigms, amply recorded in *Politics, Language, and Time*, to wane. Certainly it figured in the *Machiavellian Moment* where patterns of ideas are sometimes called paradigms, sometimes other things. Six years after the publication, he was ruefully admitting that the use of paradigms had been a mixed blessing though he continued to see value in some applications.[44] It continued, then, to serve as the banner that flew over the Cambridge camp in a publication of 1983 entitled "Cambridge Paradigms and Scotch Philosophers." Interestingly, the paradigm, wielded on the whole by arms other than Pocock's, did not work very well for purposes of conquering North Britain for civic humanism. When Boucher, two years later, published his respectful but critical account of Pocock's method,[45] he had little reason to assume that the paradigm was no longer central to it.

---

44. Pocock, "The Reconstruction of Discourse: Towards the Historiography of Political Thought," *Modern Language Notes* 96 (1981): 964.

45. David Boucher, *Texts in Context: Revisionist Methods for Studying the History of Ideas* (Dordrecht: M. Nijhoff, 1985), ch. 4.

A sort of recantation came in 1987 with the allowance, surely a monument to understatement, that the paradigm had proven an "uneconomic term" and inapt for recording political discourse. The same essay admitted the degree to which that discourse was "typically polyglot,"[46] which in the context can only have meant that recourse to the expectation that one was dealing with paradigms was likely to lead to imperfect intellectual tellectual history and had done so. With the disavowal of the paradigm as a helpful tool in reconstruction, the term "tradition," which had figured in the subtitle of the *Machiavellian Moment,* also fell out of favour, for it turned out that these too were units that were given to disaggregation under the stress of real-world political argument. This noun, in company with the corresponding adjective, faced its comeuppance with the casual observation that it served ill for purposes other than simple transmissions of discourse and that nothing was to be gained by its retention.[47] Now it was no accident that these changes in emphasis and conceptual vocabulary accompanied a complex process of retreat and the emergence of some degree of syncretism in the business of defining Locke's place in eighteenth-century political language on both sides of the Atlantic. It is undoubtedly true that Pocock withdrew, albeit slowly and reluctantly, from the exposed position that had allowed Locke a less than marginal place in the Country-party language that he had seen as central to political thought in the Thirteen Colonies.[48] There, surely, he was wrong, the victim not so much of his own sure touch as of a too-trusting reliance on evidence assembled by others. That is not to say, as some have, that Pocock had ever been wholly incautious in denying Locke's importance to several controversies. Typically, he said that the role previously assigned to Locke had been an excessive one and that, pending further inquiry, that role should be considerably reduced. I have already documented misreadings of his position on the part of several scholars who differed with his views. After the weight of evidence by some time in the 1980s dictated revision of Pocock's strong stand,

---

46. Pocock, "The Concept of Language and the *métier d'historien.*Some Considerations on Practice," in *The Languages of Political Theory in Early-Modern Europe,* ed. Anthony Pagden (Cambridge: Cambridge UP, 1987), p. 21.

47. Pocock, "Modernity and Anti-Modernity in the Anglophone Political Tradition," in *Patterns of Modernity,* ed. S. N. Eisenstadt (New York: New York UP, 1987), 1:45–46.

48. Pocock, "The Book Most Misunderstood since the Bible: John Adams and the Confusion about Aristocracy, in *Fra Toscana e Stati Uniti: il Discorso politico nell' Etá della Constituzione Americana* (Florence: Leo S. Olschki, 1989), pp. 196–201.

he has continued to call for further research the better to map Locke's place.[49]

My point in recalling these matters—both of substantive historical interpretation and of changing vocabulary of method—is that the two are part and parcel of a single process. The truth is that the Cambridge people sent the writers of the history of political thought to school to learn their lessons and the lessons to be learned are still uncertain. Paradigms and traditions both proved more porous than had been expected and both came to be discarded in the protracted controversies that continued a good fifteen years after the publication of the *Machiavellian Moment*. The favoured replacement—apart from language, which had long been in the picture—was "discourse," a terms that came to be distanced—though perhaps not enough—from its trendy continental connotations.[50] Given his penchant for borrowed theory, Pocock has consorted with some of those views that contemplate the death of the author as significant agent, now replaced by discourse or language. What difference, some of us have asked, what one calls the object of attention, for does the proof of the pudding not lie in the rightness or wrongness of the historical judgments that are made? The best answer to this lingering concern that I can find comes when Pocock repeats the view that "the history of an idea" might not be the sort of entity that could be traced down "through the ages" but that "linguistic structures" which were "communicable social practices" could be so treated.[51] Here at last is an answer to my puzzlement born with Skinner's ukase against the pursuit of ideas over time. Pocock had never, seemingly, denied that some sort of intellectual tuff might be so pursued, but it mattered a lot how the stuff was

---

49. On the retreat of the republican interpretation, see Rodgers, "Republicanism," pp. 35–38; on Locke's place, see Pocock, "Negative and Positive Aspects of Locke's Place in Eighteenth-Century Discourse," in *John Locke und Immanuel Kant: historische Rezepione und gegenwärtige Relevanz*, ed. Martyn P. Thompson (Berlin: Duncker & Humblot, 1991), p. 60, and his "The Problem of Political Thought in the Eighteenth Century: Patriotism and Politeness," *Theoritische Gescheidenis* 9 (1982): 9.

50. Pocock, "Modernity and Anti-Modernity," p. 44, and Introduction to *Varieties of British Political Thought*, Pocock (ed.), p. 1. For evidence of a move in the direction of literary theory, see Pocock, "Texts as Events: Reflections on the History of Political Thought," in *Politics of Discourse: The Literature and History of Seventeenth-Century England* (Berkeley and Los Angeles, U of CA P, 1987), pp. 21–34.

51. Pocock, "Between Gog and Magog: The Republican Thesis and *Ideologica Americana*," *Journal of the History of Ideas* 48 (1987): 33.

packaged. In place of those individual locutions and intentions that had been of concern to Skinner, Pocock had always written in more holistic terms of languages or discourse that might themselves be treated as a sort of agent, speaking through people. An individual's intentions were to be subordinated then to the modes of speech supposedly available. That seems a pity, for I'd always hoped that the quick fix of fashionable theory would be left for those who lacked Pocock's superb command of hardwon substance. I share then the sense of loss of Michael Zuckert who complained of the lack of human content in a vision of "colorless and odorless 'paradigms,'" coupling and decoupling silently in the night.[52] Before Pocock had made his best-known statement that pointed in this direction, Skinner had already sounded the alarm in relation to this sort of scheme when he suggested that one might thereby mistakenly as-similate a writer to "a completely alien political tradition." With all the chummy chat about the Cambridge school, it is too little appreciated how diverse their individual methods can be.[53] It is also true, however, that Skinner's recent efforts to distinguish between liberal and republican tra-ditions encounter some of the same problems as did Pocock on an ear-lier and similar venture.[54]

It had long been said in some quarters that neither Pocock nor Skin-ner was offering an operational method and to this opinion Charles Tarl-ton had added that John Pocock was misleading in his recurrent claim that the linguistic paradigms that have existed limit our means of say-ing things.[55] Still less, I would insist, was it persuasive to say, as Pocock did in 1972, that "men cannot do what they have no means of saying they have done." Whatever became of unintended consequences? By 1987, this claim seems to have given way to the cheerful admission that authors don't have to know what they are doing, and this is part of the replacement of the author and intention by discourse. All these claims raise ontologi-cal issues that deserve closer scrutiny than I can offer here. What seems certain, however, is that reliance on paradigms, or discourse if you will,

---

52. Zuckert, p. 175.

53. Pocock, *VCH*, pp. 4–5, and Skinner, "Some Problems in the Analysis of Political Thought and Action" (1974), in *Text and Context: Quentin Skinner and his Critics* (Cambridge, 1988), p. 106. On the divergence here, see Mark Bevir, "The Errors of Linguistic Contextualism," *History and Theory* 31 (1992): 277–78.

54. See my review of Skinner's *Renaissance Virtues* in *Philosophy in Review* 24 (2004): 293–96.

55. Tarlton, "Historicity, Meaning and Revisionism in the Study of Political Thought," *History and Theory* 12 (1973): 312, 317.

betrayed Pocock's ambitious reconstruction at a number of points and that Skinner's professed concern for individual intention might have been a better guide. The problem was not, as some had wrongly argued, that Pocock had tried to banish all paradigms but one. Rather, it was that thinkers such as Harrington, Sidney and 'Cato' spoke more than one political language and so the effort to reveal a particular political tradition was fraught with difficulties. It might work with distinction, as when Pocock unerringly found the echo of Harrington in a speech of 1675 by Shaftesbury; too often, it worked less well.

Watching fascinated if not always convinced, as Pocock sought both to argue a particular historical case and to set the standards for such performances, some of us have learned a great deal and are properly grateful. Nor is it any rebuff to the grandeur of the scheme if, sometimes, we are inclined to say, with M. Jourdain, that all along we had been trying to speak prose. One can do good intellectual history even when in the grip of the impression that one is studying ideas, just as a disavowal of that focus cannot guarantee success. That does not mean that the lessons were unwelcome, especially when Pocock has always presented himself, in that search for genuinely historical principles, as committed to discovering a truth and showing it. In a world where so many thinkers have disavowed truth itself, either of coherence or correspondence, arguing still with Pocock is not the worst of fates. Reading him always forces his readers to think hard about what they believe. I'm led to recall the advice of Hilaire Belloc about relations with another figure of authority: "And always keep ahold of nurse / For fear of finding something worse."

5. Topical Satire Read back into Pocock's Neo-Harringtonian Moment

D.N. DELUNA

> What is a King unless he have Power to
> Reward and Punish?
> *The Case of Forfeitures in Ireland Fairly
> Stated*...(1700)

J.G.A. Pocock's *The Machiavellian Moment* (1975) offered a fable for the times. Pocock has himself hinted that it should be understood in the context in which it was written, namely, that of political unrest in the High Sixties. His *Politics, Language, & Time* (1971)—featuring essays that formed the germ of this capstone book on civic humanism—concludes revealingly with his "On the Non-Revolutionary Character of Paradigms," in which that era's anti-Establishmentarians are exhorted to conduct their political activism in a mode polemically civil and hence non-revolutionary. What is now needed, Pocock declares, is not more zeal to usher in the Aquarian Age, but rather conformity to civilized norms of protest within "a theory of romantic politics which passes beyond revolution into polity" (*PLT*, p. 289). In this volume's second edition, Pocock in a new preface recalls having produced his writings on civic humanism under these disturbing circumstances:

There were Red Guards in those days, real as well as theoretical; and if it was one's business to conduct the academic polity and its civility, Weatherman might not be worse than the Ohio National Guard but was more often on one's doorstep, pressing demands which more obviously arose from within one's own values and perverted them. (*PLT*, p. xi)

I am grateful to Perry Anderson, Leon Guilhamet, and Ronald Paulson for their comments on earlier versions of this essay.

He also remembers having responded to the situation with the gnomic retort that "politics and language need time and history in which to make and to know what they have made, while and before they set about changing it" (*PLT*, p. xi). In this perhaps imaginary recollection of an exchange, Pocock cryptically puts counter-demands to Weatherman: one, invest in reading my scholarship on civic humanism (*you* need time and history), and, two, confront in it the force of my pointed aphoristic statement fleshed into parable.

Indeed, Pocock in the *Machiavellian Moment* indulges an analogical bent of mind to tell the story of a group of utopian thinkers that critiqued our modern military-fiscal state. In his narrative, bipartisan "Country" neo-Harringtonians came together in England in the 1690s to denounce it. Historically obsessed and given to view this complex as a decline from government by native militias and citizen councils, these utopians attacked its supposed infrastructure of parliaments under executive control. They accordingly cherished a Machiavellian ideal of virile republican service to the military and senate, and they shared James Harrington's sense of ills wrought by monarchies in crisis, ever desperately propped by janissaries and courtiers. Their leading spokesmen were rhetorically engaged "coffeehouse intellectuals," notably the Tory Charles Davenant and the Whig John Toland (*PLT*, p. 138). A remarkable result of this protest movement was, in Pocock's view, the production of a shrewd diagnosis of the constitutional vulnerabilities of modern oligarchy, defined as an elitist state power-structure that can readily exploit the ideological deadweight of greedy war financiers and dishonest bureaucrats.

Thus a didactic mirror for Sixties' radicals, Pocock's civic humanist movement in 1690s England is, however, the stuff of historical fiction. In this essay I expose it as false myth. When the phenomenon of Country Party politics in the reign of William III is recovered in its immediately contemporary character, no neo-Harringtonian coalition comes into view, of "the first intellectuals of the Left," who "denounced as beings below the level of the political animal" "the rentier, the officer and the bureaucrat...intruded into government where they could only have a corrupting effect" (*MM*, p. 477; *PLT*, pp. 93–94).[1] It even happens that the

---

1. Pocock is more responsible than any other modern historian for the uncontrolled meaning that continues to bedevil our use of the party-label 'Country' in scholarly work on seventeenth- and eighteenth-century English politics, notwithstanding some corrective adjustments by David Hayton and Jonathan Clark: see, e.g., Hayton, "The 'Country' Interest and the Party System, 1689–*c.*1720," in

historical Country Party movement bears no strong analogical resemblance to anti-Establishmentarianism of the late 1960s and early 1970s. Country partisans would have been branded by Countercultural radicals as racists and sexual puritans. Nor do the rhetorical maneuvers of the Party's leading writers fit Pocock's description of their normative orientation in polemic civility. Rather, these propagandists indulged a penchant, so very familiar to the day's readers of political editorial journalism, for the subtle obliquities and grotesque imagery of satire.[3]

My account of the historical Country Party differs from Pocock's didactic narrative by attending to the detailed particulars of the controversy over royal grants it raised, scrutiny of which, I submit, will compli-

---

in *Party and Management in Parliament, 1660–1784,* ed. Clyve Jones (Leicester: Leicester UP, 1984), pp. 37–85; his "Sir Richard Cocks: The Political Anatomy of a Country Whig," *Albion* 20 (1988): 221–46; his "Moral Reform and Country Politics in the Late Seventeenth-Century House of Commons," *Past & Present* 128 (1990): 48–91; his introduction to *The House of Commons, 1690–1715,* ed. Eveline Cruickshanks, Stuart Handley, and David Hayton, History of Parliament ser. (Cambridge: Cambridge UP for The History of Parliament Trust, 2002), 1:489–99; hereafter *Parliament Trust Commons, 1690–1715;* and Clark, "A General Theory of Party, Opposition and Government, 1688–1832," *The Historical Journal* 23 (1980): 295–326; his "The Decline of Party, 1740–1760," *English Historical Review* 93 (1978): 508–9; his *Revolution and Rebellion: State and Society in England in the Seventeenth and Eighteenth Centuries* (Cambridge: Cambridge UP, 1986), pp. 111–55; and consult his *Samuel Johnson: Literature, Religion and English Cultural Politics from the Restoration to Romanticism* (Cambridge: Cambridge UP, 1994), pp. 152–53. Pocock, in one essay, even lures readers into hermetically sealing off his own use of the label in his writings on civic humanism: "[T]he commonwealth and country ideologies," he asserts, "[are] more or less[,] synonymous terms" for the "rediscovery of neo-Harringtonianism," "a language of thought and debate which occupied minds from the late seventeenth century to the end of the eighteenth," "[a] language of debate [that] offers keys to a great deal that was going on in the social and political theory of the period"("The Myth of John Locke and the Obsession with Liberalism," in *John Locke Papers Read at a Clark Library Seminar 10 December 1977* (Los Angeles: William Andrews Clark Memorial Library Publications, 1980), pp. 11, 13).

2. I do not mean to suggest that these are necessary traits of satire in general. They are, rather, familiar components of both the period's journalistic political satire and of this particular polemic corpus of texts, a corpus whose satiric identity corresponds to Edward Rosenheim Jr.'s well-known definition of satire as "*an attack by means of a manifest fiction upon discernible historic particulars*" (*Swift and the Satirist's Art* [Chicago: U of Chicago P, 1963], p. 31).

cate his and others' discussions of early modern English constitutionalism by contributing to due study of the struggles over state patronal
power—thus adding to work hitherto focused on the growth of parliamentary legislative sovereignty. As we will see, the Country Party was
organized in England's postwar years (1698–1701) as a movement aimed
at legislative and judicial redress of King William's alleged abuse of his
prerogative of Crown patronage. Defined by this project, the Party drew
in Whigs and Tories. To those in its ranks, the royal patronage miscon-
duct was most powerfully attested by the titles and honors William be-
stowed on fellow Dutch foreigners and supposedly on illicit sexual objects. While Country propagandists set forth the charge of abuse in numerous satiric publications, the Party's MPs proposed and won measures
for revoking various grants of military office and landed estates doled out
by William. Such an invasion of the King's prerogative—by which Country partisans carried out an experiment in divided patronal sovereignty
—provoked alarmed responses from royalist Williamites. These included satiric tracts by Jonathan Swift and Daniel Defoe, in which the
epithet 'parliamentary tyranny' was directed at allegedly corrupt Country MPs, and wherein these authors expressed royalist constitutional
thought that turned paradigmatic upon arrival.

In documenting my account of the Country movement, I rely heavily on interpretive procedures that, by virtue of their alertness to habits
of verbal duplicity in contemporary satiric political propaganda, pose
methodological challenges to Pocock's 'linguistic' hermeneutic. These
challenges can be enumerated as cautionary reflections. First, my account
affords a notable example of how the Pocockian project of an archaeol-
ogy of political languages can lead historians to misconstrue documents
if pursued as a methodology in itself. As Quentin Skinner has put it, "There
is an obvious danger that if we merely focus on the relations between
the vocabulary used by a given writer and the traditions to which he may
appear connected by his use of this vocabulary, we may become insen-
sitive to instances of irony, obliquity, and other cases in which the writer
may seem to be saying something other than what he means."[3] In the
case of the Country assault on William, we have an instance of Pocock's
failure, through inadvertence to verbal cunning, to detect partisan satiric
attack in an entire corpus of texts—which include Charles Davenant's

---

3. Quentin Skinner, "Some Problems in the Analysis of Political Thought
and Action" (1974), in *Meaning and Context: Quentin Skinner and his Critics*, ed. James
Tully (Princeton: Princeton UP, 1988), p. 106.

An Essay upon Grants and Resumptions (1699), Dr. Robert Brady's *A Continuation of the Complete History of England* (1699), and editor John Toland's *The Oceana of James Harrington, and his Other Works* (1700)—works whose absorbed participation in the Grants Controversy he therefore fails to recognize.

Second, such insensitivity to key hermeneutic circles of satiric modality and immediate polemic context is also risked by Pocock's doctrine of the methodological autonomy of academic disciplines. In his influential essay "Languages and Their Implications," Pocock states that to emancipate the history of political thought from philosophical appropriation is to convert it into a history of "linguistic use and sophistication" which, however, is not to be accomplished by literary scholars. For, "the techniques which critics and students of literary expression employ to uncover the full wealth of association, implication and resonance, the many levels of meaning, which a living language contains when used by those who are masters of its powers of expression," finally belong to "an altogether a-historical discipline," "[which] schools of 'new criticism' insist that theirs is and must be" (*PLT*, pp. 12–13). Pocock here confuses the disciplinary skills of technique and of application. And surprisingly, he makes no mention of the pioneering New Critical *and* historical work of Earl Wasserman, his near-colleague in humanities at Johns Hopkins, whose techniques of close reading that recovered contemporary political meaning in seventeenth- and early eighteenth-century English poetry were later plied by Michael McKeon and Steven N. Zwicker in booklength studies of the political poetry of John Dryden.[4] Pocock in his "Texts as Events"—a companion-essay to "Languages and Their Implications," in *Politics of Discourse* (1989) edited by Kevin Sharpe and Steven Zwicker—again lumps literary scholars together with philosophers as ahistorical appropriators of texts. "It should be obvious by now," Pocock remarks toward the close of this essay, "that the actions of philosophers and New Critics are wholly legitimate, that the actions of historians are wholly legitimate…[I] quarrel with nonhistorians only when the latter are stupid enough to deny the legitimacy of what we are doing or think

---

4. I refer to: Earl Wasserman's political readings of poems by John Denham, John Dryden, and Alexander Pope in *The Subtler Language: Critical Readings of Neoclassic and Romantic Poems* (Baltimore: Johns Hopkins UP, 1959), chs. 2–4; Michael McKeon, *Politics and Poetry in Restoration England: The Case of Dryden's "Annus Mirabilis"* (Cambridge, MA: Harvard UP, 1975); Steven N. Zwicker, *Politics and Language in Dryden's Poetry: The Arts of Disguise* (Princeton: Princeton UP, 1984).

we are denying the legitimacy of what they are doing."[5] What Pocock denies is historical method to any and all literary scholars, even in this volume devoted to the interdisciplinary enterprise of repatriating classics of seventeenth-century English literature into the age's common culture of polemic political discourse.

Third, my account of the historical Country Party movement furnishes an example of how Pocock's work of excavating political languages can result in the scholarly failing of insufficient analytic distance if practiced on texts of polemic satire which are not however recognized as such. The risk is that of unwittingly ventriloquizing a satirist's fictions and tropes, such as hu gloomy or shocking exaggerations or hu self-proclaimed role of ethical hero. Pocock, in describing Country discourse as motivated by apprehensions of modern oligarchy, in fact seizes on satiric hyperbole unawares. As if taking up the Country Party's cause out of vicarious interest, he re-rehearses its satirists' work of inflating the petty putative scandal of William's grants into the fictive scenario of a tyrant divvying the nation among hu cronies. This scenario was popularized by the Country writer John Tutchin, who in his verse-pamphlet on the Grants Controversy, *The Foreigners* (1700), lamented that, as a result of William's patronage abuse, "The State declines by Avarice and Pride; / Like Beasts of Prey they ravage all the Land, / Acquire Preferments, and usurp Command."[6] It is only by emptying this hyperbole of its particularized satiric meaning that Pocock is able to make it recount "the neo-Harringtonian version of English history," claiming it for the 'language' of civic humanism, that "staple of English political rhetoric" and "paradigm of virtue" (*MM*, pp. 147, 525; *VCH*, p. 107).

I

The reign of William and Mary was widely regarded by those who welcomed it as a godly Protestant settlement announced by the Providential wonder of regal apposite opposites paired—religious warrior and pious wife. While William pursued Allied victories against Catholic France

---

5. Pocock, "Texts as Events: Reflections on the History of Political Thought," in *Politics of Discourse: The Literature and History of Seventeenth-Century England*, ed. Kevin Sharpe and Steven N. Zwicker (Berkeley and Los Angeles: U of CA P, 1987), p. 32.

6. John Tutchin, *The Foreigners* (1700), p. 5.

in what would stretch on to be the Nine Years War (1689–97), Mary acted as a figurehead of the Latitudinarian campaign for moral reform, whose chief theological exponent was Archbishop John Tillotson, her close advisor.[7] However, by 1693 substantial numbers of rural gentry had become tax-weary of the war, and Mary's death in 1694 left a vacuum in Crown sponsorship of the reform effort. Consequently, after mid-decade the charmed spell cast by the sovereigns' concomitant European military interventionism and domestic religious crusade was broken.[8]

Just after the war's conclusion, finalized by the Treaty of Ryswick in September 1697, William attempted to remake his public image, with the unexpected result of providing a handle by which emergent Country partisan MPs sought to legitimize parliamentary monitoring of his patronage conduct. In a speech delivered in Parliament in December, William announced two Crown agendas, both of which would downplay his war-fevered image. One was postwar correction of administrative financial corruption, which would place him in the role of national husbandman. The other was the discouragement of vicious manners, by which he would assume Mary's late reformist role. He stated, "I esteem it one of the greatest Advantages of the Peace, that I shall now have Leisure to rectify such Corruptions, or Abuses, as may have crept into any Part of the Administration during the War; and effectually to discourage Profaneness and Immorality." In February, the Commons urged that he merge these agendas by assuming the role of a good patron. In an Address commend-

---

7. On this contemporary perception of William and Mary, and its propagation by court publicists such as Bishop Gilbert Burnet, consult Tony Claydon, *William III and the Godly Revolution* (Cambridge: Cambridge UP, 1996), chs. 2, 3, 5, and Craig Rose, *England in the 1690s: Revolution, Religion and War* (Oxford: Blackwell, 1999), pp. 19–28, 41–42, 203–5. On contemporary visual and literary iconography expressing this providentialist view of the sovereigns, consult Earl Miner, introduction to *Poems on the Reign of William III*, Augustan Reprints, no. 166 (Los Angeles: William Andrews Clark Memorial Library Publications, 1974), pp. ii–vii; Lois G. Schwoerer, "The Queen as Regent and Patron," in *The Age of William III & Mary II: Power, Politics and Patronage, 1688–1702*, ed. Robert Maccubbin and Martha Hamilton-Phillips (Williamsburg: The College of William and Mary Publications, 1989), pp. 217–24; Claydon, *William III and the Godly Revolution*, pp. 72–73.

8. The late providentialist view of the dual monarchs was nevertheless remounted in 1697 in these tomes: Sir Richard Blackmore's *King Arthur*, the second edition of Samuel Wesley's *The Life of Our Blessed Lord & Saviour Jesus Christ*, and the Reverend William Turner's *A Compleat History of the Most Remarkable Providences*.

ing moral reform, it was proposed that,

Since the Examples of Men in high and publick Stations have a powerful
Influence upon the Lives of others, we do humbly beseech your Majesty, that
all Vice, Profaneness, and Irreligion, may, in a particular manner, be discouraged in all those who have the Honour to be employed near your Royal Person; and in all others, who are in your Majesty's Service, by Sea and Land...
And that your Majesty would upon all Occasions, distinguish Men of Piety
and Virtue by Marks of your Royal Favour.[9]

This recommendation was a gesture of bad faith, as many attending
Commoners would have been quick to glean. Its true purport was to dis-
miss William's new project of public self-fashioning as an impossibility
given his patronage track-record. Since the early 1690s, adversarial Commoners who served on the Commission of Public Accounts had made
careers playing the part of state husbandmen themselves, by conducting
cynical probes into suspected abuses of wartime expenditure. This
squadron of Commissioners—the first post-Revolutionary politicians to
label themselves "Country" patriots—included the Tories Christopher
Musgrave and Thomas Clarges and the Whigs Robert Harley and Paul
Foley. They wielded anti-court rhetoric of managerial counsel while
performing as inquestors into the possible maladministration of Crown
financial resources, such as William's grants of office and title to Dutch
soldiers.[10]
     At mid-decade, their rhetoric and cause were taken up by the so-called
"Cambrio-Britons" in the Commons, who sought on moralistic grounds
the revocation of William's Welsh land-grant to his Dutch favorite Hans
Willem Bentinck, Earl of Portland. In December 1695, the Tory MP
Robert Price[11] delivered an inflammatory speech in the lower House
moving that William revoke this bounty. In his oration—which was calculated to stir feelings of resentment over the King's alleged nativist
nepotism and his homosexual bias in conferring the grant—Price portrayed William as being, so far from the good national husbandman and
moral exemplar, a Dutch alien who had squandered the nation's tax eq-
uity on his sodomitical consort Portland.

---

    9. *CJ*, 12:1–2, 103.
    10. On these "Country" colleagues of the Commission of Public Accounts,
see J. A. Downie, "The Commission of Public Accounts and the Formation of
the Country Party," *English Historical Review* 91 (1976): 33–51, and consult Claydon, *William III and the Godly Revolution*, pp. 195–209.

A simulated version of Price's speech later appeared in print, entitled *Gloria Cambriae* (1702). In this tract, a satiric 'Price'[11] decries William's grant to Portland as an overlavish gift that, if not recised, must bring the nation to economic ruin. He ultimately holds that this patronage transaction among Dutchmen — about which he quips, "this Great Man makes us little" (referring ambivalently to William as well as Portland)[12] — has so financially impoverished the nation as to have compromised it to Dutch interests. His peroration raises the spectre of England's colonial enslavement by its commercial enemy the United Provinces, a scenario he suggests is rendered almost inevitable by the coinciding circumstances of the nation's economic downfall and William and Portland's ascendancy of power. He asks rhetorically, "If these Strangers...should be of a different Interest, as most plainly they are in point of Trade; To which Interest is it to be supposed these great Foreign Councils would adhere?" "So that I see," he continues, "when we are reduc'd to extream Poverty, as now we are very near it, we shall be supplanted by our Neighbours, and become a Collony to the *Dutch*" (p. 6).

'Price' concludes by enjoining, "[C]onsider we are *English* men, and must like Patriarchs, stand by our Country, and not suffer it to be Tributary to Strangers" (p. 6).[13] In context, this exhortation not only bristles with misoxenous sentiment but contains sexual innuendo directed at William. Earlier in the speech, patriarchal Cambrio-Brits are pitted against the "Strangers" William and Portland, and William is refused the customary royalist epithet of national father (e.g., "Far be it from me to think or speak any thing in Derogation of His Majesty's Honour or Care for Us; It cannot be expected He should know our laws, who is a Stranger to Us, and we to Him" ([p. 4]). And these insults retroactively pack a familiar homosexual slur against William (already a staple of Jacobite satire[14]), which is initially activated when Portland's grant is explained

---

12. My candidate for the true author of this tract is Charles Davenant.

11. *Gloria Cambriae; Or the Speech of a Bold Briton in Parliament, Against a Dutch Prince of Wales* (1702), p. 6. Further references to this pamphlet appear parenthetically in my text.

13. The 1702 text reads "Stranges."

14. For example, *Suum Quique* (1689), in vol. 5 ("1688–1697") of *Poems on Affairs of State: Augustan Satirical Verse, 1660–1714*, ed. William James Cameron (New Haven: Yale UP, 1971), pp. 121–22; John Dryden, 'trans.,' "The Third Satyr of Juvenal," in *The Satires of Decimus Junius Juvenalis* (1693); John Sergeant, *An Historical Romance of the Wars, between the Mighty Giant Gallieno, and the Great Knight Na-*

as a case of a king "being clothed with frail Nature, and apt to yield to the Importunities of their Favorites and Flatterers" (p. 5). In a subsequent historical portion of the oration, ancestral Britons in Edward II's reign are praised for having divested of royal bounty and banished the foreign *and* ho-mosexual "Lineage of *Gaveston* and his *Gascoiners*" (p. 5). 'Price' goes on to declare that ancestral patriots upheld the heroic principle "that *England* was able to Foster none but her own Children," thereby hinting that William's paternalistic love reaches only to Dutchmen, if not only to Dutch children of his sodomitical lust like Portland (p. 6).

The Country Party was born in the wake of Price's original speech. Its simulation's endorsement of patriarchal ancestral Britons' misoxenous and anti-licentious deprivation of Edward II's favored "Lineage of *Gaveston* and his *Gascoiners*" imaginatively compassed (or summed up in retrospect) what would become the Party's programmatic effort to rectify William's alleged pattern of royal patronage abuse by legislative and judicial means.[15] Meanwhile, the motion Price advanced, calling for an Address that would urge the King to revoke Portland's grant, passed unanimously. In January 1696, William responded: "I should not have given him these lands, if I had imagined the house of commons could have been concerned; I will therefore recall the Grant, and find some other way of shewing my favour to him."[16] Laced into this response of submission was William's rebuke to the Commons, admonishing them against meddling in his patronage affairs ("if I had imagined the house of commons could have been concerned"; "I will…find some other way of shewing my favour to him"), which, nonetheless, was disguised in an interjection that, by one construction, does not *not* concede the legitimacy of their interference ("*if* I had imagined…"). This equivocation can be seen to presage the constitutional conflict that, in the Grants Controversy, would engage the polemic energies of Country theorists of parliamentary patronal sover-

---

sonius, and his Associates ("Dublin," 1694). Consult also Paul Hammond, *Figuring Sex between Men from Shakespeare to Rochester* (Oxford: Clarendon, 2002), pp. 171–83.

15. I concur with Craig Rose's statement that the "Country" Accounts Commissioners did not comprise a distinct Country Party — "[A] Commission of Accounts does not a party make" (*England in the 1690s*, p. 282 [n. 109]). And I would add that neither was a 'Country moment' fully identical with the emergence of the Cambrio-Brit politicians, since for one thing the Party came to be defined by an agenda which was more sweeping than the particular matter of revoking Portland's Welsh grant.

16. *The Parliamentary History of England…*, ed. William Cobbett and T. C. Hansard, 36 vols. (1806–20), 5:986; hereafter *Cobbett's Parliamentary History.*

eignty and of Williamites who, alarmed by Country MPs' work of running interference with the Crown's exercise of patronage, diagnosed that, because this prerogative right was an attribute of sole regal authority beyond which there was no appeal, the Party's program constituted a dangerous experiment in divided patronal sovereignty.

The Country Party was launched as an organized movement in 1698. Its assault on William as a royal patron was pursued by legislative means in his 4th Parliament (1698–1700). Just earlier, during the General Election of July and August 1698, its canvassers bandied the slogan "No Courtiers" and placarded the badge "New Country Party." "A strange spirit of distinguishing between the Court and Country party visibly discovers itself in several elections," Secretary James Vernon noted about the event. Portland later recalled, "New Country party so-called" rallied against "the Courtiers so-called."[17] Ensuing parliamentary sessions extending through William's 5th Parliament (1701) saw the Party's sponsorship of four major initiatives:

1) Into the Disbanding Bill of 1699, which reprised recent Commons resolutions for the reduction of peacetime land forces, Country partisans intruded the stipulation that the retained army in England be limited to natural-born subjects, William's elite Blue Guards not excepted.[18] When William addressed both Houses to beg permission to keep this special

---

17. On the contest between "New Country" and "Courtier" during the Election, see Henry Horwitz, *Parliament, Policy and Politics in the Reign of William III* (Newark: U of Delaware P, 1977), pp. 237–39. *Letters Illustrative of the Reign of William III from 1696 to 1708 Addressed to the Duke of Shrewsbury, by James Vernon, Esq.*, ed. G. P. R. James (1841), and *HMC Portland*, 8:54—quoted in Horwitz, p. 238.

18. The Whig parliamentary diarist William Cowper thought of this stipulation as a new disbanding measure within the Bill: "Nota, this day ['17 December']...they ['the House'] agreed to the resolution of the committee of the day before, and gave an instruction to the persons who were appointed to bring in the bill, to insert a clause for the disbanding of all foreigners; and so likewise this day, in relation to the Irish forces, the committee came to a resolution that all should be disbanded but natural born subjects to the King of England" ("Debates in the House of Commons, 1697–1699," ed. David Hayton, in *Camden Miscellany, Vol. 29*, Camden 4th ser., vol. 34 (London: Royal Historical Society Publications, 1987), p. 367. Support for the Bill's provisions for reducing the standing armed forces was bipartisan but not Country, drawn largely from the ranks of Whig libertarians and Tory blue-water boys. On its Whig support, see Quentin Skinner, "Augustan Party Politics and Renaissance Constitutional Thought (1974)," in *Visions of Politics* (Cambridge: Cambridge UP, 2002), 3:356–62, pp. 360–61 esp.

Dutch regiment, his plea was rejected in the Commons with the explanation that he had been given the opportunity to contribute to the nation's happiness by "intrusting Your Sacred Person to Your own Subjects, who have so eminently signalized themselves, on all Occasions, during the late long and expensive War."[19] This explanation was an infradig, since it alluded to the Dutch stock of his Guards and more generally to the prominent Dutch, French Huguenot, and German composition of his military officers, while suggesting that such privileged employments had been denied to worthy 'born' Englishmen. And it was a tacit prescription, warning William away from non-nativist military patronage in the future.

2) The Party successfully proposed and guided passage of the Resumption Bill of 1700, which mandated the revocation of William's gifts of the confiscated Irish lands of Jacobites. Among the most generously doled recipients of this bounty were the King's great favorites, Portland and Arnold Joost van Keppel, Earl of Albemarle; his ex-generals, Godard van Reede-Ginckel, Earl of Athlone, and Henri de Massue de Ruvigny, Earl of Galway; and his reputed former mistress, Elizabeth Villiers Hamilton, Countess of Orkney. Orkney's grant consisted of the captured Irish estate of James II, but Country partisans charged with inquiring into the forfeitures nevertheless included it in their reconnaissance report, and the grant came to be comprehended within the measure's specified resumption of the Crown's gifted "forfeited and other Estates and Interests in *Ireland*."[20] The Bill made many Country converts in the Lords, despite if not because of the fact that the foreign-born Portland, Albemarle, Athlone, and Galway were fellow nobles.

3) Late in the last session of this 4th Parliament, Country Commoners resolved that William remove all foreigners from his inner-councils (other than Prince George of Denmark). This resolution went uncontested, but no further moves toward enactment followed (owing to the prorogation of Parliament the next day, then its dissolution in December 1700). But Country MPs in William's 5th Parliament secured provisions

---

19. *CJ*, 12:603.

20. Commissioners charged by the Commons with assessing the size and worth of the Irish forfeitures produced *The Report Made to the Honourable House of Commons, Decemb. 5 1699* (1700), in which their value was greatly inflated, estimated to total £2,685,138 ("worth per annum £211,623, which by computation of six years purchase for a life, and 13 years for the inheritance"). The claimed size of the substantial Irish grants to the Dutch favorites and to Orkney, as given in this *Report*, was 135,320 acres to Portland, 108,533 acres to Albemarle, 276,480 to Athlone, 36,148 acres to Galway, and near 95,649 acres to Orkney.

in the Succession Act of 1701 for excluding foreign subjects from royal conciliar office in future reigns.

4) The more momentous Country initiative of this 5th Parliament, however, was the Impeachments of the Four Lords, which lasted from April through June (1701), and saw the Party's demise. Sponsored by Country MPs, this assault on the King's patronage conduct was newly pursued within the context of the parliamentary High Court. Among the articles brought against Portland, Somers, Edward Russell, Earl of Orford, and Charles Montague, Earl of Halifax, were numerous charges implicating them in what Country partisans now held to be the criminal scandal of William's Irish grants.[21] But the difficult progress of the proceedings had the unforeseen consequence of exposing the lack of legal standards by which Country MPs had (all along, it now seemed) arrogated to themselves the judicial power of determining William guilty of patronage abuse and finding this conduct to be in need of corrective legislation.

Coincident with the Party's initiatives of 1698–1701 was a spate of satiric Country propaganda in print. Designed to influence MPs, it often vividly and sensationally represented William's patronage conduct as repeated violations of the principles of patriotic nativism and sexual virtue, by which the movement justified itself. For example, such propaganda missives published during or immediately surrounding the 4th Parliament's third session of 1699–1700, in which the Resumption Bill carried, included John Tutchin's *The Foreigners* (1700), Charles Davenant's *A Discourse upon Grants and Resumptions* (1699), Dr. Robert Brady's *A Continuation of the Complete History of England* (1699), and John Toland's *The Oceana of James Harrington, and his Other Works* (1700).

Tutchin's poem — a six-penny pamphlet — appeared in August 1700, four months after this parliamentary session had been prorogued, in April. *The Foreigners* recycled the fabling device of Old Testament allegory by which John Dryden had so famously excoriated Exclusionist MPs in his *Absalom and Achitophel*, but now in order to applaud Country MPs' gains of the Disbandment and Resumption Acts and to recommend the Party's pending cause of excluding all foreigners from royal councils. In the work's inset lampoon on "Bentir" — who is compositely William (bent-ear) and Portland (Bentinck) — a satiric Tutchin depicts in condensed allusive fashion the appalling scenarios addressed by such legislation. He exclaims, "How ill do's *Bentir* in the Head appear / Of Warriours, who

---

21. On the role of the Partition Treaty in the Impeachments, consult my n46 below.

do *Jewish* Ensigns bear?"; "By lavish Grants whole Provinces he gains, /
Made forfeit by the *Jewish* Peoples Pains; / Till angry Sanhedrims such
Grants resume"; "Must we by Foreign Councils be undone?...in our
Princely Palaces do's sound; / The self-same Language the old Serpent
spoke, / When misbelieving *Eve* the Apple took." Tutchin then amplifies
his glancing reflection on Eve-like William's sodomitically 'fallen' condition in a concluding inset lampoon on "Keppech"—both a sexually
panting William (peching) and his young favorite Albemarle (Keppel)
—it begins, "*Keppech* the Imperious Chit of State, / Mounted to Grandeur
by the usual Course / Of Whoring, Pimping, or a Crime that's worse."[22]

Unlike *The Foreigners*, the publications of Davenant's *Grants and Resumptions*, Brady's *Continuation of the Complete History*, and Toland's *Oceana*
were time-released to coincide with the parliamentary session of 1699–1700.
Grants and Resumptions and the *Continuation of the Complete History* were
published in November 1699, just before Parliament convened.[23] The
Oceana appeared in March 1700, just prior to the session's heated debate
over the Resumption Bill. These works of topical satire wrapped Country polemic in the expressive guise of bookish intellectualism, partly to
elude censorship controls but primarily to appeal to the political elite
through display of its shared educational capital.

Yet, Pocock treats such purveyed disguise and exploited cultural
capital as if they communicated these publications' most profound
meaning. He, in discussing Davenant's writings of the late 1690s, proposes
to penetrate to "an intellectual scaffolding [which] can be discovered in
his thought." The "theme" of *A Discourse upon Grants and Resumptions* is, as
he would have it, the danger of oligarchy, developed through Davenant's
notion that those who gain by the public debt "must cease to disturb the

---

22. Tutchin, *The Foreigners*, pp. 7–8, 10.

23. *A Continuation* and *A Discourse* were advertised in the Michaelmas Term
Catalogue of Books, issued in November 1699; see Edward Arber's *Term Cata-
logues*, 3:153, 158–59. Brady's *Continuation* was later advertised in the *London
Gazette* for 15 January 1700. Davenant's *Discourse* was subsequently advertised in
the *Post-Man*, which announced: "To Morrow the 1st of *December* will be published" (28–30 November 1699), "This day will be published" (30 November–2
December), "This day being the 16th of *December*, will be published, The Second Edition" (14–16 December). Additional advertisements appeared in *Post-Man*
issues of 23–26 December, 2–4 January 1700, 9–11 January, 20–23 January,
23–25 January, 9–11 April 1700; and *Post-Boy* issues of 5–7 December 1699, 21–23
December.

balance of the Ancient Constitution... [by] forms of corruption." The book, asserts Pocock, constitutes Davenant's "major essay" envisioning utopian conditions for virtuous political life within a modern credit economy (*MM*, pp. 437, 441). Of Brady's *Continuation of the Complete History*, Pocock states absurdly that Brady's "partisan instincts found no formula" after 1688, since "this second volume of his *Complete History*, published in the year of his death, contains chronicle matter only without interpretative comment."[24] Similarly, Pocock shows no alertness to the satiric wiles of Toland's edition of Harrington. In his own *Political Works of James Harrington*, he claims descent from Toland, whom he characterizes as a scrupulous scholarly father of modern critical editors of Harrington. The dedication of his edition reads, "To the memory of John Toland, H.F. Russell Smith and S.B. Liljegren, pioneers in Harringtonian scholarship" (*PWJH*, [p. v]).

II

Davenant's *Grants and Resumptions* was a work of Country propaganda which—like Brady's *Continuation of the Complete History* and Toland's *Oceana*, as we will see—would have engaged the interests of readers who may not have shared its author's doctrinal partisan commitments, whether Tory or Whig. Davenant's Toryism only strongly asserts itself in *Grants and Resumptions* in his opening chapter on resumed royal grants in English history, where William the Conqueror is idealized in both crypto-Jacobite and Country terms. That provident "Founder of our present Government," Davenant relates, "got quiet Possession of the Crown" and left to his Anglo-Norman royal successors a quasi-sacred "fair Inheritance" that true Britons have ever since "held Impious" to squander.[25] The rhetorical heart of *Grants and Resumptions*, however, is exclusively Country, as the work's polemically explicit subtitle indicates: "*that the Forfeited Estates Ought to be Applied towards the Payment of the Publick Debts.*"

This particular Country agenda was highlighted in a new introduction to the book's expanded second edition, which appeared in December 1700. Herein Davenant states, "The writer of these Papers thought it might not

24. Pocock, "Robert Brady, 1627–1700. A Cambridge Historian of the Restoration," *Cambridge Historical Journal* 10 (1951): 201, 203.

25. Charles Davenant, *A Discourse upon Grants and Resumptions...*, 2nd edn. (1700), pp. 104–106. Subsequent citations are to this edition.

be unseasonable to publish a Discourse upon *Grants*" given that, "the Parliament having last Sessions *Constituted Commissioners for Inquiring into and Taking an Accompt of all such Estates, both Real and Personal*" and that, "Mankind also abhorring to behold a Few inrich'd with the Spoils of a whole Country" and consequently "the Universal Voice of the People seeming to call for some kind of *Resumption*."[26] Also in this introduction, Davenant attempts to have his fellow MPs stand ready and willing to coerce William's assent to the anticipated Resumption Bill:

Heroick Kings, whose high Perfections have made 'em awful to their Subjects, can struggle with, and subdue the Corruption of the times; A *Hercules* can cleanse the *Augean* Stable of the Filth which had not been Swept away in thirty years…[and] pull down Ministers and Favorites, Grown formidable…they know that these Top-heavy buildings, rear'd up to an invidious height, and which have no solid Foundation in Merit, are in a Moment blown down by the breath of Kings.[27]

Davenant plays subversively with panegyrists' familiar identifications of William with Hercules.[28] The scenario he shadows is one in which a most non-heroic William must be pressured into assenting to the Resumption Bill by a Country Parliament. Davenant suggestively pictures corruption at court as an edifice that Country MPs will undertake to topple, for it is to these partisans that he assigns a Herculean part—the biblical Samson's destruction of the Philistine Temple. William, by contrast, is a king at the crossroads who has yet to live up to Hercules' Choice of Virtue by assenting to the Bill or to show himself a Hercules antitype by vetoing it ("in a moment blown down by the breath of Kings"). Davenant hints, though, that William will assert his character of the latter, making the negativing Choice of Vice if not coerced otherwise. For, to begin with, "awful" is his punword in a passage that ultimately deflates courtesy descriptions of royal patronage ("heroick," "high Perfections," "Corruption," "Filth," "invidious height"). What is more, a patronal William is implicated in the reviled evil of corrupt court government, (which a virtuous Herculean king can nevertheless "struggle with"), whose beginnings Davenant with crypto-Jacobite innuendo dates not from the Restoration

---

26. Davenant, *Discourse upon Grants and Resumptions*, pp. 42, 43.

27. Davenant, *Discourse upon Grants and Resumptions*, pp. 17–18.

28. See Stephen Baxter, "William III as Hercules: The Political Implications of Court Culture," in *The Revolution of 1688–1689* (Cambridge: Cambridge UP, 1992), pp. 95–106.

but from William's rise to power in the United Provinces in 1670 ("Filth which had not been Swept away in thirty years"). And Davenant again suggests that William is part of this "Corruption of the times" through his literary allusion to a Hercules manqué cleaning the Augean stables: recalling the mock-heroic use of the topos in Samuel Butler's *Hudibras* to describe the mighty (loutish) labors of bear-baiting Colon (i.e., John Des-borough), that farmer turned Cromwellian army officer.[29]

Like Davenant's *Grants and Resumptions*, Robert Brady's *Continuation of the Complete History* is a work of Country satire in which Jacobite Tory commitment is expressed. In this *Continuation*, however, the Jacobite expressions are flamboyantly seditious and tightly confined to framing sections of the work, where they are transfused with Country propaganda that is couched throughout the book's annalistic histories of the Plantagenets. Brady in this last work of his polemic career lives up to his reputation for delivering Juvenalian "*sagacious Inventions*,"[30] herein producing both Jacobite and Country satiric fictions in erudite discursive guise. But, it is to the Country inventions that he devotes himself at every turn. His genre of exercise is satiric parallel history, in which urgently topical applications are signaled through verbal queuing, such as anachronistic reference, and through Brady's main subject of the conflict over royal patronage conduct between the first Plantagenet kings and England's "Great Men and Commons."[31]

Brady's opening chronicle on the life and reign of Edward I culminates in an account that furnishes a satiric parallel to the Country assault on William: the Carlisle petitions of the nobility against abusive royal papal patronage. Brady tells the story of the eventual triumph of the petitioning noblemen, who pass ordinances prohibiting "the best Spiritual Preferments given to *Italians*, other Foreigners, and Non-Residents" by "Master *William*," and who beseech William "to *revoke* and make *void*" these dispensations, including "First Fruits of vacant Benefices reserved

---

29. On the identification of Colin with Desborough, consult John Wilders' commentary in the Oxford *Hudibras* (Clarendon, 1967), pp. xxxix, 350 (n441). In 1690, there appeared *Collin's Walk Through London and Westminster*, a Williamite adaptation of *Hudibras* by the Church Whig Thomas Durfey.

30. William Atwood, *A Speech, according to the Answerer's Principles*, in *Jus Anglorum ab Antiquo* (1681), pp. 1–3.

31. Robert Brady, *A Continuation of the Complete History of England: Containing the Lives and Reigns of Edward I. II & III. and Richard II* (1700), p. 311 (compare, also in "The Reign of Edward III, pp. 193–205, 219, 294, 297, 300, 312, 313). Further references to the *Continuation* are given parenthetically in my text.

to the Pope" (Brady's analogue to William's Irish land-grants) (pp. 88–89). "Master *William*," the focus of the noblemen's protest, is William Testa, a papal agent in Edward I's England, who functions here as a screen-figure for Catholic James II as well as William III. For Brady—who in his account of the nobles' moment of triumph records that Testa was "called into *full Parlement*, and *Convicted*" (p. 89)—conjures and mockingly dismisses the anti-Catholic reflections on James II embodied in provisos in the 1689 Bill of Rights, his serious joke being that the Convention parliamentarians unintentionally directed these reflections at the right man, 'William.' Hence, the scene projects an idealized Country Parliament's redress of grievances against 'popish' King William's patronage conduct, his best favors going to aliens and sodomitical 'Italians.'

The final sentence of Brady's history of Edward I, which records the King's death by "*Disenterie* or *Bloody Flux*," foreshadows the secret regicide of his son by "a red-hot Iron, thro' a Ductil-pipe, into his Guts at his Fundament" (pp. 92, 164); and Brady more than explains this uncanny symmetry in his succeeding history of Edward II. This chronicle begins with the story of the Prince's youthful homosexual attachment to Piers Gaveston ("curious in his Behavior," "fine Body"). In launching this William-Portland parallel, Brady stresses the "great *Familiarity* there was *between* the *Prince*, and *Piers Gaveston*," then proceeds to tender a cautionary tale of how such "Intimacy" combined with royal favors showered on a sodomitical consort plunged England into civil war—nobles against a "*King in his Folly*" (pp. 91, 101, 119). A brief eulogistic description of the Order of the Garter in Brady's subsequent history of Edward III contrasts starkly with what in this chronicle is a long account of the papal Templars, which is contrived as a satiric parallel to William's distribution of honors. Brady dwells on how the Templars' popish inductees in England and France "*kissed* those which received them on the *Breech*, the *Navel*, and *Mouth*, and then *obliged* themselves, and *made* a Vow to *expose* themselves one to another for the *Exercise* of the *Execrable* Sin of *Sodomy*" (pp. 168, 247).[32]

In his final history of Richard II, Brady persistently alludes to William's Irish grants while again furnishing a William-Portland parallel. The propagandistic center of this chronicle is an account of the grievances redressed by the Lords Appellant concerning Richard's bounty to his reputed homosexual favorite Robert de Vere, Duke of Ireland. William's

---

32. On English nativist sentiment attached to the Order of the Garter in early modern royalist mythology, consult Peter Heylin, *The Historie of that Most Famous Saint and Souldier of Christ Jesus; St. George of Cappadicia*...(1631), pp. 283–318.

Irish grants are evoked in a lengthy representation of these Lords' successfully waged treasons case, tried in Richard's 10th, 11th, and 13th Parliaments, which included Article 5 charging de Vere and other royal minions with procuring to themselves "the Land of *Ireland*," "whereby they are greatly enriched, and the *King* become poor," and Article 11 accusing them of having "excited" the King to seek papal ratification "that *Robert de Vere* should be King of *Ireland*" (pp. 373, 374). Brady goes on to portray Richard's deposition in 1399 as a happy sequel to these parliamentary gains, an outcome enabled by the former Lord Appellant Henry Bolingbroke's return from exile "to *demand* his Inheritance" and to witness the King's "*Renunciation*" (pp. 420, 422). Brady invests this moment with the twofold meaning of 1) Bolingbroke's recapture of his presumed patrimonial hereditaments, including his title Duke of Lancaster, which an abusively patronal Richard had confiscated after his father John of Gaunt died, and 2) Bolingbroke's rightful succession to a "*Throne being vacant*" staked on his dynastic status as grandson of Richard Crouchback, fabled eldest son of King Henry III (p. 433). In this final section of the chronicle, a Jacobite Brady echoes repeatedly the bandied pro-Revolutionary terms of William III's accession in 1689 ('abdication,' 'vacant throne'), but only to explode them as false legitimist fiction and to encourage a Stuart invasion modeled on his own panegyric parallel of Lancastrian "*Restitution*" (p. 420). At the same time, the episode's Country message — which is intended to sum up dramatically Brady's constant theme in the *Continuation* of the wrongs of royal patronage abuse and their warranted, and inevitably successful, parliamentary challenge — is no less loudly and brazenly sounded. Brady even highlights that Richard II renounced the throne in Latin, whereas Bolingbroke formally claimed it before Parliament "in his Mother Tongue, (*lingua maternal*)" (pp. 421, 422, 432), thus embellishing his story of rightful succession with a detail laden with Country resonance for MPs resentful of William and his foreign ministers' management of state affairs in Dutch.[33]

III

The Oceana of James Harrington, and his Other Works, edited by John Toland, was part of a flood of republican historical books published during the

---

33. For this expression of resentment in other works of Country propaganda, see Tutchin, *The Foreigners*, pp. 8–9, and 'Price,' *Gloria Cambriae*, p. 4.

years of the Country movement by the Whig bookseller John Darby Sr.
Toland had a hand in preparing some if not most of these publications,
which included Henry Neville's *Plato Redivivus* (1698), *The Life and Works
of John Milton* (1699), *The Memoirs of Edmund Ludlow* (1698–99), and *Discourses concerning Government by Algernon Sidney* (1699). Common to them
all was, in addition to an obvious interest in promoting republican doctrine, the use of editorial maneuver for the purpose of persuading MPs
to support the Country movement.[34] The Darby Harrington is largely
comprised of reprints of Harrington's writings, concerning which Pocock
states that Toland handled them "on the whole both carefully and honestly, making few emendations which cannot be justified or at least understood" (*PWJH*, p. xii–xiii). Pocock, however, fails to remark and is
apparently unaware of the ways in which this edition is deviously spiked
with Country propaganda—in Toland's preliminaries, in the frontispiece satirizing William, and most transparently in Toland's insertion of
a reprint of Harrington's broadside *The Manner and Use of the Ballot* (n.d.)
into the body of the text of *Oceana*, intruded at a point where it adds rhetorical ballast to Harrington's declared institution of popular patronage
in his utopian commonwealth ("This freeborn Nation lives not upon the
Dole or Bounty of one man, but distributing her annual Magistracys and
Honors with her own hand, is her self King PEOPLE").[35] And there is
the edition's reprint of John Hall's anti-Orangist *The Grounds and Reasons
of Monarchy* (1650), which Toland took the license to foist between preliminaries and his reprint of *Oceana*.

Toland in preliminaries makes specific appeals to a governing elite
to whom he recommends the edition for its wealth of political knowledge in general. Harrington's *Oceana*, he announces, not only distills "the
most perfect Form of Popular Government that ever was... [but] this, with

---

34. On these Darby publications, consult A. B. Worden, introduction to his
partial edition of Edmund Ludlow's *Memoirs*, in *A Voyce from the Watch Tower, Part
Five: 1660–1662*, Camden 4th Series, vol. 21 (London: Royal Historical Society
Publications, 1978), pp. 1–80; and Justin Champion, *Republican Learning: John Toland the Crisis of Christian Culture, 1696–1722* (Manchester: Manchester UP, 2003),
ch. 4. Worden and Champion are, however, un-alert to these works' extensive
satiric attacks on William.

35. John Toland, 'editor,' *The Oceana of James Harrington, and his Other Works
...* (1700), p. 100. Subsequent references to Harrington's writings and to John
Hall's *The Gounds and Reasons of Monarchy...* (1650) are to this edition and will
be cited parenthetically in my text and notes. In quoting from Toland's "Preface"
(pp. vii–x), I have reversed the italics.

his other Writings, contain the History, Reasons, Nature, and Effects of all sorts of Government, with so much Learning and Perspicuity"; "Heaven is duly prais'd, Learning begins to flourish again in its proper Soil among our Gentlemen, in imitation of the *Roman* Patricians" (pp. ix, x). This outreach additionally extends to Jacobites wishing for the accession of the Young Pretender. After proffering the Country rhetoric that "in a well constituted Commonwealth there can be no distinction of Party's" (i.e. Whig and Tory), Toland points out that, if Harrington's idea of a republican commonwealth should be implemented in England, it would bring Jacobites "to injoy equal Privileges with others, and so be deliver'd from their present Oppression." He further insists that Harrington's writings are nevertheless valuable, since as regards his theory of the ideally balanced socioeconomic class foundations of national power, "if the Prince should happen to be restor'd, his Doctrin of the Balance would be a light to shew him with what and with whom he had to do, so either to mend or avoid the Miscarriage of his Father." "[A]ll that is said of this doctrine," he adds, "may as well be accommodated to a Monarchy regulated by Laws, as to a Democracy or more popular form of a Commonwealth" (p. 19). Toland's broad appeal to the nation's patriciate—Whigs, Tories, and all supporters of English monarchy and lawful government, not excluding Jacobites—indicates his recognition that republicanism was an unpopular cause among political elites of the late 1690s.

His appeal to Jacobites, moreover, underwrites a Country strategy of caricaturing William's grants of military office and land to foreigners. For Toland borrows the old Jacobite slur likening William to his putative counterpart in unrightful military conquest, Oliver Cromwell ('P.O.' Prince of Orange, 'O.P.' Oliver Protector) in order to conflate representations of patronal William with images of his violent and arbitrary rule in England's newly new-modelled tyrannic regime. Nudging readers so to proleptically construe while topicalizing Harrington's damaging descriptions of monarchy, Toland claims that *Oceana* originally met with hostility from supporters of the Protectoral "Commonwealth, which was the specious name under which they cover'd the rankest Tyranny of OLIVER CROMWEL." And he goes on to note:

By shewing that a Commonwealth was a Government of Laws, and not of the Sword, he could not but detect the violent administration of the Protector by his Bashaws, Intendants, or Majors General, which created him no small danger. (pp. xviii)

This reflection on the Protectorate doubles as a covert Country assault on the Revolution Settlement, wherein Toland calls up the Jacobite pairing of William and Cromwell through his reference to the tyrant's "Bashaws," i.e., foreign guards whose more literal application is to William, not Cromwell. The pronoun in his sentence "…he could not but detect the violent administration of the Protector by his Bashaws…" therefore has triple meaning, by which Toland 1) asserts Harrington's oblique exposé of a tyrannic Cromwell, 2) remarks his own discovery of this design (he could not but detect), and 3) guides the reader ("he") to sift both it and its applicability to William, whose patronage to Dutch and sodomitical "Bashaws, Intendants, or Majors General" was so much the focus of Country partisan attack.

Moments later, Toland reactivates the Jacobite similitude when he seconds Harrington's supposed condemnation of Cromwell. He declaims, in what is a retrospective on the Protector's usurpation and a veiled prospective on William's: "he dy'd abhor'd as a monstrous betrayer of those Libertys with which he was intrusted by his Country, and his Posterity not possessing a foot of what for their only sakes he was generally thought to usurp. But this last is a mistaken Notion, for som of the most notorious Tyrants liv'd and dy'd without hopes of Children; which is a good reason why no mortal ought to be trusted with too much Power on that score." In this searing obituary on Cromwell, Toland targets William indirectly by mentioning other "most notorious Tyrants" and by alluding to William's childless condition and to his lack, from republican and Jacobite perspectives, of a right of rule. The harangue concludes with Toland's unnamed memorialization of William within a castlist of "JULIUS CAESAR, OLIVER CROMWELL, and such others as at any time inslav'd their fellow Citizens," "who will be for ever remember'd with detestation, and cited as the most execrable Examples of the vilest Treachery and Ingratitude" (pp. 20–21).

Read through Toland's satiric lens, Harrington's descriptions of monarchy in Oceana yield images of an orientalized William, one whose conduct as a royal patron shows a lack of affection for his native-born English subjects and whose rule imitates the tyrannic oppression of an Asian despot — Harrington's symbol for government in a pure monarchy. In *Oceana*, the figure of the Asian despot is that of a tyrant who upends that working principle of English kingship, 'he who sways the scepter holds the sword.' Ruling with lawless abandon in a "Monarchy by Arms," he is exemplified by the Ottoman sultans Selim and Suleyman. His military juntos are synecdoches for his subhuman character, such bashaws, janissaries, sipahis, timariots being "a Beast that has a great belly," hell-hounds "liquorish after his Blood" and "frequent Butchers of their Lords," and "bestial executioners of their Captain's Tyranny" (pp. 53, 62, 63). In 1744, as if possibly indebted to Toland's anti-Williamite hermeneutic here, James Ralph in his *History of England* editorialized on the Commons' rejection of William's plea to retain his Blue Guards. After blasting William's "shameful" new concept that "[foreign] kings should have Guards of their own native subjects" as an "undue preference…[which] had blunted the zeal of his national troops, and almost deprived him of the hearts of his people," Ralph applauds the Commons for having forceful-ly severed his attachment to "this body of Dutch Janizaries."[36]

In the Darby *Oceana*, an orientalized William is additionally adum-brated through the figure of Julius Caesar, whom Harrington represents as a monarch in the Asian despotic mold and whom Toland gleans to be a Cromwell prototype. As we know, Caesar's role in Rome's transition from republican to Imperial government is treated as pivotal in *Oceana*. A monarchical ruler so much "the same with that at this day in *Turky*," Caesar is said to have succeeded to the office of perpetual dictator estab-lished by Sulla, whose rule by the sword was accomplished through his planting of colonies of soldiers beneficed with confiscated lands. Accord-ing to Harrington, Sulla seized lands "not now of Enemys, but of Citizens," thereby innovating upon the practice in the time of the Gracchi, when lands "were taken from the Enemy and, under color of being reserv'd to the Public use, were thro stealth possest by the Nobility," a practice ca-lamitous in its own right however, since "Laws offer'd…such as drove at dispossessing the Nobility of their Usurpations, and dividing the *common purchase of the Sword among the People*, were never touch'd but they caus'd Earthquakes" (pp. 61, 62).

Toland discerned both contemporary and current topical signifi-cance in this Roman narrative, which Harrington overprotested had nothing to do with Protectoral England ("quite contrary to what hath happen'd in *Oceana*," "[where there was] the balance changing quite con-trary to that of *Rome*" [pp. 61, 73]). Specifically, Toland discovered in it Harrington's submerged parallel to the transition to Cromwell's Protec-torate from England's democratically disposed landocracy that had first obtained in Henry VII's reign, so memorably sketched in *Oceana*. What Toland celebrates in preliminaries as *Oceana's* modeled "Government of

---

36. Quoted in *Cobbett's Parliamentary History*, 12:1194–95.

Laws, and not of the Sword," (a misprision of the Harringtonian antithesis favoring a republican government of laws, not of men), perfectly describes Harrington's idealization of the Roman Republic, which in his de-
clinist narrative sinks into crisis in Gracchan times then grossly corrupts
into a government of the sword under Caesar.[37] As glossed by Toland,
the scenario shadows forth the troubles caused by Cromwell's confisca-
tions of royalist lands in Scotland and Ireland, seizures that provoked widespread accusations by its victims and by republicans (like Harrington)
of Cromwell's resort to a military reign of terror.

And Toland "could not but detect" in this scenario a ready-to-hand
parallel to the Country furor over William's Irish grants. By this lami-
nation, the provoked Cavaliers are the equivalents of Jacobites, who share
with current-day republicans (like Toland) a view of the lawless nature
of a Cromwellian military administration under William. For, from the
Jacobite perspective, the forfeited Irish estates were loyalist lands ("not
now of Enemys, but of Citizens") which had been seized by a bloody
usurper, while for republicans they were assets (properly "reserv'd to
the Public use") which a tyrannically patronal William had misused to
enrich his Dutch associates-in-arms. Not just by chance, the Darby *Oceana*
was released in late May 1700, just before the Resumption Bill carried,
on 9 April.[38]

In preliminaries, Toland even follows Harrington's Roman narrative further so as to continue to satirize Dutch William's dole of the Irish
estates, caricaturing it as a prelude to England's subjugation by barbarian Nordic invaders. In *Oceana*, the violent regimes of Sulla and Caesar are
linked to the Nordic takeover of Rome through the theme of military
colonization. As Harrington presents it, the provincial planting of military colonies by these Roman dictators gives a view in microcosm of the
impending Nordic feudalization of the Roman Empire. Significantly, Harrington invokes a flexible definition of 'feudum' which brings his account
of the rise of Imperial Rome into descriptive symmetry with his representation of the sack of Rome and its aftermath: "it is taken either for *War*,
or for a *possession of conquer'd Lands, distributed by the Victor to such of his Cap-
tains and Soldiers as had merited in his Wars, upon condition to acknowledge him*

---

37. Detailed source-and-influence study of this Roman narrative is provided
in Pocock, *BR 3*, chs. 3, 8–10, 13.

38. Advertised as "This day is published" in the *Post-Man*, 23–26 March, and
as "Newly published" in the *Post-Man* 26–28 March (1700).

to be perpetual Lord, and themselves to be his Subjects" (p. 63). Yet Harrington emphasizes that the Nordic conquest was an invasion of unmatched cataclysmic proportions by geographical and cultural aliens, to wit, "[by] a People that, deriving their Roots from the Northern parts of *Germany*, or out of *Sweden*... [fill'd] every part of the *Roman* Empire with Inundations of *Vandals, Huns, Lombards, Franks, Saxons, overwhelm'd antient Languages, Learning, Prudence, Manners, Citys, changing the names of Rivers, Countrys, Seas, Mountains and Men*" (p. 63).[39] Toland signposts this horrific event, while keeping in play his own recalled satiric identification of William with Cromwell. He claims that one reason Harrington wrote *Oceana* was to furnish Englishmen with the means to reconstruct a polity "if it should ever be the fate of this Nation to be, like *Italy* of old, overrun by any barbarous People, or to have its Government and Records destroy'd by the rage of som merciless Conqueror" (p. xix). Thus Toland, having discerned in Harrington's climax to his Roman narrative a futuristic vision of England's fate following the accession of Cromwell—who in *Oceana* is given the fictive name "Olphaus" and dubbed "the most victorious captain" (p. 77) —would have readers imagine that this vision now predicts England's enslavement by the Nordic Yoke of a Cromwellian William.[40]

---

39. Compare Harrington's equally chilling but less sublimely castastrophic portrait of monarchic takeover in *The Prerogative of Popular Government*, which draws on 1 Samuel 8: "*SAMUEL* declar'd to the People concerning the manner or policy of the King, saying '*He will take your Fields and your Vinyards, and your Oliveyards, even the best of them, and give to his Servants* (which kind of proceding must needs create the Balance of a Nobility;) over and above this, *he will take the Tenth of your Seed, and of your Vinyards, and of your Sheep* (by way of Tax, for the maintenance of his Armys) and thus your *Daughters shall com to be his Cooks and Confectioners, and your Sons to run before his Chariot.* There is not from the Balance to the Superstructures a more perfect description of a Monarchy by a Nobility" (p. 293).

40. Toland, in his *Anglia Libera* (1701), satirically traces the House of Nassau back to a barbarian military commander named "Nasua" who may have helped to lead the the sack of Rome. Herein seizing on a passage in Julius Caesar's *De Bello Gallico* in which the Emperor relates of ambassadors having relayed to him the news "*that a hundred Squadrons of the* Suabians *had incamp'd on t'other side the* Rhine, *and would attemt to pass the River under the Command of two Brothers* NASUA *and* CIMBERIUS," he adds, "Now I think it very plain that NASUA is NASAU, the last Letters being only transpos'd to give it a softer Termination after the Manner of the *Romans*...besides that the City of *Nassau* (whether it gives the Family its Name, or rather receives it from this or som other Hero) is exactly situated according to CAESAR'S Geography" (pp. 62–63).

Toland's Country assault in the Darby Oceana is reinforced by icon-ographical cunning in the edition's frontispiece engraving of the Tem-ple of Liberty, in which the head of William appears, in a medallion, madeover as a Caesarian emperor—see illustration. Physiognomically so cloned, wearing a laurel wreath over short hair, and collar of Roman military costume, the portrait is inscribed "GVLIELMUS III" and hangs from the Temple's lower façade, below an emblem in medallion that, on inspection, represents Luxury. Lady Liberty occupies the central niche, while a replica of her body appears in an ornamental dome comprised of classical and modern military paraphernalia, here symbolizing a native citizen-militia. In the center of the upper façade is a head portrait of Con-fucius, Asian antitype of the Asian despot, who is flanked by medallions of Moses, Solon, Lycurgus, and Numa, founding fathers with supposedly republican values.

This satiric engraving makes use of the moral symbolism of right and left positionality to represent William as a personification of monarchic evil. His portrait hangs to the sinister left of the Temple and at a straight diagonal from Lady Liberty's lower left arm. He is pictured in left pro-file, unlike the full-face portrait of Confucius, who seems to eye read-ers directly, and unlike the heads of the founding fathers in right pro-file. His portrait is paired with that of a composite head, in medallion, of the legendary tyrannicides, the Bruti—Brutus the Elder cloned as the Younger, the portrait inscribed "L. JVNIVS BRVTVS"—which hangs parallel to William's picture, at the right of the Temple and in right pro-file. The Bruti and William (now a type of Tarquin the Proud as well as Caesar) seem to look one another in the face, thereby telescoping the artist's topos of the Combat of Virtue and Vice evoked by the juxtapo-sition of Lady Liberty, her national arms, and her republican heroes with a tyrannic William.[41] Directly below the portrait of the Bruti, on the right side block of the Temple's base, is the name of another Junius who enlists against William—John Toland.[42] The full inscription across the base

41. This telescoping, moreover, is signposted and developed through medal-lions that appear below the Bruti and William, which in context show, respec-tively, a thriving 'free' commercial nation (under republican leadership) and an enslaved brutalized herd (under William).

42. As Pierre Desmaizeaux recorded in his "Some Memoirs of the Life and Writings of Mr. John Toland," "He [Toland] had the Name of JANUS JUNIUS given him at the font, and was call'd by that name in the school-roll every morning: but the other boys making a jest of it, the Master himself order'd him

Frontispiece to the Darby Harrington (1700). Courtesy of the Milton S. Eisenhower Library.

implicates his editorial work on the Darby Harrington in the combat: "M.DCC. I. TOLANDVS LIBERTATI SACRAVIT."

Toland's Country propaganda in the edition intersects with his own divulged republican principles in the work's reprint of John Hall's *Grounds and Reasons of Monarchy* (1650), intruded immediately after preliminaries. Another anti-tyrannical 'John,' another satirist, another young learned wonder, Hall is Toland's alter ego; who "dy'd before he was full Thirty, lamented as a Prodigy of his Age," reflects Toland (p. xxviii; "I but this present day beginning the thirtieth year of my Age... *Novemb. 30.* 1699" [p. x]).[43] Hall's pamphlet inveighs against scandalous royal patronage conduct and its posited corollary of despotic rule, while repudiating monarchy in general as a form of government that invites such corruption. The Houses of Stuart and Orange are adduced as examples. The defeat of Stuart tyranny in '48, we hear, was about rescuing a body-politic diseased by patronage sins — racial and sexual. Bloody Mary's carnal "Exhorbitancys," James I's "sloth and cowardice," the "ease and luxury of those times" — rails Hall in the tract's appended "Instance of the preceding REASONS out of the SCOTISH HISTORY" — "fomented and nourish'd those lurking and pestilent humors, which afterwards so dangerously broke out in his Son's Reign" (pp. 28, 31).

More provocatively, Hall suggests that the contagion of this anti-heroic magistracy is the problem of monarchy itself over time ("Monarchy being truly a Disease of Government" [p. 15]).[44] In his view, the monarchical system, if durable, will have subjects suffer the "eternal Inconvenience" of "Founders being braver than any that follow after them,"

---

to be call'd JOHN for the future; which name he kept ever after" (*A Collection of Several Pieces of Mr. John Toland*, ed. Desmaizeaux, 2 vols. (1726), 1:v; see also 1:78).

43. See John Davies' panegyrical biography of Hall prefixed to Hall's translation, *Hierocles upon the Golden Verses of Pythagoras: Teaching a Vertuous and Worthy Life* (1657), sigs. B3r–B4v.

44. Compare Toland, *Anglia Libera*, pp. 19–21: "No sooner did the Commons begin to discover their own Strength...but our Kings redoubl'd their Efforts to grasp at an arbitrary and unlimited Power...I shall not mention what Progress was made by the Kings of the *Scottish* Race in this impious and accurst Design, nor the treacherous Assistance they receiv'd from several Order of Men among us who depended on their Liberality or Power; neither will I revive the odious Memory of those monstrous, absurd, and abominable Doctrins which were then coin'd, publicly spread with the greatest Industry, and under the most awful Impression, to infect the Understandings of the People, and to make them eternal Slaves by their own Concurrence as well as Consent."

"bad Governors...grow too big and formidable," "Governors themselves growing in Interests, increasing in Alliances and Forces." Hall rants on about "the Fallacy, with which the Asserters of Royalty have so flourish'd, that an Agreement between a People and one Man should descend to his Posterity":

Suppose a second Generation should accept the Son, and a third a Grandson, yet this confirms not a fourth; and the People very impoliticly Strengthen and confirm the Power by continuance, and in a manner with their own hands lay the Foundation of Absoluteness...and leave nothing of Liberty except the Name, and (if they be less cunning) not that. A pertinent Example of this, and so near us that I cannot pass it, we see in young ORANGE and the Low Countrys at this day, who continuing his Progenitors for their signal Services, and him for theirs, are now punish'd for their generous and indiscrete rewarding of Virtue, that their Liberty was lately almost blown up before they well perceiv'd it to be undermin'd, and they are now at a charge to maintain their own Oppression. (p. 10)

Willem II, Prince of Orange and Stadholder, is set in opposition to the Virtue, Liberty, and the People of the United Provinces. In support of this antinomy, Hall alludes to the crisis of Orange Party hegemony in the late 1640s and to the young Willem's botched siege of Amsterdam in 1650 ("their Liberty was lately almost blown up").[45] And Toland, while he thus holds up the mirror of Orange tyranny in the Dutch Republic, points a lesson in escaping William's in England now. So speaks Hall's ghost, a mouthpiece by which Toland enjoins Country partisans to erect safeguards against William's patronage abuse by adopting the prudential political creed held by Loevesteiners, especially their anti-dynastic tenet grounded in the assumption of an original popular power of patronage which would vest the monarchic office itself in the people's gift.

Toland's rhetorically manipulative entwining of republican doctrine with Country propaganda in the Darby Harrington stems from his shrewd perception of the Party's hitherto largely unacknowledged work of constitutional alteration in constraining William's grants. In his preface to *Oceana*, he interjects a momentary apologia for his own identity of political reformer into what in context is a commendation of the innovative

---

45. For background on Hall's English republican interpretation of these setbacks to Orange hegemony, see Steven Pincus, *Protestantism and Patriotism: Ideologies and the Making of English Foreign Policy, 1650–1668* (Cambridge: Cambridge UP, 1996), pp. 15–24.

practice of parliamentary regulation of royal patronage effected by Country legislation. "I am not so blinded with admiring the good Constitution of our own ['Government']," he states, "but that every day I can discern in it many things deficient, som things redundant, and others that require emendation or change. And of this the supreme Legislative Powers are so sensible, that we see nothing more frequent with them than the enacting, abrogating, explaining, and altering of Laws, *with regard to the very Form of the Administration*" (p. viii, my italics). Thus a sense of Country partisans' and English republicans' common pursuit of parliamentary patronal sovereignty lay behind Toland's editorial work on the Darby *Oceana*.

IV

The Country Party movement ended in 1701, when the legal proceedings in the Impeachments of the Four Lords (April–June) afforded an angle of vision which caused its legislative work to be seen as having been improperly guided by a presumption of the King's guilt. Only in pretext were the Impeachments about bringing charges against Lords Somers, Orford, Portland, and Halifax. It was William who was the real object of the prosecutorial effort, the monarch's fictive innocence being the thinnest of fictions on this occasion. MPs were, therefore, made to recognize that the accusations against him, which had supplied Country legislation with a moralistic basis, had not, in point of fact, passed standards of judicial proof. What evidence had demonstrated that William's grants were motivated by racial nepotism and scandalous sexual interest? What in general defined monarchic patronage abuse? Suddenly many MPs recognized that Country legislators had acted upon mere assertions about the unpatriotic and sinful nature of William's grants, and that parliamentarians could not plausibly claim to have formally appealed to legal prescriptions in alleging patronage abuse—no judicial deliberations having entered into play until now. In retrospect, then, the Party's legislative conduct itself looked scandalous to many, seeming to have foreclosed on the possibility of William's innocence and on his right of due process. This optic was, besides, no doubt motivated by the new hawkish climate—on the eve of the War of the Spanish Succession—within which so many MPs now looked to William to replay his role of godly warrior-king.

In reckoning with the Impeachments, MPs assumed the role of guarantors of justice. They shared responsibility for a House of Commons tasked with drafting and exhibiting the impeachment articles, both for a full Parliament made to sift and weigh the prosecutorial evidence of high crimes and misdemeanors and for a House of Lords charged with rendering verdicts at trial if proceedings advanced that far. Owing to the enlistment of these protocols and practices by parliamentary justiciars, William's controversial patronage conduct (refracted through the Impeachments of his ministerial proxies) was reassessed, almost inevitably.

And, that no such legal safeguards had previously been applied by Country legislators in his case was registered (again, through this juridical perspective) in other ways as well. In April, shortly after all the resolutions for the impeachments had carried, a Lords Counter-Address challenged the justice of a Commons Address urging William to remove the Four Lords – pre-trial — from his councils forever. More friction between the Commons and Lords ensued, notoriously; and in mid-June it reached a crisis-point when John Thompson, Lord Haversham, insinuated at a Joint-House Conference that the multitudinous impeachment articles concerning William's Irish grants embodied a Country agenda that, although newly punitive, was still underwritten by mere allegations based on unfounded belief that the King had committed patronage abuse.[46] Later in June, the trials of Somers and Orford dramatized the implications of Haversham's point. For the prosecution's case had literally dwindled to absence. Only a scattering of Commoners defied the orders of their Speaker and attended the events, albeit strictly in the capacity of onlookers. Peers in attendance and a vast crowd of spectators were, as a result (it happened), provoked to quizzical laughter when the Lord Keeper directed empty benches to argue their evidence.

The acquittals met with wild cheers and City bonfires. Easy dismissals of the charges against Portland and Halifax took place in Parliament on 24 July. On this last day of the session, William arrived hoping to mediate the ongoing dissentions between the Houses, but ended up thanking Members "both for your dispatch of those necessary Supplies, which you have granted for the public occasions, and for the encouragements you have given me to enter into Alliances for the preservation of the Liberty of Europe."[47] As MPs were well aware, Party gains made during the

---

46. Haversham thus reflected on William's Irish grants obliquely, through his suggestion that the impeachment articles dealing with the Partition Treaty masked anti-Whig political maneuver by Tory Commoners who believed the Lords to be innocent of diplomatic malpractice. Consult *CJ*, 13:629.

47. *Cobbett's Parliamentary History*, 5:1323.

progress of the Disbanding Bill in 1699 had left William so discouraged about prospective Anglo-European resistance to French aggression as to threaten to give up his kingship and enjoy retired private life in Holland. His Speech also in effect commended the judicial outcome in the Impeachments, final verdicts that tended to discredit the Country view of his patriotism.

Although the Country movement did not survive beyond July, a handful of adherents later took to print to vindicate its conduct in the Impeachments. In defensive pamphlets that began appearing in August, they professed reverence for the constitutional forms that Country MPs had manipulated in challenging William's grants. In so doing, they theorized parliamentary patronal sovereignty, consequently adding to Toland's Party literature of reformist constitutional thought. MP Sir Humphrey Mackworth's *A Vindication of the Rights of the Commons of England* (August 1701) was the first of the tracts, and proved the most explosive, in this wave of retrospective propaganda.[48] Like much Country polemic, it satirically exaggerated the size and scope of William's grants, and like the Darby *Oceana* it hitched this hyperbole to constitutional theory that in effect lodged powers of Crown patronage in Parliament.

Mackworth's peroration in this pamphlet, for example, introduced that hyperbole before transitioning into a constitutionalist justification of the Country attack on William. The turning-point comes when Mackworth pleads on behalf of Country Commoners, "What would you have the *House of Commons* do in such a Case? Would you have them sit still and see the Nation brought to Ruine and Desolation? Would you have them betray their Trust and act contrary to their Judgments? "No!" This moment immediately follows a satiric assault on William's patronage conduct:

[G]ive me leave to suppose (*for a Wise Constitution of Government provides a Remedy for all Distempers and Accidents in the Body Politick*) that in any future Reign, a Great and Powerful Minister of State having the Command of many Millions of Money rais'd for the necessary Occasions of the *King* and Kingdom…[undertook] such a Scheme of Management of the Publick Affairs, that the Nation should not only be brought under a vast Debt, whilst the Managers got vast Estates, but should be Involv'd in such Unhappy Circumstances, and so reduc'd to the last Extremity, that the Representatives of the People should be

---

48. Other such tracts included *The Taunton-Dean Letters, from E.C. to J.F. at the Grecian Coffee-house* (1701), *A Letter from the Grecian Coffee-house, in Answer to the Taunton-Dean Letter*…(1701), James Drake, *The History of the Last Parliament* (1702), and *The Source of our Present Fears Discover'd* (1703).

entirely convinc'd that either that Publick Manager must be remov'd from the Publick Ministry, or the Nation be utterly Ruined and Undone.[49]

Mackworth in this passage pursues his target of patronal William, while his designations of "a Great and Powerful Minister of State" and "that Publick Manager" also comprehend any one of the impeached Lords. His discussion of ruinous patronage abuse is pretendedly hypothetical, by which he maneuvers to boost the credibility of his exaggerated attack on William (and to prudently disguise it). But, also, the academic register of his discussion is part of his pamphlet's sustained venture in apologizing for the Country movement by asserting a theory of parliamentary patronal sovereignty. Mackworth accordingly argues for the people's right to depose kings in cases of patronage malpractice, one calculated effect of which however is to commend the Party's less extreme interventions of law-making and impeachment. Only superficially anomalous is the fact that he makes his case within the context of an ambivalently worded scenario that sanctions Jacobite legitimism as well as Whig populism as justifications for deposition. (For instance, the mismanaged millions otherwise due "the *King*" for necessary occasions invites readings that assign the money to a Stuart Prince *or* to a regal office which is by definition forfeited by tyrannical occupants.) Mackworth's object is to suggest that Country MPs happily accommodated these doctrinal perspectives within a non-revolutionary theoretical framework, namely, parliamentary patronal sovereignty, envisaged as a fundamental constitutional tenet that has guided the Party's legislative and judicial initiatives. Hence Mackworth defends a Country Parliament that saved England from "Unhappy Circumstances, and so reduc'd to the last Extremity," through application of this constitutional "*Remedy.*"

The Impeachments, however, brought to a close the experiment in divided patronal sovereignty entailed by the Party's legislative successes — its theoretical ratification by Toland, Mackworth, and others notwithstanding. The work of these Country publicists did not go unanswered in any event, but rather met with hostile replies from royalist Williamites, notably Jonathan Swift and Daniel Defoe.

Swift's *A Discourse of the Contests and Dissensions between the Nobles and the Commons in Athens and Rome* (October 1701) and Defoe's *The Original Power of the Collective Body of the People of England* (November 1701) — a pen-

---

49. Humphrey Mackworth, *A Vindication of the Rights of the Commons of England* ...(1700), p. 25.

dant to his anti-Country *True-Born Englishman* (1700)—went on the satiric counterattack, redirecting allegations of corrupt patronage onto Country MPs and denouncing as tyrannical their interference with William's grants. These tracts participated in the groundswell of royalist fervor that accompanied the theatrical trials of the impeached Lords. Moments of skillfully crafted panegyric affirm the excellence of monarchy while enshrining the view that Crown patronage is a power held indivisibly by the king alone, who dispenses royal bounty through extra-parliamentary exercise of his prerogative will. And in this panegyric the emotive force of emblematic royalist icons is tapped: William is cast as the benevolent Hand of Divine Providence and as Lady Justice in *Contests and Dissensions*, and as the Fountains of Favor and Justice in *The Original Power*.

Thus we can witness the late slide toward parliamentary patronal sovereignty being written out of eighteenth-century constitutional thought. But Pocock in *The Machiavellian Moment* and *The Political Works of James Harrington* labors to build a case for the "Country" neo-Harringtonian triumph of mixed legislative constitutionalism by the end of William's reign, and even misguidedly extrapolates from rhetorical surfaces of counterattack in "*Discourse of the Nobles and Commons*" and *The True-Born Englishman* to credit Swift and Defoe with advancing into Queen Anne's England this "science of virtue," of which Harrington was "the fountainhead" (*MM*, pp. 481, 484; *PLT*, 108).[50]

V

Rather, Swift's *Contests and Dissensions* is a patchwork of satiric allegories in which the learned historical drapery wheeled out by Country propagandists like Davenant and Toland is parodied in general, and its true

---

50. On this proclaimed 'Country' triumph, Jonathan Clark has been duly skeptical, but the corrective adjustments accomplished by his work pay no attention to the fact or implications of the *return*, after 1701, to a constitutional framework significantly defined by royal patronal sovereignty. Clark has even remarked that late Georgian parliamentarians accepted closeted high-political maneuvers used to form teams of royal managerial elites "because they concerned so wholly the King's prerogative, as yet unchallenged in theory, to choose his ministers" (*The Dynamics of Change: The Crisis of the 1750s and English Party Systems* (Cambridge: Cambridge UP [1982], p. 421).

polemic tenor subversively recast to serve Williamite ends.[51] Consider the first of Swift's many specimens culled from Roman history to illustrate "Oligarchy, or Tyranny of the *Few*" — all of which are intended to vilify Country MPs.[52] Swift in this initial specimen draws a parallel between the rule of the Decemvirs and Country partisans' incursions into royal patronage made through their input into the Act of Settlement of 1701:

> These very Men, though chosen for such a Work, as the digesting a Body of laws for the Government of a free State, did immediately usurp Arbitrary Power, ran into all the Forms of it... One of them proceeding so far as to endeavour to force a Lady of great Virtue: the very Crime which gave Occasion to the Expulsion of the Regal Power but sixty years before. (p. 7)

Through manipulation of his analogy, Swift tacitly refutes the Country Party's satiric portrait of William as a sexually licentious tyrant and shifts its terms of attack (disguised as grounds for animadverting on the Decemvirs) onto Country Commoners — who had recently exploited the urgent need for the succession bill by proposing under its title such Party provisions as the prohibition of royal grants to foreigners, which were represented by their leading architect the Tory Country partisan John Grobham Howe as libertarian safeguards to supplement the Bill of Rights. Swift in the passage takes particular aim at Howe. His lines that refer to Appius Claudius' rape of Virginia embed an allusion to the sexual advances Howe reputedly made to William's Queen Mary. Further, through the technique of a double parallel time-scheme, Swift satirizes Howe as one who has "endeavour[ed] to" reenact Tarquin the Sixth's Rape of Lucrece ("the very Crime ..."), as did the Stuart politician Thomas Wentworth, Earl of Strafford, who was rumored to have sexually harassed the Irish Lord Chancellor's wife, Lady Loftus, prior to his impeachment and execution in 1641, near the start of the first Civil War ("the Expulsion of the Regal Power but sixty years before").[53] Through these allusions to

---

51. I am grateful to A.C. Elias, Hermann J. Real, and Michael Seidel for advice on my specific queries about Swift's *Contests and Dissensions*.

52. Jonathan Swift, *A Discourse of the Contests and Dissensions between the Nobles and the Commons in Athens and Rome* (October 1701), p. 7. Subsequent references are taken from this issue, citations to which will appear parenthetically in my text.

53. On Howe's reputed sexual overtures to Queen Mary, see *Parliament Trust Commons, 1690–1715*, 3:417.

the crime of rape and its furious avengement, Swift casts William as a victim of Country depredation, which among other things is figured as a reprise of late Cavalier and Roundhead atrocities combined.

In his Chapter III, "*Of the Dissensions between the Patricians and Plebeians in Rome*," Swift strikes at Country pseudo-populism and the tyrannic horrors supposedly unleashed by it. Herein he reduplicates Toland's work of linking the Gracchi's agrarian law to the affair of William's Irish grants, although his comparison is between this redistributive law and Gracchan Country partisans' reconveyance in the name of plebeian welfare of the "*Conquered Lands*, to be divided, beside a *great private Estate left by a King*" (p. 34). While developing this parallel that decries the Resumption Act of 1700 as the Party's oligarchical scheme to recapture power through "such an Addition of Property," Swift at one point celebrates the few "wisest among the Nobles" who attempted to block its passage, especially "the *Appian*" — i.e. John Lowther, Viscount Lonsdale. We hear that this noble, "having made a Speech against this Division of Lands, was Impeach'd by the People of High Treason, and a Day appointed for his Tryal; but disdaining to make his Defence chose rather the usual *Roman* Remedy of killing himself: After whose Death the Commons prevailed, and the Lands were divided among them" (p. 29). Lonsdale had indeed strongly opposed the Bill's passage in the Lords. He was one of the signatories to the recorded protest, which pronounced that "the lords can by no means consent, that the commons shall take upon them to dispose of any of the said forfeitures to any private persons, it being the sole and undoubted right of the crown to be the distributors of all bounties."[54] Lonsdale — who had succeeded Somers as Lord Privy Seal in 1696 — is fictiously a fifth Impeached Lord here in Swift's allegory: he had recently spent months at *Bath* dying of a fatal illness (thus "disdaining to make his Defence chose rather the usual *Roman* Remedy," of suicide).

In Swift's story, Lonsdale and his protesting Peers challenge the machinations of an anti-patrician faction in the senate whose aggressions have advanced to the point of naked usurpation. We are told that, "by procurement of the elder *Gracchus*" and his "younger Brother [who] pursued the same design," it was "declar'd by their Legislative Authority" that the confiscated lands "were not to be disposed of by the *Nobles*, but by the *Commons*" (pp. 34–35). It is the Country Commoners of Dissenting heritage, Robert and Edward Harley, who are Swift's equivalents of the Gracchi.

---

54. Cobbett's Parliamentary History, 5:1219.

Through this specific parallel, they are tarred as a more destructive version of the Old Puritan rebels; for Swift through allusion compares them to parliamentary revolutionaries in the Civil Wars and Interregnum: "from the expulsion of the Kings; tho' the People…sometimes [went] so far as to pull and hale one another about the *Forum*; yet no Blood was ever drawn in any popular Commotions till the time of the *Gracchi*" (pp. 31–32). But, Swift suggests, Oliver Cromwell and cohorts' violent diminution of the Long Parliament to the Rump supplies no close analogue of sanguinary Gracchan times, including Harleyite days at hand. For, Swift in this passage additionally alludes to the execution of Charles I, but the reference is satirically euphemized (at one level) as "the expulsion of the Kings" because he is hinting that the times in England produced no great bloodbath when compared to Lonsdale's Williamite martyrdom, to its heroic replications to be expected from the Impeachments of his Peers, or to a predictable repetition of the grisly murders of the brothers Gracchi by popular reactionary rage.

Numerous images of atrocities, all blamed on the Country initiative, appear throughout *Contests and Dissensions*, functioning to heighten Swift's almost continuous metaphorical descriptions of violent Party tyranny. At one key point, however, his satire is directed at the Party's own patronage relations, which supposedly underpin its Crown patronal encroachments. Swift paints these relations as vilely corrupt. "While *Rome* was governed by Kings," he relates at the opening of Chapter III in his account of the reign of Romulus, "its people were divided into patricians and plebeians":

The former were like the Barons of *England* sometime after the Conquest; and the latter are also described to be almost exactly what our Commons were then. For, they were Dependants upon the Patricians, whom they chose for their Patrons and Protectors, to answer for their Appearance, and defend them in any Process: They also supplied their Patrons with Money in exchange for their Protection. This Custom of *Patronage*, it seems, was very antient[.] (pp. 25–26)

With characteristic Swiftian irony and satiric indirection, feudal England's royal High Court, from which plebeians were excluded but able to purchase influence, is nostalgically recalled and favorably compared to a Country-led Parliament, where similar exchanges are still practiced but which now includes Commoners, who pay venal Lords whom they retain as Party collaborators.

This attack on corrupt Country MPs imparts crucial topical material back into Swift's arresting definition of political tyranny in Chapter I, which contains his illustrative figure of twin scales thrown out of equipoise when the balance breaks between their equal weights measuring divided patrician and plebeian power. Swift uses this illustration to attack Country Commoners, who are portrayed by allegorical and allusive means as grasping plebs engaged in violently usurping the authority of their social superiors. And it is used, when re-stocked with Swift's material on corrupt Country MPs, to pursue this attack coherently through the focal-point of satire leveled at the Party's patronal claims. Through art of juxtaposition, this satire works in tandem with Swift's adumbrated panegyric in the passage, which at once celebrates William as a pattern of virtuous patronage and as England's sovereign force of stabilizing concord.

Swift's rhetorical carapace here is that of a lecture on the Whig constitutional ideal of a Polybian balance between monarchical, aristocratic, and democratic institutions of government. "The true Meaning of a Balance of Power, either without or within a State," he writes, "is best conceived by considering what the nature of a Balance is":

It supposes three Things, First, the Part which is held, together with the Hand that holds it; and then the two Scales, with whatever is weighed therein. Now consider several States in a Neighbourhood: In order to Preserve Peace between these States, it is necessary they should be formed into a Balance, whereof one or more are to be Directors, who are to divide the rest into equal Scales, and upon Occasions remove from one into the other, or else fall with their own Weight into the Lightest. So in a State within it self, the Balance must be held by a third Hand... When the Balance is broke, whether by the Negligence, Folly or Weakness of the Hand that held it, or by mighty Weights fallen into either Scale, the Power will never continue long in equal Division between the two remaining Parties, but (till the Balance is fixed anew) will run entirely into one. This gives the truest account of what is understood by the word *Tyranny*[.] (pp. 5-6)

Swift takes aim at Country partisans' gains in Parliament by depicting them as weights falling into twin scales to crash a system of balanced government. His description is rendered more grotesquely fanciful still when these "mighty Weights" take on human form, becoming the bribing Commoners and venal Lords of his later sketch on intra-parliamentary patronage. These MPs now appear as the moral antitypes of 'the hand that holds the balance'—who is William, invoked by the title for which he was hailed for concluding the Treaty of Ryswick. In Swift's domestic version of this international heroic role, a colossal William is suggestively pictured palming a set of twin scales containing the corrupt diminutive partisans. Already, the future author of *Gulliver's Travels* is comically equating ratios of human physical and moral size.

In Swift's fantastic scene here, the binned Country MPs engage in dirty patronage relations, with hands that sell out the nation and eyes blind to the common good. William, by contrast, is portrayed fulfilling his obligation to act as the nation's hands and sight; indeed, he is cast as the living image of the traditional royalist icons of the Hand of Providence ("a third hand")[55] and Blind Justice ("the two Scales"). Swift's multiple conflations of William's roles of patron and monarch not only counter the satiric Country depictions of his patronage as the plunder of a tyrant, but they also reject the theory of parliamentary patronal sovereignty, so recently propounded by the defensive Party propagandists. Swift, by commingling representations of William's dispensations of patronage with his broader exercise of kingship, stigmatizes this theory as an argument against monarchy itself. Moreover, to attend to the symbolic imagery of his Williamite panegyric is to see his own constitutional thought running in a wholly opposite direction, toward an assertion of the excellence of feudal English monarchy. The royalist emblems of the Providential Hand and Lady Justice had, in Norman and early Angevin times, exalted the king's patronal power, which functioned both as a preventative against blood feuds waged over national honors and as a gifting policy that unified local chieftains under the more pacific banner of eligible contestants and recipients of royal bounty.[56] Implicit in that emblematic art, now revived by Swift, was a theory of monarchical sovereignty which almost wholly defined the concept as the godly king's exercise of patronage.

To turn from Swift's *Contests and Dissensions* to Defoe's *The Original Power of the Collective Body of the People of England* is to see yet another superfi-

---

55. Swift here embeds a literal allusion to the Stadholder's *main de justice.*

56. On such feudal patronal power, consult Peter Brown, "The Rise and Function of the Holy Man in Late Antiquity" (1971), in his *Society and the Holy in Late Antiquity* (Berkeley and Los Angeles: U of California P, 1982), pp. 103–52; Linda Levy Peck, "'For a King Not to be Bountiful Were a Fault': Perspectives on Court Patronage in Early Stuart England," *Journal of British Studies* 25 (1986): 31–61; her Court Patronage and Corruption in Early Stuart England (Boston: Unwin Hyman, 1990), ch. 1.

cial but polemically manipulated exposition of a familiar component of
Whig constitutionalism—resistance doctrine—together again with
Williamite panegyric that conflates the roles of patron and monarch for
purposes of attacking Country MPs and rejecting on royalist grounds the
theory of parliamentary patronal sovereignty.

VI

In *The Original Power*, it is the Whig doctrine of justified popular resistance to tyranny that functions as a rhetorical pretext by which Defoe attacks a Country-led Parliament and extols William as a patronal king.
Defoe in this tract postures as a political thinker seeking to correct Humphrey Mackworth's theory of parliamentary sovereignty, to which this resistance doctrine had formed the linchpin. Mackworth, he insists, failed
to consider the matter of the people's right to resist the lawless proceedings of MPs, and so did not duly distinguish between the collective
body of English freeholders and its abridged form of lesser and greater
propertied representatives in Parliament, who are but "the Nations Servants."[57] "Had Sir *H. M.* gone on to have Recogniz'd the Peoples Right,
to preserve their own Liberties in case of failure in any, or in all the Branches of the Constituted Power," we hear, "he had completed his *Vindication of the Commons of England*, which no Man could have done better than
himself" (p. 12).[58]
    With ironic sensibility, Defoe turns Whig resistance doctrine against
a Country-led Parliament that he accuses of maladministrative tyranny,
while tacitly parodying this doctrine's pseudo-hypothetical application
in Mackworth's pamphlet: "*if* the Male-Administration of Governours have
extended to Tyranny and Oppression, to Destruction of Right and Justice,
overthrowing the Constitution, and abusing the People, the People have
thought it Lawful to Re-assume the Right of Government into their own
Hands" (p. 5–6, my italics). Writing in the wake of the acquittals of the

---

57. Daniel Defoe, *The Original Power of the Collective Body of the People of
England, Examined and Asserted* (1702), p. 23. Subsequent citations appear parenthetically in my text. Italics have been reversed in my quotations from the
work's dedication to Parliament (sigs. A2r–A3v).

58. Repeatedly in *The Original Power*, Defoe refers sarcastically to Humphrey
Mackworth by his initials, which are also those of 'His Majesty.'

Four Lords, Defoe claims that the delays in their trials, ostensibly caused by conflicts over procedure, inflicted great damage to these English freeholding nobles and hence to "the Subject in general." "[T]o see Disputes between the Two Houses about Punctilios of Form," he retrospects, "interrupt the due and ordinary Course of Justice; so that a Criminal cannot be Detected, nor an Innocent Man be Justified, but such Impeachments shall lie as a Brand upon the Reputation of an Innocent Person... *is a Punishment worse than his Crime deserv'd, if he were Guilty*" (p. 15). Equally egregious, Defoe suggests, was the injustice that Country legislators perpetrated on William by their "manner of fixing Guilt upon a Person or Party by Vote," as when they cast imputations on his Irish grants, bounty which had so reasonably matched Lordships to great freeholds: "if the Royal Favours of Princes has Dignified Families, it has always been thought fit to bestow or to enable them to Purchase some Portion of the Freehold of *England* to be annexed to the said Titles, to make such Dignity rational" (sig. [A2r], p. 15).

Midway through *The Original Power*, Defoe develops an analogy that likens such betrayals of English liberties to the legalistic manipulations of James II's Catholicizing policies; and at various points he satirically qualifies this satiric parallel by suggesting that the Country proceedings were tyrannical ("*this noble well-contrived System has been Overwhelmed*; the Government has been Inverted"), whereas James' indulgence of his Popish "inclination" never extended so far ("I presume I may affirm, That the Deposing King *James* was founded upon his Deserting the Nation, not his Male-administration" [pp. 8, 21]). The pamphlet's "Conclusion" celebrates William's recent dissolution of his 5th Parliament in terms meant to recall his Revolutionary intervention in 1688, Defoe finding in the King's Proclamation of 11 November 1701, declaring his subjects' fresh "*Opportunity to chuse such Persons to Represent them in Parliament, as they may judge most likely to bring to effect their just and pious Purposes*," a "glorious Recognition," "from the Restorer of *English* Liberty," of the populist principles that have ever compelled William to harken to "the Voice of the People," and so "to depose *for them* a Power which they saw going to be misapplied to the Ruine of those from whom and for whom it was appointed" (p. 24). In speaking of England's plaintive subjects who witnessed power "going to be misapplied" to their ruin, Defoe alludes ambivalently to James' Popish designs and to Country tyranny.

The royalist Williamite twist of this "Conclusion" is, while unexpected in a tract so apparently committed to asserting popular power, subtly prepared earlier, when Defoe exclaims against the Church Tory tenet

of non-resistance but only to assert another theory of divine right king-
ship, one which postulates a bulwark of conjoint monarchical and popular sovereign power in the event of failed representative institutions of
English government. In the pamphlet's dedicatory preface "To the King,"
Defoe blasts Tory belief in that "preposterous and inconsistent Forgery"
of "The Authority of Governours *Jure Divino*," but he then interjects,
"And yet, if the *Vox Populi* be, as 'tis generally allow'd, *Vox Dei*, your Majesty's
Right to these Kingdoms *Jure Divino*, is more plain than any of Your Predecessors" (sig. A1v). In the tract proper, he goes on to provide two examples of this imagined conjunction of William's monarchical authority and God's vocalic instrumentalization of the English people. They
are proffered in a passage that (which, while again ironically mimicking
Country hyperbole about royal patronage abuse) reintroduces, but satirically underscores the inexactness of, the analogy between tyrannical
Country proceedings and James' aborted Catholicizing designs. For Defoe suggests that, in the case of Country MPs' maladministration, "the
Peoples Liberties have been trampled on, and Parliaments have been ren-
dred useless and insignificant: and *what has restored us?* The last resort has
been to the People; *Vox Dei has been found there*, not in the *Representatives*,
but in their Original the *Represented*" (p. 8). In context, Defoe hints that ruinous Country proceedings culminated in populist tyrannicide (if however bloodlessly performed by William's dissolution of his 5th Parliament;
"*Vox Populi* has been found there"), in contrast to the Revolution of 1688,
which ended not in deposition (since James' Popish design failed before
extending to tyrannic maladministration), but in populist election (which
saw William accept the offer of James' vacated throne from the people's
delegates at the Convention), and thus in a less extreme assertion of the
original power of Whig libertarianism ("*Vox Dei* has been found there").

   Defoe's representation in his "Conclusion" of a second glorious revolution in 1701, brought off by a godly prince and a divinely possessed
people, is bolstered by his ontotheological theory of the virtuous irre-
sistibility of monarchy in England. At the core of Country anti-Williamite
oratory, he finds the masked voice of viciously corrupt politicians, who
have bartered their way into the House by "*private Briberies* and Clandestine
Contrivances"; "*No Man would give a Groat to sit where he cannot get a Groat
honestly for sitting, unless there were either Parties to gratifie, Profits to be made,
or Interest to support*" (p. 14). But at the heart of England's rightfully resisting people, who supposedly appealed to William to depose these governors turned tyrants, is its monarchical disposition; in Defoe's words, "The
Genius of this Nation has always appear'd to tend to a Monarchy" (p. 13).

In his anti-Country *True-Born Englishman*—to which *The Original Power* is a pendant—William is pictured as this philo-monarchical people's ideal symbiotic object. In the poem's panegyric section "Britannia's Song," William plays the Messiah to Britannia's Angel of the Apocalypse, who announces:

> My Hero, with the Sails of Honour furl'd,
> Rises like the Great Genius of the World.
> By Fate and Fame wisely prepar'd to be
> *The Soul of War, and Life of Victory.*
> He spreads the Wings of Virtue on the Throne,
> And ev'ry *Wind of Glory* fans them on.
> Immortal Trophies dwell upon his Brow,
> Fresh as the Garlands he has won but now. ([ll.] 905–12)[59]

This verse-'character' is full of elevating descriptions of royal bounty in courtesy language ("Honour furl'd," "spreads the Wings of Virtue on the Throne," "Glory fans them on," "Immortal Trophies"). Consequently, William's monarchical rule and patronage conduct are exalted in terms of one another. And underlying these doubled panegyric terms is the polemic strategy of suggestively deeming Country critics enemies of monarchy in general. In lines 909–10, for example, Defoe employs obverse statement to insinuate that they spread false rumors about William's munificence, ingloriously defaming the excellence of monarchy itself. But additionally, (as in Swift's *Contests and Dissensions*) this oblique satire is presented within a context of constitutional thought, imagistically expressed, which is decidedly hostile to any and all Country claims of parliamentary sovereignty. Significantly, Defoe's attack on inglorious Country enemies here is immediately framed by his vision of William as a cosmogonic patronal king and by his identification of William in the "Song" as the millennial Christ—images that by implication idealize monarchical omnipotence.

In the *Original Power*, moreover, such idealization continues when Defoe lays down certain maxims that are seemingly only in elaboration of the concept of the popular *vox dei*, but which in context, and viewed in the light of his theory of English subjects' philo-monarchical genius, evoke the traditional royalist emblems of the sovereign king as a Fountain of Favor and Fountain of Justice. Defoe writes: "Power which is Original, is Superior; *God is the Fountain of all Power*"; "Now it cannot be sup-

---

59. Defoe, *The True-Born Englishman. A Satyr* (1700), p. 53.

pos'd this Original Fountain should give up all its Waters, but that it re-
serves a Power of supplying the Streams"; "Nor has the Streams any power to turn back upon the Fountain, and invert its own Original. All such
Motions are Eccentric and Unnatural" (p. 9). In context, these maxims
invite a topical allegorical reading that at once assigns deific authority
to William and his freeholding loyalists and attributes the evil of rebel-
lious anarchism to Country MPs, whose activities are likened to motions
"eccentric and unnatural" which self-destructively subvert the order of
divine bountiful Nature. At the same time, they figure forth a conception of constitutional formation in which Defoe envisions the hierarchical ideal of an English monarch and His People concurrently efflu-
escing supreme divine power by which parliamentary functionaries are
controlled and subsist.

In his mock-epic *Jure Divino* (1706), Defoe continues to embrace this
constitutional ideal, while he again attacks Country MPs as sacrilegious
rebels against deific William and His People. In Book 11, he petitions his
satiric muse, "Sing monstrous Births, and unforeseen Events, / Of Patriot
Kings, and Tyrant Parliaments; / Such Wonders startled Nature never
saw, / Submissive Crowns, and tyrannizing Law…Forbear to write, for
who without a Tear, / Can injur'd *William's* dying Hist'ry hear; / How conquer'd by Ingratitude he fell." In preceeding stanzas, Defoe eulogizes a
Christic William, who "show'd all Kings how they might be Divine: /
Open'd the Gate of Honour to their View"; "Constitution's built upon
his Name." In a footnote Defoe adds that kings in William's Glorious line
"reign for Heaven, and are instructed from thence, and claim a Divinity
of Honour, tho' not of Person."[60]

Unsurprisingly, a different conspectus was tendered by the Whig ex-
Country MP, Richard Cocks. In his parliamentary diary entries for February 1701, Cocks reflected gloomily on England's declined monarchy
and instanced as his main case in point the late Country perceptions of
a patronal William and his most favored grantees. After lamenting how
in post-Restoration times "we lost the right names of things and at last
the things themselves," he imputes to false courteous glosses of "royall
bounty and Princely munificence and Generosity" what he speaks of as
"the extravagant luxury of our kings their great grants" and "those that
by pimping…Like the harpyes devoured all that was in their way." He
then proceeds to single out as particularly vicious William's Irish grant
to Lady Orkney, since, "worth about 10000 li. Per annum," "this was a lit-

---

60 Defoe, *Jure Divino. A Satyr. In Twelve Books* (1706), 9:20, 26–27.

tle to[o] much to be granted to one mistris it was used to be the establishment and provision for them for all king Jameses were provided out of
it."[61]

That these Whig coevals in Defoe and Cocks should thus argue versions of the king's two bodies was endemic to an ideological universe
that had taken a royalist turn, to a point where the conception of a divine
patronal king 'above the Parliament' was, after the Impeachments of 1701,
no longer a preoccupation but a common presumption. It was a world
with no close parallels in Pocock's neo-Harringtonian version of English
history of the 1960s.

61. Richard Cocks, *The Parliamentary Diary of Sir Richard Cocks, 1698–1702*,
ed. D. W. Hayton (Oxford: Clarendon P, 1996), pp. 210, 214.

6. Pocock's History of Political Thought, the Ancient Constitution, and Early Stuart England

GLENN BURGESS

The human experience of time has always been at the centre of J.G.A. Pocock's attention. One of his favorite metaphors for the historian, drawn from the "Preface" to Hegel's *Philosophy of Right*, likens hu to the owl of Minerva, whose flight at dusk provided the setting for mature reflection on the day that had passed.[1] At one level, the comparison might suggest no more than the obvious point that the historian's subject matter is always in the past. But it does more than that. It suggests also that the historian is a participant in the day's events. Hu might not fight battles in the noonday sun, or labour in the fields from dawn; but hu is there, alert and reflective, at dusk. There is no discontinuity between the time of the owl's flight and the rest of the day: the historian is immersed in the flow of time that also forms hu subject matter. A sense of this predicament has been an emphatic presence in Pocock's work. The historian's present there-

---

1. For example, see Pocock, "On the Non-Revolutionary Character of Paradigms," in *PLT*, p. 291 esp., and his "The Owl Reviews his Feathers," in *J.G.A. Pocock's Valedictory Lecture: Presented at The Johns Hopkins Univeristy, 1994* (Baltimore: Archangul, 2006). *Hegel's Philosophy of Right*, ed. and trans. T. M. Knox (Oxford: Clarendon P, 1952), pp. 12–13: Hegel was, of course, talking of the role of the *philosopher*, and explaining why the philosopher's understanding of the actual world was doomed always to arrive too late to provide effective advice on how that world ought to have been.

fore becomes important to hu understanding of the past. This, the inescapable 'presentism' of historical inquiry, does not open the floodgates
to the irrationalist tide.[2] But the interconnectedness of past and present
does mean that the past as constructed (formed) by historians will vary
with the circumstances in which its construction (formation) occurs.[3] Pocock has had no doubt, for example, that the entry of the United Kingdom into the European Economic Community has altered profoundly
the way that historians have approached its history, leading to efforts of
various sorts to Europeanise the history of Britain.[4] There are those who
would claim that to place British history in European context is to re-
alise that British history has no identity apart from its place in a European
narrative. Against these simplicities Pocock has urged us to see European
history not "as a single process" but "as many processes not all leading
the same way: a cavalcade of foxes rather than of hedgehogs."[5] As a result, the Europe whose history we might strive to write must be seen as
fluid, its nature and identity changing as our sense of its constituent parts

---

2. Consult Pocock, "Notes of an Occidental Tourist II," *Common Knowledge*
2 (1993): 16: "One can never eliminate oneself as interpreter, or the language one
uses, from the accounts one gives of who they [i.e. people in the past] were and
what they did and said and experienced; the blood one gives the ghosts must be
one's own, or the blood one shares with others; but it is possible to reason about
the ways in which this must be so, and to give discussable accounts of one's reasons for holding that they were as one has described them."

3. For Pocock's preference for "formation" over "construction, see the open-
ing paragraph of his "The Treaty between Histories," in *Histories, Power and Loss:
Uses of the Past—A New Zealand Commentary*, ed. Andrew Sharp and Paul McHugh
(Wellington: Bridget Wills, 2001), ch. 4.

4. Pocock, "History and Sovereignty: The Historiographical Response to Europeanisation in Two British Cultures," *Journal of British Studies* 31 (1992):
358–89. Pocock has mounted a considerable campaign to mitigate the worst excesses of this development, especially a tendency to assert that the Europeanisation
of British (or English) history must mean that neither of those subjects can have
an identity of their own. See, for example, Pocock, "Enlightenment and Counter-
Enlightenment, Revolution and Counter-Revolution: A Eurosceptical Enquiry,"
History of Political Thought 20 (1999): 125–39; his "Some Europes in Their History," in *The Idea of Europe: From Antiquity to the European Union*, ed. Anthony Pagden (Cambridge: Cambridge UP, 2002), ch. 2; his "Deconstructing Europe," in
DI, ch. 15. And note particularly the strength of feeling behind the remarks in
his "*Vous autres Européens*—or Inventing Europe," *Filozofski Vestnik/Acta Philosophica*
14 (1993): 141–42.

5. Pocock, "Notes of an Occidental Tourist I, *Common Knowledge* 2 (1993): 5.

changes. "Europe" is an open and indeterminable concept, without natural frontiers, whose present structure and usable past history must necessarily be modified each time a new partner is admitted to the program of its integration."[6] It is not just that the owl of Minerva flies always at dusk: its flight today may be over a Europe differently configured from yesterday, and no doubt the territorial landscape will be different again for tomorrow's flight.

In another key phrase Pocock has talked of himself as an historian "working on ideas in time." Again, "in time" can be a location for the historian as well as for the ideas that he studies.[7] This thought has led Pocock to ask how it is that some societies and not others pursue an approach to their pasts that is historical rather than traditional. This contrast identifies the historian as "something more than the expositor of a traditional relationship with the past." Historians, at least those who pursue the Rankean objective of "describ[ing] the past 'as it really was,'" exist in societies whose traditional relationship with the past has been "ruptured."[8] It is important to note that in this the historian is a figure whose connectedness with the past takes a particular form. Hu may come into existence "when the traditional statements of such continuities [between past and present] are exposed to challenge…[and] may in certain circumstances be restated in the form of authentically historical explanations."[9] Note the force of the word "restated" in this: Pocock has not altogether abandoned the view that even an authentically historical historian might, in sophisticated ways, be as much "entrusted [with] the keeping of the useful myths" as are the guardians of traditional accounts of the relationship between past and present.[10]

In more recent work, he has continued this early interest in the comparative study of understandings of time and history with particular reference to the way in which the Maori, the *tangata whenua* ("people of the land," or indigenous inhabitants) of *Aoteoroa*/New Zealand, have under-

---

6. Pocock, "Occidental Tourist II," p. 138.

7. The phrase is taken from Pocock, "Working on Ideas in Time," in *The Historian's Workshop: Original Ideas by Sixteen Historians*, ed. L. P. Curtis (New York, 1970), pp. 151–65.

8. Pocock, "The Origins of the Study of the Past: A Comparative Approach," *Comparative Studies in Society and History* 4 (1962): 215, 217.

9. Pocock, "Origins of the Study of the Past," p. 243.

10. The quoted phrase is from Carl Becker, "Everyman His Own Historian," *American Historical Review* 37 (1931–32): 231. I do not intend to suggest that Pocock accepts this view in the same way that Becker does.

stood their past, and how this differs from the approach to history dominant in the intellectual world of the *pakeha* (New Zealanders of European
origin). In contemporary New Zealand we can see a collision between
different conceptions of time that has had the impact to make of the
country "the only sovereign state in the English-speaking world that has
chosen to acknowledge a history in which its sovereignty is conditional
upon the performance of promises entailed by a treaty with an indigenous people more than a century and a half ago [the Treaty of Waitangi,
1840]."[11] The Treaty brought face to face two very different histories, and
these "alternate histories are contesting for authority; not simply alternative accounts of the same events, but alternative cultural codes which
give conflicting accounts of what authority is, how it is generated in and
transmitted through time, and how time and history are themselves struc-
tured by the authoritative systems set up by humans existing in them."
New Zealanders, living in a world shaped by the Treaty and its subsequent reception, are "trying to live in two histories simultaneously pen-
etrating one another."[12] In this context Pocock has found it useful to contrast the "dreamtime" of some aboriginal peoples, which folds space and
time into a sense of relationship with the cosmos, with the linear time
of (Western) history.[13] This approach to an understanding of contemporary New Zealand politics thus continues an inquiry that has always been
at the very heart of John Pocock's work, understanding in comparative and
social context the ways in which human societies locate themselves in
time. This has been a highly self-reflective inquiry, for the 'history' that
Pocock practices is, as he has been the first to note, but one of many possible ways of forming a usable relationship with the past. Thus, he has
acknowledged in the New Zealand context "that 'history' is a heavily
freighted Pakeha term which we may never be able to separate from its
Pakeha meanings, and that to include Maori in it may be no less an attempt at domination than to exclude them from it."[14] This sensitivity
comes both from Pocock's powerful imaginative capacity — if asked to
choose one word that characterised the power-source of his historical

---

11. Pocock, "The Uniqueness of Aoteoroa," *Proceedings of the American Philosophical Society*, 145 (2001): 485.

12. Pocock, "Law, Sovereignty and History in a Divided Culture: The Case
of New Zealand and the *Treaty of Waitangi*, in *DI*, p. 231. See also p. 246 for a powerful contrast between the histories of the Maori and the pakeha.

13. Pocock, "Law, Sovereignty and History," pp. 251–52.

14. Pocock, "Treaty between Histories," p. 81.

writing I would opt for "imagination"—and from an acceptance of the fact that our social need for a relationship with the past is far from exhausted when we acquire the ability to make (or, rather, to assert and to discuss) truth claims about it.

But "working on ideas in time" more obviously refers to an intellectual activity that concerns itself with the study of past ideas. For Pocock's work, the phrase has a stronger, more precise meaning that makes it more than just another label for what we call "intellectual history."[15] From his earliest work on 'the common law mind' to his most recent on Gibbon, Pocock's subject matter has been the ways in which people in the past think about time. Perhaps that puts the matter in a way that too much suggests deliberate reflection. Pocock's interest has above all been in the paradigms or languages that convey or contain assumptions about the location of political communities in time. "Political discourse," Pocock tells us, may be considered "the intellect's attempt to construct an intelligible world out of political experience," while his own work has shown greatest interest in political discourse conducted through "modes of thought which entail an image of a past and its relation to the present."[16] "There is a point," he has said, "at which historical and political theory meet," and it is at this point that much of his own research has taken place.[17]

Thus Pocock has shown greatest interest in those political writers for whom reflection on time was most important. Machiavelli could be understood in relation to differing conceptions of time, as a man "refusing to live in Christian time governed by redemption, [who] must therefore live in pagan time governed by *fortuna*."[18] More startlingly, perhaps, Pocock has also introduced us to the wonderful spectacle constituted by the efforts of the supposedly 'secular' Thomas Hobbes to tinker with the work of the great watchmaker himself, and produce a reading of Christian time compatible with the verities of Hobbesian civil science.[19] In some of his

---

15. Compare the comment on intellectual history in Pocock, "Treaty between Histories," p. 155.

16. Pocock, "Treaty between Histories," pp. 154, 157.

17. Pocock, "Time, Institutions and Action: An Essay on Traditions and their Understanding," in *Politics and Experience: Essays presented to Michael Oakeshott on the Occasion of his Retirement* (Cambridge: Cambridge UP, 1968), p. 209.

18. Pocock, "Machiavelli and the Rethinking of History," *Il Pensiero Politico* 27 (1994): 221.

19. Pocock, "Time, History and Eschatology in the Thought of Thomas Hobbes," in *PLT,* ch. 5.

earliest remarks on a political writer who was to play a central role in his own work, and whose writings he was to edit, Pocock has said of Harrington's *Oceana* that it was "a Machiavellian meditation upon feudalism."[20] Thus a central feature of Harrington's thought was the way in which it understood the present in relation to historical change. Little needs to be said about his most recent work on Gibbon, for its concern with another thinker who wished to illuminate the present by recounting its relationship to the past is unmistakable.

II

The attempt just made to delineate the continuities of interest and inquiry that underlie all of John Pocock's work is important for a proper understanding of his first book (*The Ancient Constitution and the Feudal Law*) and of the work that surrounds it. The book is concerned very much with those ideas in time that are also ideas about time. It explores — as its subtitle makes explicit — "English historical thought" considered as a form of political thought. Pocock's account in this work of the "common law mind" — a label chosen "perhaps rashly," he now suggests[21] — has recently been forcefully challenged by J.W. Tubbs. Tubbs's work is important and enlightening as an account of common law thinking in late medieval and early modern England, and modifies much earlier work (including some of my own); and he appreciates that Pocock is concerned with historiography more than with theories of law.[22] Nonetheless, the criticisms he advances have only limited force against Pocock's work, which (as we will see more fully soon) is essentially an account of the contested emergence (and equally contested endurance) of what has come to be known as the Whig interpretation of history. Tubbs's central claim is that "although one may find references to the antiquity of the common law, or to the common law as the common custom of the realm, scattered through the seventeenth-century case reports, [any]one who systematically reads all those reports and the legal treatises of the time cannot avoid the impression that the things [Sir John] Davies emphasized about common law were not central to the leading common lawyers' vi-

---

20. Pocock, *ACFL*, p. 147.

21. Pocock, "Treaty between Histories," p. 82.

22. J. W. Tubbs, "Custom, Time and Reason: Early Seventeenth-Century Conceptions of the Common Law," *History of Political Thought* 19 (1998): 364.

sion of the common-law."[23] In particular, leading lawyers tended to see the common law as reason rather than as custom.[24] As is so often the way with debates amongst historians, views are not always as opposed as they seem.[25] Tubbs carefully acknowledges the existence of claims for the antiquity of English law even in the writings of those lawyers who are inclined to see law primarily as reason and not as custom, but he tends to marginalize these claims. There were various ways of combining the two perspectives in the period.[26] Whatever his valuable modification of the details (and I would not minimize the importance of these), Tubbs leaves largely unscathed two essential claims. (a) Amongst common lawyers and others there took shape a particular way of locating the present in time, one that was inclined to stress *continuity, repetition* and *precedent.* A jurisprudence that emphasized the character of law as reason could, in some circumstances, actually reinforce such a view. (b) This way of locating the present in history acquired considerable, though contestable, political importance in seventeenth-century England, and has continued to be of mythical importance, in the form of the Whig interpretation, as an account of the continuities of English law and institutions. Tubbs, while acknowledging the lip service paid by many lawyers to the importance of the antiquity of the law,[27] does not ask why they felt inclined to pay such lip service. On what grounds are some of the things people in the past say deemed to be less significant than other things? In any case it is perhaps of less significance for the way in which Pocock has developed his account of the 'common law mind' that many professional lawyers did not conform to the account than that it became one of the predominant ways in which a whole society located itself in time.

---

23. Tubbs, "Custom, Time and Reason," pp. 375–76.

24. Tubbs, "Custom, Time and Reason," p. 406.

25. As Tubbs himself is aware—"Custom, Time and Reason," p. 383.

26. This was, indeed, the essential point of my own account in *The Politics of the Ancient Constitution: An Introduction to English Political Thought, 1603–1642* (Basingstoke: Macmillan, 1992), Pt. 1. Subsequent work has modified some of this argument—it is clear, for example, that I was rather too inclined to connect John Selden into a 'standard account' of the history of English law. But the book does, at least, try to understand why so many lawyers, who often understood the law to be reason, were also willing to emphasise its antiquity or even its customary authority.

27. For more detail, see also J.W. Tubbs, *The Common Law Mind: Medieval and Early Modern Conceptions* (Baltimore: Johns Hopkins UP, 2000), p. 149.

III

Particularly revealing are those moments in which political communities confront challenges to the ways in which they have habitually located themselves in time. At such moments, when the disturbing must be faced, communities may well find themselves renewing and reinventing the ways in which they relate to their pasts. An example of this sort of moment that Pocock has briefly discussed came in 1554 when Mary Tudor married Philip of Spain. The so-called *Machiavellian Treatise*, which was written to advise Philip at this time, "assumed that he will be a *principe nuovo* in England and need all the Machiavellian arts proper to that condition, for no other reason than that the English have customs of their own, by which they must be governed but to which Philip will never be able to frame his own statecraft." We are here in a world "where custom directly confronts innovation."[28] The Machiavellian new prince must secure his throne by innovative means, rejecting customary approaches and ways (covertly if not overtly).

The present essay will explore another of these moments (only very partially Machiavellian) at which a new prince came to the English throne with habits of thought and action that were unlikely to adapt fully to English ways of rule. This moment plays an important role in linking together two subjects of central importance to John Pocock's historical work, 'the ancient constitution' and 'the new British history.'[29] He has remarked that any "community which has generated an image of its own identity as existing over time requires two kinds of history: the one autocentric, a record of how its inhabitants have dealt with one another over time, and the experiences they have undergone in establishing the bases of their

---

28. Pocock, "Machiavelli and the Rethinking of History," p. 222. In *A Machiavellian Treatise by Stephen Gardiner,* ed. Peter Donaldson (Cambridge: Cambridge UP, 1975), the attribution of the treatise to Gardiner is extremely doubtful: see Dermot Fenlon, review in *HJ* 19 (1976): 1019–23; Sydney Anglo, "Crypto-Machiavellism in Early Tudor England: The Problem of the *Regionamento dell'Adventimento delli Inglesi, et Normanni in Britannia," Renaissance and Reformation,* n.s. 2 (1978): 182–93; Glyn Redworth, *In Defence of the Catholic Church: The Life of Stephen Gardiner* (Oxford: Blackwell, 1990), p. 308 (n. 93).

29. Pocock, "The Limits and Divisions of British History: In Search of the Un-known Subject," *American Historical Review* 87 (1982), pp. 311–36; his "The New British History in Atlantic Perspective," *American Historical Review* 104 (1999): 490–500; his "British History: A Plea for a New Subject," in *DI,* ch. 2.

existing community; the other heterocentric, a record of how encounters with others, whom they have ruled or been ruled by, have contributed to the shaping and present character of both the 'self' community and the 'others,' autonomous or not, now contiguous with it."[30] I shall suggest that the idea of an insular ancient English constitution, which might itself seem the very model of an autocentric history, actually took the shape that it possessed for early Stuart Englishmen as an episode in a history decidedly heterocentric.

It may be, as Pocock has said, that much recent historical writing about Stuart England has been the "rendering contingent of a history formerly written as self-explanatory [which] has sometimes been intended to deprive it of any meaning of its own."[31] Part of this process has been framed as an attack on the Whig interpretation of history — an interpretation that Pocock has helped to explain and explore, the uses of which he has keenly appreciated, and to the demise of which he has contributed while still appreciating the value of that which he exposes to critical scrutiny.[32] The Whig interpretation, the roots of which are explored in *The Ancient Constitution and the Feudal Law*, provided the English with a 'self-explanatory' history, an autocentric history, for several centuries. This essay will attempt to show that at least some of the roots of this history extended beyond English soil: at a crucial point they grew into and drew sustenance from the soils of surrounding lands, most notably those of Scotland.

In works subsequent to *The Ancient Constitution and the Feudal Law*, Pocock has sketched something of the development of Whig historiography. Challenged by Filmer and Brady in the seventeenth century, and by Hume in the eighteenth, it still flourished in the nineteenth.[33] Pocock him-

---

30. Pocock, "The Third Kingdom in its History," in *DI*, p. 95.

31. Pocock, "Occidental Tourist II," p. 18.

32. Some of Pocock's relationship to Whig history can be appreciated from his brief remarks on the work of his own teacher and famous critic of Whig history, Herbert Butterfield; see his "The Varieties of Whiggism from Exclusion to Reform: A History of Ideology and Discourse," in *VCH*, pp. 215–16, 304–5. There was a complex ambivalence in Butterfield's attitude to the Whig tradition, and it is perhaps shared in certain respects by Pocock himself. For the most recent attempt to capture the complexity, see Keith C. Sewell, "The 'Herbert Butterfield Problem' and its Resolution," *Journal of the History of Ideas* 64 (2004), pp. 599–618.

33. Esp. Pocock, "Varieties of Whiggism" in *VCH*, pp. 362–87. Also important is the account of the relationship between Hume and ancient constitutionalism in Duncan Forbes, *Hume's Philosophical Politics* (Cambridge: Cambridge UP, 1975), ch. 8.

self has shown the connection between Burke and Coke;[34] others have shown the important place that Burke has in forming the historical thinking of some exemplary Whig historians, notably Macaulay and Acton.[35] Much less has been done to examine the early development of ideas of the ancient constitution—Tubbs's work discussed above contains important material though its focus of interest is elsewhere.[36] Clearly, the elements from which Edward Coke and Sir John Davies constructed their own views had a long pre-history, but it does seem that a new configuration of ideas about the past takes form at the beginning of the seventeenth century. Few, if any, of the elements in this configuration are new, but it comes to play a very powerful role in political argument during the seventeenth century, and thus an important role in laying the foundations for the dominance of Whig history. This essay will try to take a closer look at the circumstances in which this fresh configuration was formed.

IV

Scholars have identified a number of key themes in the ancient constitutionalist myths by which early Stuart Englishmen located themselves, their institutions and their laws in time. It should not be supposed that this was the only way that they had of understanding their place in time. There were others, some of which John Pocock has written about.[37] But it is with that cluster of ideas that formed the myth of the ancient constitution that I am here concerned. Paul Christianson has suggested that

---

34. Pocock, "Burke and the Ancient Constitution: A Problem in the History of Ideas," in *PLT*, ch. 6.

35. J.W. Burrow, *A Liberal Descent: Victorian Historians and the English Past* (Cambridge: Cambridge UP, 1981), esp. chs. 1–2; John Clive, *Not by Fact Alone: Essays on the Writing and Reading of History* (New York: Knopf, 1989), pp. 125–34; Gertrude Himmelfarb, *Lord Acton: A Study in Conscience and Politics* (London: Routledge, 1952); Hugh Tulloch, *Acton* (London: Weidenfeld and Nicolson 1988), p. 28, though Tulloch contests Butterfield's (early) identification of Acton as the highest form of Whig historian.

36. There is important material in Annabel Patterson, *Reading Holinshed's "Chronicles"* (Chicago: Chicago UP, 1994), and in Janelle Greenberg, *The Radical Face of the Ancient Constitution: St. Edward's "Laws" in Early Modern Political Thought* (Cambridge: Cambridge UP, 2001).

37. Esp. in Pocock, *MM*, ch. 10.

these ideas were first coherently and elaborately expressed by Thomas Hedley in the Impositions debate of 1610.[38] This, at any rate, seems a good place to look for the distinctive features of ancient constitutionalist thinking.

There are three themes in Hedley, and in ancient constitutionalism, to which I wish to draw attention. First, *immemoriality*. The common law was the product of "reason and time," "such time wherof the memory of man is not to the contrary, time out of mind." It was "a reasonable usage, throughout the whole realm, approved time out of mind in the king's courts of record which have jurisdiction over the whole kingdom, to be good and profitable for the commonwealth."[39] The term immemorial could have a technical legal meaning, with the limit of legal memory fixed at 1189; but it is not so clear that those who wrote more generally of the history of common law meant it to be taken in that sense. Even in specific matters, the term could be taken literally to refer to things beyond the memory of any living person. Debates amongst historians, lawyers and antiquaries showed little concern simply to prove usage as far back as 1189 and no further. The most significant implication of this understanding of law was that it left no room for a *law-maker*, either original or continuing. Laws evolved without being made by any authority. Strik-

---

38. Paul Christianson, "Ancient Constitutions in the Age of Sir Edward Coke and John Selden," in *The Roots of Liberty: Magna Carta, Ancient Constitution, and the Anglo-American Tradition of Rule of Law*, ed. Ellis Sandoz (Columbia MO: U of MO P, 1993), ch. 3, pp. 90, 97–102. Recent work has also explored the ways in which Hedley's speech is in important ways reliant on the vocabulary of Roman law; and it is important to recognize, not only that there was no inherent connection between Roman law and absolutism, but also that the languages of Roman and common law were by no means incompatible. Often they could interpenetrate. See Markku Peltonen, *Classical Humanism and Republicanism in English Poltical Thought, 1570–1640* (Cambridge: Cambridge UP, 1995), pp. 220–28, and Quentin Skinner, "Classical Liberty, Renaissance Translation and the English Civil War," in *Visions of Politics: Renaissance Virtues* (Cambridge: Cambridge UP, 2002), 2: ch. 12. The only thing to which I might object in some of these accounts is the suggestion that if arguments are neo-Roman or Roman law in character, then they are not anything else. Hedley, for example, is using a Roman law vocabulary to talk *about* the common law, and to provide a set of arguments to buttress a particular understanding of English common law and its political implications — see also Tubbs, *Common Law Mind*, pp. 149–51. There seems little point in asking whether he was a common law or a civil law thinker: he was both.

39. Elizabeth Read Foster, *Proceedings of Parliament, 1610*, 2 vols. (New Haven: Yale UP, 1966), 2:175; hereafter *PP 1610*.

ingly, that implication told against the authority of king-in-parliament as much as against the authority of the king alone. As Hedley put it, the Parliament may "amend" defects in the law," "[b]ut that the parliament may abrogate the whole law I deny, for that were includedly to take away the power of the parliament itself, which power it hath by the common law."[40] As a set of ideas, this was — to say the least — not well-shaped to serve as the ideology for parliamentary criticism of royal policy.

A second feature of ancient constitutionalism is its emphasis on the *perfection* of English law. Custom was a "second nature," and therefore the customary law of England was perfectly fitted to *English* circumstances.[41] Hedley was careful to avoid going too far, but even he could not resist saying that the common law of England "excellently performed" what was needed for the "felicity and happiness of *all* kingdoms" [stress added], by balancing "the blessings and benefits of an absolute monarchy and of a free estate."[42] Others were even more careless about using an argument showing the perfect fittedness of English law to English circumstance in order to demonstrate that the law possessed a more abstract and universal perfection. Sir John Davies in 1616, in the midst of extending common law tenures to Ireland, said more than his reasoning entitled him to say when he declared of the common law "that it does excel all other laws in upholding a free monarchy, which is the most excellent form of government,"[43] and that "the judgment and reason of it is more certain than of any other human law in the world."[44] The conclusion seems blatantly to conflict with the very idea of a customary law. How could the custom of a particular place achieve a perfection that justified imposing it onto a very differently circumstanced kingdom? That is an interesting question, but so too is another. Why did ancient constitutionalists try so often to hold together two ideas that are often in tension with one another, the idea that law is custom, and the idea that English law was per-

---

40. *PP 1610*, 2:174.

41. *PP 1610*, 2:180.

42. *PP 1610*, 2:191.

43. Sir John Davies, "Preface" to *Le Primer Report des Cases et Matters en Ley* (1615), in *Divine Right and Democracy: An Anthology of Political Writing in Stuart England*, ed. David Wootton (Harmondsworth: Penguin, 1986), p. 133; Hans Pawlisch, *Sir John Davies and the Conquest of Ireland: A Study in Legal Imperialism* (Cambridge: Cambridge UP, 1985); Eugene Flanagan, "The Anatomy of Jacobean Ireland: Captain Barnaby Rich, Sir John Davies and the Failure of Reform, 1609–22," in *Political Ideology in Ireland, 1541–1641*, ed. Hiram Morgan (Dublin, 1999), pp. 158–80.

44. Davies, "Preface," p. 136.

fect in ways that other laws were not? On the one hand we have *insularity*, the view that English law was uninfluenced by external developments; on the other, something that went beyond this to claim that English law was not just different from but better than any other law.

A third feature of ancient constitutionalism is its desperate attempt to deny that the Norman *conquest* had any effect on legal and constitutional continuity. Hedley was more tolerant of interruption to legal history than most when he said of Magna Carta that it was "a restoring or confirming of the ancient laws and liberties of the kingdom, which by the Conquest before had been much impeached or obscured."[45] More common was the view that William himself had so liked English laws and customs that he had ensured their transmission through time. But even for Hedley, however delayed and violent the process might have been, over time the effects of the Conquest were irrevocably undone, and ancient laws and liberties securely retained. Why was conquest so important? Historians have much debated the question.[46] Part of the answer surely lies in the need to avoid any suggestion of a law-making, law-breaking authority at work in English constitutional history. Yet few royal policies — and certainly not Impositions, about which Hedley was debating — were defended in terms of conquest-right. Nonetheless, regardless of circumstances, conquest was discussed over and over again. It could, perhaps, be seen as a subsidiary of the perfection argument; but there are other reasons, I shall soon suggest, why a concern with conquest was pre-programmed into English ancient-constitution thinking.[47]

I have identified a number of features of ancient constitutionalism, some of them puzzling. In the remainder of this essay I will suggest that it will help to clarify the subject if we see ancient constitutionalism as a corpus of ideas that was forged initially as a weapon to resist Anglo-Scottish union. The configuration of ideas that Hedley expresses, with much help from Roman law, was given an important impetus by the way

---

45. *PP 1610*, 2:190.

46. For a summary with references to the debate, see my *Politics of the Ancient Constitution*, pp. 82–86; for criticism of the view there expressed, see J.P. Summerville, "The Ancient Constitution Reassessed: The Common Law, the Court, and the Languages of Politics in Early Modern England," in *The Stuart Court and Europe: Essays in Politics and Culture*, ed. Malcolm Smuts (Cambridge: Cambridge UP, 1996), ch. 3.

47. On the relationship between immemoriality and custom, see also Greenberg, *Radical Face*, pp. 11–35, which is not altogether satisfying in its account of why interest in the Norman Conquest was pervasive.

in which 1603 threatened to break the bonds between the English nation and its past. I shall concentrate on two themes: (a) the 'Fortescuean revival' of the 1600s; and (b) the development of the language of fundamental law.

V

The Fortescuean Moment

What use was made of Fortescue before about 1600? I do not know the answer to that question. Caroline Skeel's still standard article of 1916 tells us almost nothing about commentary on Fortescue before the seventeenth century. Clearly there are patterns, changing over time, in the use made of Fortescue. In the 1628 parliamentary debates, for example, he was cited most particularly as authority for the principle that a king should not in person perform many of the legal and administrative functions carried out in his name.[48] But in the first decade or so of the century Fortescue's name was frequently cited for a different purpose, and one that was (I suspect) rather different from any employment he may have been given earlier.

Christopher Brooks has recently, and persuasively, argued that essential features of ancient constitutionalism were not formed before about 1600. (He, too, has suggested Anglo-Scottish union debates as the most important arena within which they were formed.)[49] The 1579 edition of John Rastell's *Exposition of Certaine... Termes of the Lawes of this Realme*, for example, defined common laws simply as "such lawes as were generally taken and holden for lawe before anye statute was made to alter the same." They were "the usuall and common received lawes of the realme."[50] That may provide some of the materials with which later writers would

---

48. See the citations catalogued at *Commons Debates, 1628*, ed. Robert C. Johnson, Mary Frear Keeler, and others, 4 vols. (New Haven: Yale UP, 1977–78), 1:135–36; hereafter *CD 1628*; see also Caroline Skeel, "The Influence of the Writings of Sir John Fortescue," *Transactions of the Royal Historical Society*, 3rd ser., 10 (1916): 77–114.

49. Christopher Brooks, "The Place of Magna Carta and the Ancient Constitution in Sixteenth-Century English Legal Thought," in *Roots of Liberty*, Sandoz (ed.), ch. 2, pp. 83–88.

50. John Rastell, *An Exposition of Certaine Difficult and Obscure Wordes and Termes of the Lawes of this Realme* (1579), fol. 43b–44.

work, but Rastell showed little interest in the elaborated conceptions of custom, immemoriality and unchanging perfection that fascinated some of his successors, and became so central to their idea of the character of law. The tone was pragmatic and professional. The preface to the first edition (1527) had shown more general concerns, but they were distinctly humanist. "[A] good reasonable commyn lawe makith agode commyn pease and a comyn welth among a grete commynalte of people."[51] This dual focus on pragmatic particulars and humanist commonplaces arguably typified much Tudor legal thinking. It tended to support a view that accepted the mutability and variety of laws and customs. Laws and customs mediated between shifting circumstances and a few basic structural continuities, with the result that:

Never in all pointes one common wealth doth agree with an other, no nor long time any one common wealth with it selfe. For al chaungeth continually to more or lesse, and still to diverse and diverse orders, as the diversity of times do present occasion, and the mutabilities of mens wittes doth invent and assay newe wayes, to reforme and amende that wherein they do finde fault.[52]

The situation was transformed during the first session of James VI and I's first English Parliament (March to July 1604). Not long before, in 1602, Attorney-General Sir Edward Coke had, in a not uncommon moment of hyperbole, echoed Sir John Fortescue in declaring that the ultimate proof of the perfection of English laws lay in the fact that no conqueror had ever seen the need to alter them.[53] The laws of England were older than those of the Roman Emperors,[54] and Coke quoted Fortescue directly: "If [English customs] had not been the best, some of those kings [between the Britons and the Normans] would have changed... and totally abolished them, especially the Romans, who judged almost the whole

51. John Rastell, *Expositiones Terminorum Legum Anglorum* (1527), proemium.

52. Sir Thomas Smith, *De Republica Anglorum*, ed. Mary Dewar (Cambridge: Cambridge UP, 1982), p. 67. A sense of the differences between early Stuart doctrines of the ancient constitution and Elizabethan attitudes can also be gleaned from the interesting account of 'Holinshed's ancient constitutionalism' in Patterson, *Reading Holinshed's Chronicles* pp. 104 and following.

53. My citations to Coke's *Reports* and *Institutes*, and other law reports, follow standard legal form: Coke, 2 *Rep.*, Pref. vi. On Coke's development before 1603, see now the important work of Allen D. Bowyer, *Sir Edward Coke and the Elizabethan Age* (Stanford: Stanford UP, 2003). It has appeared too recently for me to be able to incorporate its findings into the present paper.

54. Coke, 3 *Rep.*, Pref. xviii–xix.

of the rest of the world by their laws."[55] In 1602 these points remained undeveloped, and pregnant with several possibilities. But in 1604 a real conquest was threatened, and thus fertile soil provided for Coke and others to insist that Fortescue had in fact defended the *literal* unchangingness of English law and custom. The evidence suggests that such a view was not common in the first few years of the seventeenth century, and was indeed being made less and less plausible by the increasingly sophisticated legal antiquarianism of the age.[56] Thus Sir John Hayward in his Union tract of 1604, commenting on the parliamentary debates of that year, remarked that the view "that the lawes of *England* were never changed since the time of *Brutus*; not onely in the peaceable state of the realme, but not by any of the severall conquerors thereof: not by the Normanes, Danes, Saxones; no not by the Romanes" was not widely held. He was clear about the point of the argument: "the lawes do still remaine the same, which *Brutus* compiled out of the Trojan lawes; and therefore it is not fit they should *in any point* be altered" [stress added]. This was, said Hayward, an argument "not commonly received"; it was "fabulous." Hayward was careful to deny that he was "derogating any thing from the true dignitie of the common law"; but to accept the argument from immutability was, he said, the same as "esteeming hyperbolicall praises now out of season; as never sutable but with artlesse times."[57] Artless times they may have been, for Hayward was a few months out of date. In the debates of 1604 the fear of conquest began to encourage wide acceptance of exactly the view that Hayward found so rare.

The parliamentary debates on Union in 1604 focused primarily on two (interlinked) subjects: legal union;[58] and union in name, whereby Eng-

---

55. Coke, 3 *Rep.*, Pref. xxi-xxii, quoting Fortescue, *De Laudibus Legum Angliae*, ch. 17. Consult also 3 *Rep.* Pref. xl. It should be emphasised that Coke's reading of Fortescue most probably did not capture his original meaning. See the pertinent remarks by the editor of the most recent edition of Fortescue: Sir John Fortescue, *On the Laws and Governance of England*, ed. Shelley Lockwood (Cambridge: Cambridge UP, 1997), p. xxxi (the passage quoted by Coke is at 26–27).

56. See my *Politics of the Ancient Constitution*, pp. 69–73.

57. Sir John Hayward, *A Treatise of Union of the Two Realmes of England and Scotland* (1604), p. 11 (sig. A1v).

58. This subject has been thoroughly explored in work by Brian P. Levack, esp. "The Proposed Union of English Law and Scots Law in the Seventeenth Century," *Juridical Review*, n.s. 20 (1975): 97-115; "English Law, Scots Law and the Union, 1603–1607," in *Law-Making and Law-Makers in British History: Papers Presented to the Edinburgh Legal History Conference, 1977*, ed. Alan Harding, Royal

land and Scotland would become "Great Britain." (They were linked, above all, by the fact that union in name was widely believed to imply the abolition of English law.) This focus was especially evident following the King's message of 13 April.[59] Almost as soon as debate on the two issues is recorded, conquest was mentioned: "in all Conquests," it was said on 18 April, "the Kingdom of England continued in Name." The following day it was remarked that "[t]he Conqueror did not impose the Name."[60] It was thought, Francis Bacon reported on April 25, that "[i]f a new Name [is adopted, then] a new Kingdom [is erected]," as when an unpopulated island is discovered or a kingdom is conquered.[61] In that same report, Bacon delivered a "[r]ecital of his Majesty's Promise, not to alter the Laws."[62] On the 18th April another speaker, perhaps Sir Oliver St John, tried to reassure a worried House. These were the terms by which he did so:

That the abrogatinge and takinge away of their lawes and customes was not sought and Intended [by the Union proposals] for ther wer in England diuerse lawes and customes according to the auncient use thereof... That this feare of expulsion of their nation and change of their lawes and making a conquest was put into their heads by those who had rather hazard the spoyle of their countrie then loose their estimation and desire of gouerment.[63]

What was feared, however unreasonably, was a breach in the fabric of time, the result of which would have been to destroy the identity of England as a political community.

The fullest discussion was in Sir Edwin Sandys' speech of 26 April.[64] Union came, he said, by three means, marriage (the present case), agreement and election, or conquest. Of the first two types, "there is not any

Historical Society Studies in History, vol. 22 (London: Royal Historical Society, 1980), pp. 105–119; "Toward a More Perfect Union: England, Scotland and the Constitution," in *After the Reformation: Essays in Honor of J.H. Hexter* (Manchester: U of Manchester P, 1980), pp. 57–74.

59. *CJ*, 1:171.
60. *CJ*, 1:177, 950.
61. *CJ*, 1:184.
62. *CJ*, 1:963.
63. Brian R. Dunn, "Commons Debates, 1603/4," Ph.D. thesis, 2 vols. (Bryn Mawr, 1987), 1:414 (from State Papers 14/7/41; hereafter SP), pp. 418–19 for authorship.
64. *CJ*, 1:186-87.

example of any Kingdomes wch though they have been united in the head wch is the person of the Prince have held the same course in the body by Union of Lawes, Customes, Priviledges, and Stiles of honor, as name and dignities." Only unions by conquest "hath had the union in substance, but the name hath been imposed at the pleasure of ye Conqueror." Sandys then added to Bacon's summary of objections from the previous day the point that changing the name of the kingdom would free the king from his coronation oath while still leaving his subjects bound by their oaths of allegiance to him.[65] The subject would then be worse off than if ruled by a conqueror, for "[a] conqueror may be expelled, where there is not such an oath [of allegiance], unless there be a [subsequent] yielding [to him]."[66] Even Bacon's compilation of objections had mentioned that "it was to be feared that in frameing a new name, wee should erect a new Kingdom and that the King by Force of his Proclamations might establish new Lawes as if he came in by Conquest."[67]

The Commons' fear of conquest as a result of the change in name was reflected in the pamphlet debate too. John Thornborough, Bishop of Bristol, in his response to the Commons' objections, referred to the claim that the only genuine precedent for Union was in case of conquest. In fact, he argued, the name England was itself a product of "the conquest of the Saxons," and so adoption of "Great Britain" would be no more than a restitution of the original name.[68] This argument is a sort of Saxon Yoke theory, not dissimilar in form to the idea of the Norman Yoke later to be used against common-law traditionalism by the radicals of the 1640s. The vigorous Commons' response to Thornborough's book may have had something to do with his rejection of their nascent ancient constitutionalism.[69] In contrast to Thornborough, Sir Henry Spelman expressed the same fears of conquest as those found in the Commons' debates. Union, he argued, would require that the laws be changed. He warned: "though

---

65. PRO SP 14/7/63–64.

66. *CJ*, 1:186.

67. PRO SP 14/7/57-58, calendared 25 April. This should be distinguished from the fuller compilation of reasons against union in name given by Bacon on 27 April: *CJ*, 1:188-89; PRO SP 14/7/76–77; Bruce Galloway, *The Union of England and Scotland, 1603–1608* (Edinburgh: J. Donald, 1986), pp. 28–29.

68. John Thornborough, *A Discourse Plainly Proving the Evident and Urgent Necessitie of the Desired Happie Union of the Two Famous Kingdomes of England and Scotland* (1604), pp. 2, 6–7.

69. For the record of the Commons' pursuit of Thornborough, see *CJ*, 1: 226–27, 230, 231, 232, 234, 236, 238, 244, 248, 251; *LJ*, 2:306, 309, 314, 315, 325, 332.

it be an ordinary thinge for them that enter by conquest to impose lawes at their pleasure... yet what danger it is for him that is in by lawfull succession to attempte such a matter the experience of all ages and the present case of the King of Spaine with the lowe cuntryes do well declare."[70] As Sir John Dodderidge summed up, Union would produce "a total alteracion of lawes" which might lead to "the evercion of the whole state."[71]

Union thus threatened legal change. More than that, it threatened legal change brought about by a *conquest* that would leave the law in the king's hands, regardless of his intentions, and produce the complete subversion of the commonwealth and of the liberties and privileges of its members. The past, which had bequeathed those liberties and privileges, would be wiped away, and the English would become the new people of a new prince. What counter-arguments could be used to ward off this threat?

In their search for such arguments MPs pulled together a series of claims that came to characterize the mature ancient constitutionalism of the period from 1610 to 1640. Sandys, for example, denied that even Parliament could do what was required. "[T]he house of Parliament wch was sent up according to old custome, and bounded in theyr commission within ye limits of former presidents was not capable to dispose of this matter or impose a new name without especiall commission from the country."[72] Customary law, by which Parliament existed, restricted its actions. We remember Hedley's later reworking of the point. But the case against Union did not rest with the simple argument that there was no authority capable of making the necessary changes. Debaters began to make use of what they took to be Fortescue's belief in the immutability of English law. One writer marvelled at:

what conquests soever were made in this Realm (as 5 times at least there have bin) and thereupon new Lawes, alteracions, amendments and innovations propounded by the conquerours or Commanders of those times. Yet could Englishmen never be drawn to alter the Lawes and Customes of this Kingdome:

---

70. Sir Henry Spelman, "Of the Union," in *The Jacobean Union: Six Tracts of 1604*, ed. Bruce Galloway and Brian Levack (Edinburgh: Scottish Historical Society, 1985), pp. 180–81.

71. John Dodderidge, "A Brief Consideracion of the Unyon of Twoe Kingdomes," in *Jacobean Union*, Galloway and Levack (ed.), p. 146.

72. PRO SP 14/7/74–75, calendared *CSPD*, 1603–10, p. 101 as 27 April; Galloway, *Union of England and Scotland*, pp. 20–21, 26 (n35), takes this to be a speech of 20 April.

which if they could have needed bettering by change, some of those Kings (moved eyther with Justice or with reason of their own, especially the Romans, who judged all the rest of the world (England Excepted) by their own Lawes and Ordinances, only preserving the English Customes entire and untoucht, as more agreeable to this Country and Common-Wealth then any other, and more willingly obeyed then any other.... [73]

What was to become one of the great catch-cries of ancient constitutionalism — *nolumus leges Angliae mutare* [we do not wish the laws of England to be changed] first uttered by the barons at Merton in 1236 — was heard again in this document,[74] was mentioned by Nicholas Fuller in the Commons on 25 April, and even adapted to *nolumus nomen Angliae mutare*.[75]

The Fortescuean perspective which seems to have been deployed so effectively in debate during 1604 was then promulgated in the Speaker's Address at the close of the session (7 July 1604). Sir Edward Phelips had given King James at the beginning of the session a beginner's guide to English law and government.[76] In July the tone was significantly different. His more specific remarks carried unmistakable resonances of the Union debates:

The Laws, whereby the Ark of this Government hath been ever steered, are of Three Kinds, the first, the Common Law, grounded or drawn from the Law of God, the Law of Reason, and the Law of Nature, *not mutable* [emphasis mine]; the second, the positive Law, founded, changed, and altered by and through the Occasions and Policies of Times; the third, Customs and Usages, practiced and allowed with Times Approbation, without known Beginnings: Wherein although we differ from the Laws of other States Government, yet have the authors thereof imitated the approved Excellency of *Plato* and *Aristotle*, framing their Laws according to the Capacity, Nature, Disposition, and Humour of the Place and People; by the Level of whose Line this State hath been com-

---

73. BL Harleian MS. 1314, fol. 14b, clearly echoing Fortescue, *De Laudibus*, ch. 17; hereafter Harl. MS. There appears to be no foundation to the claim made by Levack that this is from a 1604 Commons speech: Brian P. Levack, *The Formation of the British State: England, Scotland, and the Union, 1603–1707* (Oxford: Oxford UP, 1987), p. 89. Harl. MS 1314 is an interesting analysis of the 1704 English and Scottish acts appointing Commissioners for Union, and of the Instrument of Union that those commissioners produced in December 1604. It describes itself as a "treatise." See also Galloway, *Union of England and Scotland*, p. 64.

74. BL Harl. MS. 1314, fol. 16.

75. *CJ*, 1:185, 957.

76. *CJ*, 1:146–49.

manded, governed, and maintained these *** Years, not inferior, but in equal
Balance with any confining Regiment whatsoever; and have by the Touch-
stone of true Experience, approved to be to the King his Scepter, to the Senate
the Oracle of Counsel, to the Judge the Rule of Justice, to the Magistrate the
Guide of Discipline, to the Subject the School-mistress of Obedience, to the
Multi-tude the Preventer of Ignorance, the Standard-bearer of Sedition, and,
generally, to all, the Bond, that tieth Men to civil and orderly Course of Life.[77]

I quote at length because it seems that this speech, especially read in the
light of the Union debates that preceded it, is the earliest expression of
something recognizably close to the elaborated ancient constitutionalism of the early-seventeenth century. It touches all the right notes: immutability, immemoriality, insularity, fittedness to circumstance; and with
the first of them betrays the general receptiveness to Fortescue — or, at
any rate, to his *De Laudibus*, chapter 17 — evident in 1604. In England, custom ("Experience") rather than a law-maker produced laws fitted to the
"Nature, Disposition, and Humour of the Place and People," and for that
reason those laws were "not mutable," and were the equal of any laws
anywhere. Their construction had been, in effect if not by deliberate design, in accordance with the wisdom of Plato and Aristotle.

Thus threatened with a Scottish conquest — albeit a surreptitious and
unintended one — the English responded by claiming that their immutable laws and glorious name had never been tainted by conquest. Furthermore, because laws were the product of customary development, there
was no authority capable of altering them. As one anonymous manuscript
tract put it, English laws were not "declared in writing," as some were,
but the product of "tradicion." Such laws were changed only "by full conquest" and "at the Princes pleasure."[78] It may have been true, as was suggested, that "this feare of…makinge a conquest was put into their heades
by those who had rather hazard the spoyle of their countrie then loose
their estimation and desire of government";[79] but the threat of conquest nonetheless produced an interesting body of argument. That body
matches closely the pattern found in Hedley's 1610 speech. There was an
in-built antipathy to the idea of conquest, coupled with a view of the history of law that eschewed a law-making authority (even, to a considerable degree, with parliamentary law-making) and asserted both the per-

77. *CJ*, 1:254.
78. PRO SP 14/7/61.
79. PRO SP 14/7/41.

fect Englishness and the absolute perfection of the common law. Finally, in extreme cases, this body of ideas became pushed into an assertion of the historic and continuing immutability of English law. A threat to take away the past was met by the most emphatic affirmation of the continued vitality of the bonds that bound past and present together.

This pattern was clearly transmitted beyond 1604, and was closely associated with a particular reading of Fortescue. As an epilogue to the foregoing remarks, let me look forward to some evidence from 1607. In that year, Sir Edward Coke commented that not all were convinced by his argument (from Fortescue) that English law had shown itself immutable. Particularly unconvinced were "those of another profession," which can only be a reference to those pro-Union civilians who had rejected Coke's opinion, Sir John Hayward and Alberico Gentili.[80] Typically, Coke's response was to quote entirely chapter 17 of Fortescue's *De Laudibus*. In the same year the judges gave, on 26 February in a Conference of the Lords and Commons, their unwelcome opinion that the post-nati of Scotland (i.e. those born in Scotland after the accession of James VI to the English throne) were naturalized subjects of the king of England.[81] Lord Chief Justice Popham was reported to have begun his remarks thus:

That they [the laws] had continued as a Rock without alteration in all the varieties of people that had possessed this Land, namely the Romans, Brittons, Danes, Saxons, Normans, and English, which he imputed to the Integrity and Justice of these Laws, every people taking a liking to them, and desirous to continue them, and live by them, for which he cited Fortescues Book of the Laws of England.

With "people" instead of "conquerors," this was a remarkably populist rendering, a tone reinforced by the following remarks in which Popham emphasised that Magna Carta and similar concessions were "bought and purchased by the blood of our Antecessors… after long and bloody wars between the Kings and Barons of the realm."[82] That was going rather far, but it surely speaks eloquently of the way in which Fortescuean perspectives had become entrenched that Popham felt compelled to begin by making his obeisances to them.

---

80. Coke, 6 *Rep.*, Pref; Galloway, *Union of England and Scotland*, pp. 40–41.
81. Galloway, *Union of England and Scotland*, pp. 108–10.
82. *English Reports*, Moore (K.B.), 797.

Thus we witness a reception of Fortescuean notions of immutability, and the building up around them of the complex range of arguments
characteristic of ancient constitutionalism. It is notable, in particular, that
we find conjoined in this context the idea that England's legal identity
is based upon custom, and the idea that these customs are immutable. The
latter is important to the assertion that nothing should be changed to accommodate the Scots and their kings, notwithstanding the intellectual
difficulty involved in making immutability compatible with the very idea
of custom.

VI

Fundamental Law

By the 1620s the concept of 'fundamental law' had become closely associated with ancient constitutionalism, in political argument if not in legal
theory. The core belief was, in John Pym's words, that the laws "are fundamental from the very original of this kingdom and are part of the essential constitution thereof."[83] In the early 1640s that concept was the
subject of even more discussion and elaboration. How did the language
of fundamental law gain a place for itself in English political discourse
of the early seventeenth century? Again, I shall suggest that the clue, both
to the establishment of the idea of fundamental law and to its close association with the development of ancient constitutionalism, lies in the
Union debates of the early Jacobean period.

Authorities agree that the first use of the term "fundamental law" in
English was as recent as 1596. In the dedicatory epistle to his *Maxims of
the Law*, Francis Bacon said of Edward I that he "bent himself to endow
his state with sundry notable and fundamental laws, upon which the government ever since hath principally rested."[84] These fundamental laws
were statutes. However, a rather different use of the phrase, and the most

---

83. Pym, in *CD 1628*, 4:103.

84. Bacon, *Maxims of the Law*, in *The Works of Francis Bacon*, ed. James Spedding,
Robert Leslie Ellis, and Douglas Denon Heath, 7 vols. (London: Longmans,
1857–61), 7:314. J.W. Gough, *Fundamental Law in English Constitutional History* (Oxford: Clarendon P, 1955), p. 51, and Martyn P. Thompson, "The History of Fundamental Law in Political Thought from the French Wars of Religion to the American Revolution," *American Historical Revieww* 91 (1986), p. 1110 (n18).

developed English-language discussion of the subject for the entire period before the 1640s (actually originally in lowland Scots, Anglicised
for the London edition of 1603), was to be found in King James VI's *True
Law of Free Monarchies* (1598). There the term seems to have been used primarily to refer to those laws that determined the form of government,
and above all those which determined that in Scotland kings had a mo-
nopoly over the sources of public authority.[85] It was King James more than
anyone else who injected 'fundamental law' into English political thought,
though after doing so he quickly lost control over the language.

To understand the importance of these points we need to lay down
some historiographical markers. C.H. McIlwain in *The High Court of Parliament* (1910) treated the language of fundamental law as inherently constitutionalist. Fundamental law was itself, indeed, what would later be
called a constitution.[86] That explains how McIlwain was able to read Bodin, who said that kings were limited by *leges imperii* or *lois royals*,[87] taken
by McIlwain to be the same as fundamental laws, as a sort of constitutionalist. The standard authority on fundamental law, J.W. Gough, was
aware of many problems in all of this, and particularly aware of the flu-
idity in the actual usage of the term "fundamental law" before the Civil
War. Yet, in a crucial respect, if only tacitly, Gough reinforced McIlwain.

---

85. Most revealing, perhaps, is the passage on Parliament and law-making
in King James VI & I, *The True Law of Free Monarchies*, in *The Political Writings of
James I*, ed. J.P. Sommerville (Cambridge: Cambridge UP, 1994), p. 74. James's
exploitation of the term may be related to its use by Presbyterians in 1597: see Arthur H. Williamson, *Scottish National Consciousness in the Age of James VI: The Apocalypse, the Union, and the Shaping of Scotland's Public Culture* (Edinburgh: J. Donald,
1979), pp. 80–82. Elsewhere Williamson has referred to the language of "fundamental law" in the Scottish National Covenant (1638) as "unScottish" (see his "Patterns of British Identity: 'Britain' and its Rivals in the 16th and 17th Centuries,"
in *The New British History: Founding a Modern State, 1603–1715*, ed. Glenn Burgess
([London: I. B. Tauris, 1999], p. 152). UnScottish it may have been by 1638, but
in 1597–98 it was perhaps more Scottish than English. (I am grateful to Professor
Williamson for his advice on these points.)

86. C.H. McIlwain, *The High Court of Parliament and its Supremacy* (New Haven:
Yale UP, 1910), ch. 2.

87. Richard Knolles, translating Bodin in 1606, used the term "lawes royall," following the French text at this point; see Jean Bodin, *The Six Bookes of a Com-
monweale: A Facsimile Reprint of the English Translation of 1606*, ed. K.D. McRae
(Cambridge, MA: Harvard UP, 1962), p. 95 and marginal n; compare also Bodin,
On Sovereignty, ed. Julian H. Franklin (Cambridge: Cambridge UP, 1992), p. 18
(and n).

His treatment of the history of fundamental law—in defiance of chronology—moved from antecedents, through Coke (who was implicitly treated as the norm) and only then to "the claims of James I." The effect was to reinforce the idea that 'fundamental law' was *naturally* a constitutionalist idea, allied closely to the thinking of the common lawyers, the ancient constitutionalists.[88]

As Martyn Thompson has suggested, this is to read the history of fundamental law backwards. Harro Höpfl has shown for France that the term "fundamental law" (invented by Beza) had a great variety of uses, did not amount to the same thing as the idea of a 'constitution,' and was not even inherently constitutionalist.[89] All this is equally true of Britain. It was possible, as Sir Thomas Fleming did in his argument in the Case of Monopolies (1601), to use the term "fundamental laws" in a sense similar to Bodin's *leges imperii* (though, as we have seen, the 1606 translator of Bodin did not use the term "fundamental laws").[90] King James's use of the term was similar, at first; but the development of his thinking on the subject revealed a considerable adaptability.

Let me begin with a crucial passage—one of the most significant of all James's political utterances. It comes from his adjournment speech to Parliament on 31 March 1607. In the course of the speech, James came to discuss the fact that the Scottish and English Acts of 1604 establishing the Union Commission had each excepted "fundamental laws" from change (though the English Act had done so only in the preamble). What did the term mean?

Their [i.e. the Scots'] meaning in the word of Fundamentall Lawes... [was to] intend thereby onely those Lawes whereby confusion is avoided, and their Kings descent maintained, and the heritage of the succession and Monarchie, which hath bene a Kingdome, to which I am in descent, three hundred yeeres before **CHRIST**: Not meaning it as you doe, of their Common Law, for they have none, but that which is called **IUS REGIS**.[91]

---

88. In addition to Gough's *Fundamental Law in English Constitutional History*, cited already, see his "Fundamental Law in the Seventeenth Century," *Political Studies* 1 (1953): 162–74.

89. Harro Höpfl, "Fundamental Law and the Constitution in Sixteenth-Century France," in *Die Rolle der Juristen bei der Entstehung des modernen Staates*, ed. Roman Schnur (Berlin, 1986), pp. 327–56.

90. PRO SP 12/286/47: the king "by the fundamentall lawes of this lande hath attributed unto him plenary fullness of power."

91. James VI & I, *Political Writings of James I*, Sommerville (ed.), p. 172.

James was attempting to calm fears that had arisen — however cynical the motivation behind their expression may have been — in the natural-ization debates of February and March 1607. It had been suggested in the English Commons that the Scots had built protection of *their* fundamen-tal laws into the body of the 1604 Act appointing the Commissioners to debate Union, while the innocent and gullible English were left vulner-able, having written such protection only into the preamble of their Act, where it was of no legal force. The Scottish estates, in a letter of Au-gust 1607 to the King, seemed to endorse James's reading of what they had meant. In referring to fundamental law they rightly claimed only to be following the English statute (they had, indeed, been instructed to fol-low it); and they meant by the term only "these fundamentall lawis wher-by your Majestie, efter so long a discent, dois most happelie injoy the Crown; as lykewayes quhairby the frayme of this hole kingdome is es-tablissed, togidder with such speciall previledgeis and prerogativeis qu-hairby all distinction of rankis and ordouris is manteynit among us." The estates explicitly excluded all "perticlair Actis, or Statutis or uther lawis or customes" which "are and evir aucht to be alterable as the weele of the commounwealth and publict state sall require."[92] In spite of the loyal words, it is hard not to believe that the Scots were not here engaged in a move analogous to that made by the English lawyers. While paying lip-service to James's Bodinian view that fundamental laws were primarily laws protecting the rights of the Crown, they were enlarging the con-cept to provide protection for the privileges and liberties of subjects.[93]

James's narrow understanding of fundamental law we might call Bo-din-ian, as it was closely analogous to Bodin's *leges imperii* (which included, above all, Salic law, whereby succession to the Crown was established); and this usage of the concept came naturally to the author of the *True Law of Free Monarchies*. The term "fundamental law" does not itself seem to have much presence in Scottish political thought before James wrote. Sir Thomas Craig, the most important of the Scottish writers on Union, seems not have used the term or any close equivalent of it.[94]

---

92. *Register of the Privy Council of Scotland* (1604–7), 7:535.

93. I am much indebted here to J.H. Burns, *The True Law of Kingship: Concepts of Monarchy in Early Modern Scotland* (Oxford: Clarendon P, 1996), pp. 266, 287, which has altered my reading of this document. See also the valuable discussion in Allan I. MacInnes, "Regal Union for Britain, 1603–38," in *New British History*, Burgess (ed.), pp. 36–37.

94. Important to the civilian-trained Craig was the distinction between pub-lic and private law, and the concept of 'maxims' or 'axioms,' which included

More interesting from the English side is James's explicit recognition in 1607 that, for his subjects south of the (for James, ex-) border, fundamental law meant *common law*. Indeed, James's acceptance of that fact is absolutely central to the gradual accommodation he reached with English institutions and legal traditions, a process examined by Paul Christianson.[95] James, that is to say, came—not, of course, to possess a 'common-law mind'—but to accept the need to live and work with the political implications of ancient constitutionalist modes of thinking. In any case, this was a much broader understanding of fundamental law. How is it, then, that the English, as James recognized in 1607, came to see common law and fundamental law either as the same thing or as closely-connected things?

To answer that question we need again to step into 1604 and the legislation establishing the Union Commission. The English and Scottish Acts, as we have seen, each protected from the Commission's proposals "fundamental laws" (though, in the former case, only in the preamble).[96] There were minor differences between the Acts, the English referring significantly to "fundamentall and ancient Lawes," the Scottish to "fundamentall lawes / Ancient privilegeis, offices and liberties of this Kingdome."

The first draft of the English Commission Act, which Francis Bacon had prepared by 12 May, already mentioned that his Majesty had "no in-

---

customs. See esp. Sir Thomas Craig, *De Unione Regnorum Britanniae Tractatus*, ed. C. Sanford Terry, Publications of the Scottish historical society, vol. 60 (Edinburgh UP, 1909), ch. 6; also *The Jus Feudale of Sir Thomas Craig of Riccarton*, ed. James Avon Clyde, 2 vols. (Edinburgh, 1934), 1: Bk. 1, Tit. 7. In his reply to Doleman (the Catholic propagandist Parsons) on the succession, only published in the early eighteenth century, there is a concept of fundamental law present. For example: "There are other Laws or rights, which are so nearly allied to the royal Majesty, and are of the same date and Establishment with the Kingdom, such as those which are called Fundamental Laws, which it's evident can neither be abolish'd nor violated, without the certain and unavoidable Hurt or Subversion of the State" — Thomas Craig, *The Right of Succesion to the Kingdom of England* (1703), p. 129; consult also p. 111. This is very much a narrow view. It occurs in the midst of passages explicitly indebted to Bodin, and may represent the double influence of Bodin's *leges imperii* and of James VI's *True Law*. The catch, however, is that this 1703 publication is a translation of a Latin original, and the original MS is now lost. We do not know what Latin terminology Craig employed.

95. Paul Christianson, "Royal and Parliamentary Voices on the Ancient Constitution, c. 1604–1621," in *The Mental World of the Jacobean Court*, ed. Linda Levy Peck (Cambridge: Cambridge UP, 1991), ch. 5.

96. 1 Jac. 1, c. 2, *Statues of the Realm* 4,2:1018–19; 1604, c. 1, *Acts of the Parliament of Scotland* (1593–1625), 4:263–64.

tention to alter, change or diminish our fundamental laws, liberties and grounds of government."[97] In using that language, the Act was from the beginning reflecting James's own terminology. To calm the extravagant fears aroused by the possible changes in name and laws he had sent a message to the Commons, *via* Bacon, on 21 April. In it he stated that neither then nor later was it "My Meaning...to alter or innovate the fundamental Laws, Privileges, and good Customs of this Kingdom, whereby only the King's Princely Authority is conserved, and the People['s]...Security of their Lands, Living, and Privileges, is maintained unto them."[98] (Is that the first time that the term "fundamental law" appears in English parliamentary records?) James did not mean by fundamental law in 1604 what he was to be compelled to mean by it (in England if not in Scotland) by 1607.

So far as I am aware it was James's message that injected "fundamental law" into the debates. One of the earliest speeches to follow that lead was by none other than Thomas Hedley. "The King cannot preserve the fundamental Laws, by Uniting, no more than a Goldsmith, Two Crowns."[99] On 2 May the House insisted that the King's promise "not to alter the Laws" should be inserted into the Commission Act.[100] It took exactly eleven days for James's "fundamental laws" to become simply "the laws," a slippage that James himself would not acknowledge until his 1607 speech.

That is not the whole story about 1604. It is evident that there was a struggle for control over the meaning of the term "fundamental law." In the Commons, it quickly came to be a synonym for the laws generally or for ancient laws. But there were others who wished to insist on a narrow or 'Bodinian' understanding of "fundamental laws." Sir John Hayward, for example, whom we have already met as an enemy of immemoriality and immutability, briefly referred to "the fundamental lawes...of both Kingdomes and Crownes" in a context suggesting a rather narrow view of them. Indeed he followed this with a reference to "*other* lawes of government,"[101] a formulation suggestive of James's own earlier usage. More interesting is Francis Bacon. In his "Brief Discourse" on the Union, Bacon argued that there was no need "to extirpate all particular customs." It was

---

97. James Spedding, *The Letters and the Life of Francis Bacon*, 7 vols. (London, 1861–74), 3:204–5.

98. *CJ*, 1:180.

99. *CJ*, 1:958, 187 (26 April).

100. *CJ*, 1:197.

101. Hayward, *Treatise of Union of the Two Realmes*, p. 14 (stress added to second quotation).

enough "that there be an uniformity in the principal and fundamental laws both ecclesiastical and civil."[102] Thus in 1603, it was Bacon's view that fundamental laws were the ones that ought to change. In a later [?] document on legal Union Bacon used different terminology — *jus publicum* (government, including criminal law) and *jus privatum* (property) — but again suggested that some or all of the former, "being matters of that temporary nature as they may be altered…in either kingdom, without Parliament," ought to be made uniform.[103] The two statements together suggest that Bacon himself believed that fundamental laws were 'public,' did not concern property-rights, and were mutable. None of this is entirely clear, but it suggests a perspective rather distant from that emer-ing in the Commons' debates. Property law, it is true, was deemed unalterable; but the fundamental laws of government were not. Bacon's position, curiously, is certainly based on a narrow view of fundamental law; but, unlike James's view, it was one that was prepared to believe such laws alterable. Even though we may here be reminded of Gough's emphasis on the enormous flexibility of the term fundamental law early in its history, there is nonetheless a clear division evident between narrow and broad views of what the term meant.

It is in the debates of 1607, shaped by the terms of the Instrument of Union, which had been produced by the Commission late in 1604, that we find concepts of fundamental law becoming more prominent. It is worth remembering how the 'Fortescuean moment' of 1604 led to the expression of ideas of immutability, immemoriality and insularity. It would scarcely be surprising if this new concept of fundamental law were to be co-opted by this burgeoning ancient constitutionalism of the period. The evidence from 1607 shows that it was.

By 1607 Sir Edwin Sandys had become an advocate of a perfect, all-or-nothing Union, in which Scotland would become subsumed within an essentially English state. He now claimed that the Scottish Commission Act of 1604 was the main obstacle to such a union, because it prevented changes to Scotland's fundamental laws.[104] Sandys' position is generally interpreted as a tactical move to frustrate the naturalization recommendations of the Instrument by insisting on the prior need for union of a type

---

102. Bacon, "Brief Discourse" (1603), in Spedding, *Letters and Life of Bacon*, 3:97.

103. Bacon, in *Works of Francis Bacon*, Spedding, Ellis, and Heath (ed.), 7:731–32.

104. See *The Parliamentary Diary of Robert Bowyer, 1606–1607*, ed. David Harris Wilson (Minneapolis: U of MN P, 1931), pp. 224–45 (7 March), 238 (n) (11 March, 14 March).

unacceptable both to the Scots and the King. So it may have been; and yet there can be little doubt that, if Union had to happen, then the sort of union Sandys advocated in 1607 would have been the only one accept-able to an English parliament. Thus, however cynical Sandys' politics, his speeches of 1607 remain a good guide to his beliefs and thinking. The same point applies to those who supported Sandys' policies in the Com-mons. Laurence Hyde, for example, identified the key obstacle to Union as the Scots' attachment to "their fundamentall Lawes," arguing that, giv-en an open choice, they "would gladly yield to the Subiection of Our Lawes." *English* laws, of course, remained fundamental and immutable. It was clear, following the King's speech on 31 March, that further debate on Union simply accepted that English common law was a fundamen-tal law. Legal change continued to be envisaged only for Scotland, as was evident in speeches by Sandys, Croft, Fuller, Alford and Owen on 28th and 29th April.[105] Bacon, interestingly, reiterated his view of 1596 that most fundamental laws were the legislation of Edward I, suggesting that he still believed that they could be changed and did not apply the term "fundamental law" to the common law, whatever his king might now be prepared to do. But the more typical view was expressed by Holt. Attor-ney-General Hobart had suggested that it was self-contradictory to pro-pose perfect legal union in 1607 when it had been opposed in 1604. Not so, replied Holt, "for our first purpose was to preserve our Fundamentall Lawes, if the perfect Union proceede, wee keepe our Purpose." Yelverton, too, asserted that "this proposition taketh no fundamental lawe away" — at least, not from the English. Dudley Carleton was a lone voice straying in from 1604: "in the Word, unless in Case of Conquest, no Union was at the first perfect."[106]

Even more revealing were attitudes expressed on the debates on the recommendations made in the Instrument of Union for the repeal of hos-tile laws. Much of the debate and argument concerned precisely the ques-tion of whether *particular* measures would alter "fundamental law." When the question was tackled, it was almost always taken to mean whether a measure would alter the common law — or, perhaps alter, *significantly*, though (as always) the criteria of significance were never specified.[107] Sir

---

105. *Parliamentary Diary of Robert Bowyer*, Wilson (ed.), pp. 255–70.

106. *Parliamentary Diary of Robert Bowyer*, Wilson (ed.), pp. 269 (Bacon), 273 (Hobart), 277 (Holt), 281 (n) (Yelverton), 279 (Carleton).

107. For example, in Cotton's summary of arguments the argument that the proposal on rules concerning witnesses altered "fundamental law" was met with

Henry Montague thought it a telling argument on one point to say, "You change the Lawes so deare to our predecessors that they said *Nolumus leges Angliae mutare*."[108]

In 1607, "old," "fundamental" and "common" laws were all merging in English political vocabulary, and they were converging on the notion that none of them had been or ought to be changed. One can see over the years 1604 to 1607 a willingness to argue both that the customs of England were purely English and defined the character of the English polity, and (more abstractly) that they were so perfect that change was never needed. Both arguments, whatever their compatibility, were ideally employed against a perceived threat of the Scottification of England and its law. These arguments were all concerned to use a particular way of locating the English present in relation to the English past in order to affirm a conception of national identity.

VII

Conclusion: 1610 and Beyond

The foregoing account suggests something of the importance of *narrative* in the history of political thought. John Pocock, particularly in his earlier writings has often been interested in this dimension of the subject. "The individuals of my story," he once wrote, "are paradigms rather than people."[109] There is no reason why they should not be. Nonetheless, concentrating on the paradigm will not tell us the whole story. The history of the establishment and development of paradigms remains a story in which people have a role, and so do authors, who (like Mark Twain) seem quite perky even after their demise has been announced.

As well as this, the story I have told can tell us something of the political uses of myths of the ancient constitution, including something about the precise character of the 'constitutionalism' that they support. It is argu-

---

the response "It is no alteration of an old Law" (*Parliamentary Diary of Robert Bowyer*, Wilson [ed.], p. 316 [n]).

108. *Parliamentary Diary of Robert Bowyer*, Wilson (ed.), p. 319.

109. Pocock, "Working on Ideas in Time," p. 161; consult also William Klein, "The Ancient Constitution Revisited," in *Political Discourse in Early Modern Britain*, ed. Nicholas Phillipson and Quentin Skinner (Cambridge: Cambridge UP, 1993), ch. 2.

able, for example, that the disproportionate attention given to the best-known speech made in the Impositions debate of 1610, James White-locke's, has given a distorted impression of constitutional thinking at that time. Whitelocke's speech, we might usefully remember, began by sketching a series of problems of escalating significance (and increasing particularity—a telling correlation): the plan to change the name of the country to "Great Britain," the Union (by which he seems to have meant that naturalization of the post-nati), and Impositions. The last of these, because it concerned individual property rights, was the most serious.[110] In discussing the particular problem of Impositions, Whitelocke distinguished between "the natural frame and constitution of the policy of this kingdom, which is *jus publicum regni*" or "the fundamental law of the realm"; and "the municipal law of the land, which is *jus privatum*, the law of property and of private right."[111] This has done more than anything else to lead historians to the conclusion that fundamental law was an embryonic expression of the idea of a constitution. But Whitelocke's language is untypical and misleading. His civilian distinction between public and private law was similar to Bacon's, and reminds us that Whitelocke was a pupil of Alberico Gentili. Furthermore, in linking fundamental law to public law, Whitelocke was also following in Bacon's footsteps. All of this is at some distance from the dominant view that linked fundamental law with— if we can use these distinctions—*private* law; that is, with the common law of landed tenure. When Coke praised Littleton for his learning in "fundamental law" he can only have meant the law of landed property.[112] More commonly, Coke and Davies, like Digges and Pym in 1628, referred to fundamental *points* of the common law, a formulation in practice so flexible that it enabled the defense of virtually *any* law as fundamental. This language of the later 1620s was quite distant from Whitelocke's, which was a dying echo of the effort (largely defunct by 1610) to insist that fundamental law meant something other than the common law itself. Whitelocke's fundamental laws were *leges imperii*, as were those of James VI & I, Bacon, Fleming and others before c. 1607, and his remarks thus faced backwards to the 1600s more than they faced forward to the 1620s.

110. T. B. Howell, *A Complete Collection of State Trials*, 33 vols. (London, 1812), 2:[cols.] 477–79, and consult *Parliamentary Debates in 1610*, ed. S. R. Gardiner (London: Camden Society, 1862), p. 103.

111. J. R. Tanner, *Constitutional Documents of the Reign of James I, 1603–1625* (Cambridge: Cambridge UP, 1961 [1930]), p. 260.

112. Coke, *1 Inst.*, Pref. (1628).

If this is so, then it may be said that James VI & I saw more starkly the paradoxes of constitutionalism than did the critics of Union in his first Parliament. In a speech to Parliament on 2 May 1607, the King addressed the fear that there could be no secure guarantee for any protections of English law and liberty that might be attached to perfect union. He replied:

> To this I cannot tell what to answere; because neither I am well versed or skilled in yor common Lawe, nor you will give Credit to the Judges in the which they can say in this Point. But I will bring it to this Dilemma; either I can give Security or I cannot. If I can; why do you not yourselves enter into Consideration of it, and accept it! If I cannot, then must you leave all to me, after the Parliament, to do what I will. And if any thing light upon you other than you looked for, you must take, and bear that which your own Folly hath brought you unto, because you did not prevent in Time, when it was in your Hands... [113]

The comment was not tactful, but it correctly diagnosed the problem in the English MPs' position. They were demanding safeguards without committing themselves to the concepts that would make safeguards properly imaginable. James had already conceded to the English that, to them, "fundamental law" meant common law. He was now telling them—correctly and precisely—that that left them incapable of imagining constitutional restraints. Any protection must come from the common law itself, or trust must be placed on the king's own willingness to respect any reservations made. James was no doubt aware that his own idea of "fundamental law" could have provided another alternative. This may explain why it is, especially in 1607–8, that there was a marked tendency for English critics of Union to invoke the language of natural law. Edwin Sandys, for example, speaking on the first day of the Conference on naturalization (25 February 1607) was reported to have said that "This is a Case of the Law of Nations: There is no Statute Law for it: no express Common Law." In the same Conference, Coke (one of the judges giving their opinion) remarked that the Union could not harm England because "the king cannot change the natural law of a nation."[114] Natural law terminology was, as is well known, even more prominent in *Calvin's Case*.[115]

---

113. Huntington Library Ellesmere MS 2600, fol. 1v, checked against the generally inferior text in *CJ*, 1:367.

114. SP 14/26/54, quoted in Conrad Russell, "Composite Monarchies in Early Modern Europe: The British and Irish Example," in *Uniting the Kingdom? The Making of British History*, ed. Alexander Grant and Keith J. Stringer, p. 145.

115. Especially Polly J. Price, "Natural Law and Birthright Citizenship in

But the most important point to make concerns other uses of the ancient constitution. The myths of the ancient constitution took decisive form at the beginning of the seventeenth century because they provided a way of apprehending time that supported an insular English identity. This was an identity much contested. It was forged in debate and argument. Its importance in the period after 1603 was as a weapon in preventing the Scottish accession from undermining the identity of the English political community. Out of the Fortescuean moment and the King's concept of fundamental law was forged the ancient constitutionalist view that the common law was a fundamental law, defining prerogative and property rights, unchangeable and immune from conquest. It was a law not consciously made but the product of consensual practices; and because it was not made there was no authority above it that was capable of altering it in its entirety. A concern with conquest was pre-programmed into this language from the beginning, which is why it can seem so out of place later. Above all, because the common law was a fundamental law, it defined the essential character of the English polity. The language of ancient constitutionalism was not in its inception a constitutionalist ideology of anti-absolutism so much as it was an ideology of national identity. It should come as no surprise, then, to discover that it was invented when national identity was most threatened; still less should we be surprised by the insularity that permeated these ideas, or by the way in which Sir John Davies reached out for them to introduce his Irish Reports.

John Pocock's work has much still to tell us about this subject. And it has most to tell us when we recognize that what is central to it is a concern with time, and with those sorts of political reflection that operate by locating communities and their institutions in the flow of time. We have a fuller sense now than John Pocock had available to him in 1957 of the varieties of political thinking in early Stuart England, and of the challenges, even amongst lawyers, to what he identified as the "common law mind." But his central insight, that ancient constitutionalist myths were for many in the seventeenth century, fundamental to the Stuart perception of time, remains, if taken seriously, immensely fruitful.

Calvin's Case (1608)," *Yale Journal of Law and the Humanities* 9 (1997): 73–145.

Part Three: Ancient or Modern

7. Barbarism, Religion and the History of Political Thought

JONATHAN CLARK

The recent study of the history of political thought began in Cambridge in the late 1940s with Peter Laslett's edition of Filmer (1949) and John Pocock's Ph.D. thesis, submitted in 1952 and the basis for his book of 1957. This in turn drew on Herbert Butterfield's interest in Brady,[1] the subject of Pocock's first article in 1951.[2] The subject took off with Laslett's edition of Locke's *Two Treatises* in 1960; from there, it developed with writings on method first by Pocock, then by John Dunn and Quentin Skinner, and in work by the next generation, including Mark Goldie and Richard Tuck. It finds current expression, especially with respect to its original subjects in seventeenth- and eighteenth-century England, in the writings of a further generation, including Justin Champion and John Marshall. For so cerebral a subject, and for so theoretically-oriented a group of scholars, its is regrettable that the history of this school has not, so far, been written;[3] its antecedents, its birth, its methods and its achieve-

---

1. For Butterfield's contribution, see C.T. McIntire, *Herbert Butterfield: The Historian as Dissenter* (London: Yale UP, 2004), and Keith C. Sewell, *Providence and Method: Herbert Butterfield and the Interpretation of History* (Basingstoke: Palgrave, 2005). A study by Michael Bentley is expected.

2. Pocock, "Robert Brady, 1627–1700: A Cambridge Historian of the Restoration," *Cambridge Historical Journal* 10 (1951): 186–204.

3. For some autobiographical fragments, see the "Preface" to Pocock, *ACFL*,

ments are evidently still too vital to allow of dissection. Yet if we do not yet have a history of the movement, we are beginning to see exercises in summing up, whether in Skinner's collected essays[4] or in a multi-volume monograph by Pocock, still in progress, published under the general title *Barbarism and Religion.*[5] Perhaps we have now reached a stage at which that magnum opus can be interpreted in the light of the development of the subject itself.

Future students of the history of political thought will give much attention to a related set of innovations of which John Pocock has been a pioneer throughout his career. His writings on method,[6] initially influenced

pp. vii–xii. Pocock there traces the origin of "the historical resolution of political discourse into the idioms and 'languages' in which it has been conducted" to "the linguistic analysis of political utterances" of the contributors to *Philosophy, Politics and Society*, ed. Peter Laslett (Oxford: Blackwell, 1956). I am grateful to John Pocock for a copy of his paper "Present at the Creation: With Laslett to the Lost World."

4. Quentin Skinner, *Visions of Politics*, 3 vols. (Cambridge: Cambridge UP, 2002); importantly reviewed by David Wootton, *The Times Literary Supplement*, 14 March 2003, pp. 8–10.

5. Pocock, *BR*, separately subtitled *Volume One: The Enlightenments of Edward Gibbon, 1737–1765, Volume Two: Narratives of Civil Government* and *Volume Three: The First Decline and Fall*—all volumes hereafter cited parenthetically. The present essay began life as an appreciation of the first two volumes of Pocock's ongoing work in H-Albion. I am grateful for the comments on an early draft of Jock Gunn, Charles Prior, and John Pocock, none of whom, especially the subject of this essay, is necessarily in agreement with the views expressed here.

6. Including Pocock: "The History of Political Thought: A Methodological Enquiry," in *Philosophy, Politics and Society*, ed. Peter Laslett and W. G. Runciman, 2nd ser. (Oxford: Blackwell, 1962), pp. 183–202; "Languages and Their Implications: The Transformation of the Study of Political Thought," in *PLT*, pp. 3–41; "Verbalising a Political Act: Towards a Politics of Speech," *Political Theory* 1 (1973): 27–43; "Reconstructing the Traditions: Quentin Skinner's Historians' History of Political Thought," *Canadian Journal of Political and Social Theory* 3 (1979): 95–113; "Political Ideas as Historical Events: Political Philosophers as Historical Actors," in *Political Theory and Political Education*, ed. Melvin Richter (Princeton: Princeton UP, 1980), pp. 139–58; "The Reconstruction of Discourse: Towards the Historiography of Political Thought," *MLN* 96 (1982): 959–80; "Introduction: The State of the Art," in *VCH*, pp. 1–34; "The Concept of Language and the *métier d'historien*: Some Considerations on Practice," in *The Languages of Political Theory in Early-Modern Europe*, ed. Anthony Pagden (Cambridge: Cambridge UP, 1987), pp. 19–40; "Texts as Events: Reflections on the History of Political Thought," in *Politics of Discourse: The Literature and History of Seventeenth-Century England*, ed. Kevin Sharpe

by Thomas S. Kuhn's idea of paradigms ("controlling concepts and theories"[7]), have since come to be associated more with the characteristic idea that the task of the history of political thought is to trace the discourses, the political languages, which unified intellectual exchange into idioms with common styles, assumptions, preoccupations and results.[8] I shall consider later what one might mean by 'discourses,' and how they might be understood in *Barbarism and Religion*.

The Cambridge School, of course, was not alone. Yet not only is it lacking a history; alternatives to it have seldom been drawn into an overview. Even so, the relative weakness of several major alternatives is apparent. The historical profession of the United States has long been too positivist, and is now too postmodernist, to generate many methodologies of its own in the history of ideas,[9] but it has some. The most clearly-defined of them, Straussianism, acquired the function of providing a revised reading of the sacred scrolls of America's civic religion,[10] and it has remained within that geographically large but intellectually parochial subject. Its attention to the classic texts for their present-day lessons apparently promised what its host society required.[11] Yet its high-level preoccupation with the continuation of the message of the Founder helped to ensure that its low-

---

and Steven N. Zwicker (Berkeley: U of CA P, 1987), pp. 21–34; "Concepts and Discourses: A Difference in Culture?," in *The Meaning of Historical Terms and Concepts: New Essays on Begriffsgeschichte*, ed. Hartmut Lehmann and Melvin Richter (Washington, D.C.: German Historical Institute, 1996), pp. 47–58

7. Pocock, "Languages and Their Implications," pp. 13–15. This inclination to identify paradigms may have been paramount in Pocock's method to the publication of *The Machiavellian Moment* in 1975 and his edition of *The Political Works of James Harrington* in 1977.

8. For an earlier survey, see Iain Hampsher-Monk, "Political Languages in Time — The Work of J. G. A. Pocock," *British Journal of Political Science* 14 (1984): 89–116. That article chiefly addressed Pocock's interpretation of Harrington (which will not be examined here) but also importantly explored Pocock's and Skinner's differences of method, differences that have since become more significant.

9. Unless, of course, the jeremiad and its opposite the celebration are counted as methodologies; but this seems implausible.

10. It acquired this role, it may be suggested, by its insistence on a fall from 'ancient' virtue to 'modern' corruption, a scenario congruent with both the American jeremiad and 'modernization theory.'

11. For American political scientists' criticism of the Cambridge School as antiquarian, see Skinner, *Liberty before Liberalism* (Cambridge: Cambridge UP, 1998), pp. 106–7. It will be suggested later that this 'contextualist' variant of that Cam-

level incarnation, in Western Civ. Courses on Great Books and Great Men, is on the retreat. Recent US culture has not found in Strauss an international ambassador. As the Iraq war of 2003 revealed, Staussianism has not yielded US culture an adequate self-knowledge of its religious base, or of the problems associated with unrestrained power ('barbarism').

The most historical continental European offering, *Begriffsgeschichte*, promised a better route to self-awareness. Yet its strictly limited influence overseas had to do with more than Anglophone readers' famous difficulty with German compound nouns. The history of concepts, as practiced in Germany, was so committed to treating concepts as natural and appropriate reflexes of social change[12] that the school was largely trapped on board the sinking ship of reductionist social history. This last has everywhere been unsuccessful in establishing links with the history of ideas.[13] Even in Cambridge, links between the developing historiography of political thought and its social-structural setting in the past have been chiefly confined to Peter Laslett's work on Filmer and its implications for our understanding of patriarchalism. This is a remarkable lacuna, little remarked on. As a result of its modernist preconceptions, *Begriffsgeschichte* had almost nothing to say on religion, the theme that has returned as central to much of the subject matter of 'political thought.' By contrast, when Pocock offers a "*Begriffsgeschichte* of 'the decline and fall of the Roman empire,'" that is, an account of the formation of the concept of its decline and fall as Gibbon inherited it, he does so in discursive, not reductionist terms (*BR 3*, p. 62),[14] and terms that even owe most to "the image of the Eusebian sacred empire" (*BR 3*, p. 74); the concept of decline and fall "has as much to do with religion as with barbarism, and is entangled with the rise and character of a Christian and anti-classical perception of history" (*BR 3*,

---

bridge School was more purposive than US methodological preoccupations allowed their owners to appreciate.

12. Reinhard Koselleck, "*Begriffsgeschichte* and Social History," in Reinhard Koselleck, *Futures Past: On the Semantics of Historical Time*, trans. Keith Tribe (Cambridge, MA: Harvard UP, 1985), pp. 73–91.

13. For attempted rehabilitations, see Melvin Richter, "Reconstructing the History of Political Languages: Pocock, Skinner and the *Geschichtliche Grundbegriffe*," *History and Theory* 29 (1990): 32–70; his *The History of Political and Social Concepts: A Critical Introduction* (New York: Oxford UP, 1995); *Historical Terms and Concepts*, Lehmann and Richter (ed.).

14. Pocock's enquiries issue in "a series of layered concepts — deposited as it were by history in a sequence of surviving texts — which may be said to constitute a notion of "the decline and fall of the Roman empire" (*BR 3*, p. 203).

p. 120). Other continental European alternatives, notably deconstruction-ism, deserve more attention than is possible here; but in the case of the latter it would be difficult to point to substantive achievement in the long eighteenth century.

The track records of Straussianism, *Begriffsgeschichte* and other schools deserve to be compared in greater depth than space permits here with that of the Anglo-New Zealand school[15] conjured up by the word "Cam-bridge." Yet this itself developed two variants, related and overlapping yet not identical: Pocock's analysis of languages of discourse, and other scholars' focus on the contextual exegesis of texts (I shall refer to these as the "discursive" and "contextual" sub-schools). These have brought great gains in understanding, and I mean here to magnify rather than to dimin-ish both. Their emerging differences of method deserve consideration, however. Even in 1984, it was argued that Pocock and Skinner "are in one important sense proposing the rehabilitation of history within political thought on different principles." In Skinner's method, it was objected, "his-torical meaning is reduced to a series of discrete acts of understanding on the part of a range of authors and audiences... The continuing identity of the idea through time is in danger of being sacrificed to the particular purposes for which it is employed at any particular time"; whereas Pocock's usage "runs the opposite risk of a kind of neo-idealism through schema-tizing a transhistorical 'language' from a range of uses to which it is put."[16] These points will be considered later.

Both sub-schools are now at a mature stage of development, and invite reappraisal. A flagship of the contextualists has been the series *Cambridge Texts in the History of Political Thought*. As it draws to a conclusion, we can appreciate more clearly both its strengths and its limitations: among the latter, that the contexts normally appealed to by this sub-school still con-sist mainly of other texts.[17] Moreover, those other texts are often quite familiar ones, and their choice often silently minimizes or excludes the themes captured in Pocock's title, 'barbarism' (monarchy?) and 'religion.'

---

15. Its New Zealand contacts including also John Salmon, Glenn Burgess, and Andrew Sharp.

16. Hampsher-Monk, "Political Languages in Time," p. 104.

17. It should be recalled that 'contextual' and 'discursive' analysis are differ-ent emphases, not independent methodologies. Pocock, too, can write of texts supplying contexts (*BR 1*, pp. xii, 1). A central issue is what else is allowed to con-tribute to the creation of a 'context'; and here the contextualists have very def-inite precommitments.

Although the canon of texts appealed to has been extended by this series, and made more accessible, it is not essentially different.[18] The main additions to the canon for the long eighteenth century were Filmer (but this was Laslett's achievement in 1949, before the Cambridge School had formulated its claims on method) and Harrington (but Pocock's understanding of Harrington was formed in the 1960s within a still secular framework). Which authors were accepted into the series *Cambridge Texts in the History of Political Thought* and which were not is an important question. Many authors whose canonical status was already undeniable were included; but more interesting were the criteria for the election of new members to this club. Generally, authors in whose writings religious and legal themes predominated were omitted: to some degree, 'contexts' did not encourage the retrieval of 'discourses.' In this respect the series worked with the grain of widespread academic assumptions, and was not perceived as (and doubtless was not intended as) polemical or programmatic.

Within this 'contextual' sub-school, however, it would be difficult to point to major reinterpretations of such events (within Pocock's period) as 1776 and 1789 as a result of the contextual reinterpretation of a text, the exception that illustrates the marked lack of similar achievements since 1960 being Laslett's remarkable edition of Locke's *Two Treatises* and its wide implications for the interpretation of 1688. Although the inter-textual analysis of texts often yielded important insights into the texts being examined, those insights, when at odds with then-prevalent assumptions, were not always followed up. John Dunn's pioneering study *The Political Thought of John Locke*, published in 1969, came, unexpectedly to its author, to the conclusion that Locke's religion was central to his political writing on civil society; yet few initially developed that idea, and it was left for a later generation like John Marshall and Justin Champion to make it central to scholarship.

Instead of contextual analysis and studies of authorial intention, it has generally been (after Laslett) discursive analysis and the tracing of social constituencies that have most changed perspectives on the long eighteenth century. Discursive studies have been chiefly responsible for highlighting two themes that were often lacking not only from the texts but from the sense of relevant contexts shown by the Cambridge-based, con-

---

18. Pocock, "Languages and Their Implications," in *PLT,* pp. 3–4: "A canon of major works had been isolated by academic tradition…Alone among the major branches of historical study on the middle twentieth century, the history of political thought was treated as the study of a traditional canon."

textualist students of the history of ideas: law and religion. Law (except perhaps Roman law) had been too vulgarly implicated in the world of power and profit to feature in contextualist accounts. In respect of religion, the contextualist school has been held to be not merely secular in its assumptions, but programmatically secularizing in a way that has also been held to detract from historical understanding.[19] It should be said in defense of this methodology that that is not true of all its practitioners, although this adds importance to the question of why it might be true of some of them. It would be hard to argue that contextualization is implicitly secularizing where discourse analysis is not; rather, contextualism tends to construct contexts from already-familiar texts and so tends to reinforce existing historiographies, other late-modern, and therefore secular, ones.

The academic marginalization of law and religion dates from the late nineteenth century,[20] a time when several academic disciplines were defined by omissions (as 'English' was then defined by the omission of the classical languages). This allowed a novel genre to be constructed, known without challenge from any methodological school as "the history of political thought." The success of that genre shielded it from the historical qualification, suggested here, that until the nineteenth century Anglophone discourse lacked the independent, free-standing category 'political thought':[21] what we observe, filling the space that political thought now occupies, are impassioned and sophisticated debates over law and religion.[22] Both were, of course, conducted in the public realm (as well as in private): their status as political in the present sense is not in doubt, and they made up (a neglected) part of the content of works within the twentieth-century canon of 'political thought.' Yet the late twentieth-century exegesis of that canon contrived often to ignore them, reducing all to a sec-

---

19. Paul A. Marshall, "Quentin Skinner and the Secularization of Political Thought," *Studies in Political Thought* 2 (1993): 85–104, esp. p. 104 (n. 91). Earlier reactions normally neglected this secularizing outcome, for example *Meaning and Context: Quentin Skinner and his Critics*, ed. James Tully (Princeton: Princeton UP, 1997).

20. Especially since Leslie Stephen's ghost-laying *History of English Thought in the Eighteenth Century* (1876).

21. It is important in this context that the broad Aristotelian idea of 'politics' did not, until quite recently, generate 'the history of political thought.'

22. For an argument that the priority of these discourses means that the term "ideology" is also inappropriate for the seventeenth century, see David Martin Jones, *Conscience and Allegiance in Seventeenth-Century England: The Political Significance of Oaths and Engagements* (Rochester, NY: U of Rochester P, 1999), p. 231.

ular language of 'politics' more narrowly defined (often in functional terms). Pocock's first monograph, *The Ancient Constitution and the Feudal Law*, was in this sense prescient in its identification of one such discourse[23] that the political science of the 1950s passed over in silence, namely law.[24] The history of the historiography of political thought since the 1950s has been the history of a slow escape from the assumptions that the idea of 'political thought' embodied. In that process, Pocock's contribution has been immensely important.

The process of transcending the initial assumptions of the discipline has nevertheless been in tension with those present purposes that have sometimes come to influence the obligation equally to discuss all discourses and equally to contextualize all texts. Quentin Skinner recorded, in the printed version of his inaugural lecture of 1997, that the charge that contextual method led only to antiquarian studies of no present-day relevance "troubles me deeply," and set out, as a manifesto, a rationale of the modern application of his work.[25] It showed that the purposive content now advocated in one branch of the Cambridge School of historical enquiry had come to be expressed as the 'neo-Roman' theme of republicanism, interpreted and advocated as a view that liberty is to be understood as unconstrained self-government rather than as the absence of interference or, by implication, as public life guided by an ancient constitution.[26]

---

23. It may be that this work was, in its inception, a historiographical study in the manner of Sir Herbert Butterfield more than a study of paradigms like *The Machiavellian Moment*; but Pocock's later and clearer focus on the languages of politics has retrospectively and helpfully enlisted his earlier work.

24. From a later perspective, the book's lack of attention to religion is noteworthy; but this theme only began to secure much recognition from the mid-1980s. For a renewed attention to religion, see the Retrospect in the second edition (1987), esp. pp. 318–20: "I would now make far more of the extent—revealed by Hill's researches for Winstanley, and paradoxically (I think) by my own on Harrington—to which anti-Normanism was antinomianism, part of the Spirit's indictment of the as yet unsanctified flesh" (p. 320).

25. Skinner, *Liberty before Liberalism*, pp. 107–8. It should be noted that Skinner's work has covered many topics in many periods, and that they are perhaps not all to be subsumed in the avowed agenda of his expanded inaugural lecture.

26. For example, Skinner, *Liberty before Liberalism*: "I have never understood why the charge of utopianism is necessarily thought to be an objection to a theory of politics (pp. x-xi); and important lesson of the past is that "values set in stone at one moment melt into air at the next" (p. 111); history's social function is essentially emancipatory (p. 117). This position might, of course, subvert the

Why contextual analysis has more readily lent itself to this sort of pre-sentist use is a matter for further investigation.[27]

It need only be pointed out here that Pocock's reconstruction of the neo-Roman language of discourse we know as civic humanism, which historically carried a similar message for self-government, came in Pocock's pages with no such programmatic message.[28] The emergence of neo-Roman themes to political prominence in contextualist historiography in the 1990s thus seems not only some decades behind Pocock's reconstruction of civic humanism in discursive analysis in the 1960s and 70s, but un-necessarily normative in a way that Pocock's work was not.

Pocock's writings since the 1950s have also, importantly, evolved: whatever his enthusiastic remarks on civic humanism in *c.*1975–85, he has not urged a single model over the decades. *The Ancient Constitution and the Feudal Law* had primarily illuminated the discourse of common law thinking, and showed its close relationship to historical writing in the later seventeenth century. The recovery of the language of civic humanism was the achievement of *The Machiavellian Moment* (1975) and his definitive edition of *The Political Works of James Harrington* (1977). Subsequently, Pocock's enquiries have explored more and more of the discourses available in the English-speaking world of the eighteenth century,[29] especially Whig discourses, a diversification the need for which is acknowledged, if not fully

---

new values presently being recommended as well as the old ones that are un-willingly inherited.

27. For the allegedly unresolved tension in the work of Skinner between a 'teleological and present-centred' approach and the claims of historical-mindedness (the interpretation of texts in the light of their purposes at the time they were written), see Blair Worden, "Factory of the Revolution," *London Review of Books*, 5 February 1998, pp. 13–15: "By recovering 'lost' ideas, he [Skinner] proposes, we can supply practical alternatives to current political values. Thus, he implies, the writing of history will be an exercise not merely in scholarship but in citizenship." This argument may be compared with that of Mark Bevir, *The Logic of the History of Ideas* (Cambridge: Cambridge UP, 1999), p. 82: "because Skinner offers us his method as a logic of discovery, he necessarily fuses epistemology with methodology. His method constitutes a form of justification."

28. Even though its discussion of corruption may have drawn some inspiration from the misdeeds of President Nixon: Pocock, "*The Machiavellian Moment* Revisited," *Journal of Modern History* 53 (1981): 49–72.

29. For his recognition of the diversity of languages, see for example Pocock: "Languages and Their Implications," in *PLT,* pp. 20–22; "The Reconstruction of Discourse," pp. 963–66, 972; "The Concept of a Language," pp. 21, 23.

achieved, in *The Varieties of British Political Thought, 1500-1800,* a collection he edited with Gordon Schochet and Lois G. Schwoerer in 1994.

Pocock's expanding world of discourses has come to fill a vacuum opened up by the decentring of Locke,[30] and what used to be called Lockeian contractarianism or Lockeian liberalism, in the 1960s and 70s.[31] This was partly an unintended consequence of Laslett's work: where Laslett initially celebrated Locke as a founding father of liberalism, the effect of his profoundly important edition of the *Two Treatises* was to replace Locke in a context very close to that just outlined by Pocock in *The Ancient Constitution and the Feudal Law,* this fact being only partly obscured by the loss in the 1680s of what is now thought to have been the third of Locke's treatises, that on constitutional law. This decentring was a process that Pocock, in the 1970s and 80s, urged forward with a zeal which has revealed the extent to which Locke as a Founding Father of the United States is still essential to certain readings, not only Straussian readings, of American culture.[32]

If the eighteenth century mind could no longer be described as *Locke et praeterea nihil,* a great many other figures presented themselves as points of access to the discourses of the age. In his magisterial study *Barbarism and Religion* Pocock is drawn to Edward Gibbon, the author who best embodied in the late eighteenth century the intellectual preoccupations first surveyed by Pocock in his monograph of 1957, and many other preoccupations besides. The work therefore to some degree invites comparison with Quentin Skinner's advocacy of what in *Liberty before Liberalism* he terms neo-Roman themes.

Barbarism and Religion shows how the idea of 'context' has become something of a truism to which all now subscribe, since it presents Gibbon in the wide, and perhaps diffuse, contexts of the discourses of historical writing, religion, scholarship and politics (*BR 3*, p. 1). It situates him, in other words, in "a series of contexts in the history of eighteenth-century Europe" established by languages of discourse, challenging the idea that there was

---

30. Locke's decentring, that is, from the position ascribed to him in the USA in the early and mid-twentieth century as an inaugurator of 'liberalism' in the American sense.

31. By contrast, for example, the 'contextualist' Ideas in Context series contained one monograph entitled *Early Modern Liberalism* (1997), the anachronism revealing its normative intent.

32. Pocock, "The Myth of Locke and the Obsession with Liberalism," in Pocock and Richard Ashcraft, *John Locke* (Los Angeles: William Andrews Clark Memorial Library, 1980).

only one Enlightenment context, established by the rectitude of its content, to which to relate him. The discursive settings offered by Pocock's first volume are chiefly biographical and geographical: Putney, Oxford, Hampshire, Paris, Lausanne, Rome; they take us to the alleged moment of the conception of *The Decline and Fall of the Roman Empire* on 15 October 1764. The second volume offers a series of discursive intellectual settings in the historiography of the Enlightenment in the form of studies of historians and others who influenced Gibbon: Giannone, Voltaire, Hume, Robertson, Ferguson and Adam Smith. The third depicts the setting in which the first fourteen chapters of Gibbon's first volume were written, chapters that trace the decline and fall of "ancient, imperial and polytheist Rome" before the spread of Christianity. It is the part of Gibbon's text, moreover, that determined the shape of his *History* not as a story of emancipation from barbarism and religion by Enlightenment, but as the story of 'the triumph of barbarism and religion.' Figures illuminating this direction-setting include Tacitus, Appian, Orosius, Otto of Freising, Leonardo Bruni, Flavio Biondo, Niccolo Machiavelli and many more.

Gibbon is located, then, in an intellectual landscape much more diverse than that which Pocock first encountered in the 1950s. Even Harrington features only infrequently in the first three volumes, and civic humanism lacks an entry in the indexes of the first two ("The rise of a high-minded civic humanism was part of the story, but not the whole of it" [*BR 2*, p. 204]):[33] it re-emerges via Gibbon's indebtedness to a "Tacitean historiography of republican decay," a theme juxtaposed to the "Gracchan explanation," as in Appian and Sallust, of the republic's failure to satisfy the demands of its armies for land grants (*BR 3*, p. 14). These themes yield a less happy picture of political power than is Skinner's. For Pocock's Edward Gibbon as an MP, neo-Roman themes clearly did not produce an endorsement of republicanism at key moments like 1776 and 1789, as Skinner's analysis might lead us to expect it should have done.[34]

---

33. Pocock intends his work to show that "there is far more to the *Decline and Fall* than the tensions between virtue and commerce, ancient and modern, or even, in a sense, than Decline and Fall itself" (*BR 1*, p. 2). A standing army and public credit is presented as transforming English society at the end of the seventeenth century, but the significance of this was to create an "intellectual climate" in which "the writings of Tacitus took on renewed significances"; and Gordon's edition of Tacitus "is a narrative of exclusively moral decay, lacking a material base" (*BR 3*, pp. 304, 322).

34. Mark Philp, "English Republicanism in the 1790s," *Journal of Political Philosophy* 6 (1998): 235–62, traces this to a difference of historical method: "Whereas

When Pocock posits a 'Machiavellian moment' in the fifty to seventy years following Harrington's writings of 1656–60, he refers to liberty as containing its own tendency to self-corruption (*BR 3*, p. 310), but this harks back to a "Sallustian (it could be Polybian) moment at which the *imperium* won by *libertas* is seen subverting the *virtus* on which the *libertas* depends" (*BR 3*, p. 203). Nor is the concept of an ancient constitution prominent in this work: law has, perhaps temporarily, receded. Rather, Gibbon's family was implicated in Jacobitism, a discourse which linked barbarism not with religion but with irreligion (especially Whig irreligion).[35]

Dynastic politics are taken seriously here (indeed one of the tasks of pastor Pavillard at Lausanne was "to wean Gibbon from his persisting Jacobitism" (*BR 1*, p. 72[n]). The interconnections of dynastic politics are also rightly appreciated: discontent with the Revolution Settlement "took not only a dynastic but an ecclesiological and theological form" (*BR 1*, p. 19). *The Machiavellian Moment* identified a language of civic virtue and the anxieties expressed about its declension, latterly in the face of advancing commercial society; yet what set the main intellectual contexts for the young Gibbon were not commerce and corruption but 'barbarism' and 'religion.' Indeed the social project of *The Spectator* is now identified as precisely to secure a victory over both those things (*BR 1*, p. 107): in Pocock's work barbarism and religion now bulk large, and civic virtue is a moderate and belated response (sometimes as fragile a response as Gibbon's militia service).

Pocock proposes an intellectual setting populated by issues of theology, ecclesiology, and an historiography which often concerned itself

---

Pocock embraces the diversity of languages, idioms and rhetorics, the identification of a republican theory of politics or liberty [by Quentin Skinner and Philip Pettit] must be far more resistant to diversity…Moreover, whereas Pocock can acknowledge that republicanism is just one of several idioms or languages available, claims for the continuing influence of a republican theory of liberty imply its continuing salience in the face of such competition" (p. 237). Philp argues that republicanism was "marginal" in England in the 1790s, and that this gives "grounds for questioning the extent of its influence in earlier decades" (p. 239).

35. The trope later found an echo in Edward Gibbon: for him the decline of ancient virtue was an important cause of the decline of the ancient Roman polity, but his antipathy to Christianity meant that ancient virtue had also to be identified with pagan Roman religion. Gibbon's claim to have described, in the *Decline and Fall*, "the triumph of barbarism and religion" was too general to be a correct characterization of his argument. It was not religion as such that he deplored, but Christianity in particular.

with Biblical history and the history of the early Church (Gibbon, indeed, appears as "an ecclesiastical historian," inhabiting "a world where Enlightenment was a product of religious debate and not merely a rebellion against it" [*BR 1*, p. 5]). It is this salience of religious debate which, writes Pocock, entitles England to claim to have had *an* Enlightenment; not *the* Enlightenment, nor a prototypical Enlightenment, but its own variant, the similarities with other Enlightenments established first by the survival and intellectual force of the Church of England and second by the need for English intellectuals to challenge and rebut the theology and ecclesiology of that church. Franco Venturi's argument that Gibbon was a member of an European Enlightenment which had no counterpart in England is gently dismissed (*BR 1*, pp. 6, 292–308): Venturi was using a French model as if that were the only appropriate one.

Pocock shows, from Gibbon's earliest English and Swiss settings, "a number of ways in which he had occasion to be Enlightened"; in particular, "scholarship, we may say, was his Enlightenment" (*BR 1*, pp. 8, 10). A discourse here illuminates Gibbon, but it is a discourse echoed also in texts. Pocock finds the immediate historiographic antecedents of the attention to Byzantine history of *The Decline and Fall* in the young Gibbon's chance reading (Howel, Echard) in the library at Stourhead in 1751; and he finds in the young historian's erudition "a strong clerical component."

Gibbon's disparaging remarks on his university may be "a juvenile disappointment at finding the high-church and non-juror clerical learning, which had been the glory of Oxford, in abeyance and no longer expected of him" (*BR 1*, p. 43). Failing such enlistment, Gibbon was drawn into the debate on miracles launched by Cambridge's Conyers Middleton in 1749 and joined the Roman Catholic church in reaction against English skepticism; this choice is presented as "an expression of the Anglican predicament," caught since the sixteenth century in the tension between the claims of Rome and Geneva (*BR 1*, p. 24).

For Gibbon, Europe was not 'the Other' but a diverse series of Others. His father's reaction to his son's Roman conversion in sending him to Lausanne pitched Gibbon into a philosophical culture far more diverse than his family could have foreseen, notably the European Calvinist culture that Pocock interprets as another variant of Enlightenment. Pocock creates a richly drawn discursive setting in the theological writings of late seventeenth-century members of the French Protestant diaspora (Bayle, Basnage, Le Clerc, Jurieu), although admitting that "How far the young Gibbon at Lausanne was reading histories of this kind cannot be determined" (*BR 1*, p. 66); it seems more likely that at that time the more influential items on his reading list were Crousaz's logic and Locke's epistemology, the second interpreted by Pocock as an implicit undermining of the Roman doctrine of transubstantiation (*BR 1*, p. 75).

This tracing of languages of discourse takes Pocock on to historiography. In volume two we are introduced to a world of Enlightened historians, beginning with Giannone, who explored on a large narrative canvas the ways in which an ancient world of virtue and civil law had given way to ecclesiastical dominance, which in turn was being recast by commercial society. What engaged Gibbon in his encounters with these historians was his confidence that they had indeed outlined a defensible account of the rise and fall of clericalism. As Momigliano suggested, Gibbon combined the insights of the *érudits* with those of the *philosophes*, and added the discipline of narrative; as Pocock shows, "The marriage was not made in heaven," for Gibbon's art emerged in a complex conjuncture of contexts which generated, for him, "a narrative…of systemic change" (*BR 2*, p. 5). Gibbon became an historian, not a present-minded political scientist.

One of those systemic changes was prompted by a reflection on the civil role of religion which Pocock traces to Giannone (*BR 2*, p. 69); another was prompted by the assimilation of an historiography focused on manners, something pioneered by Voltaire. Voltaire, too, prefigured the sixteenth chapter of *The Decline and Fall* in his account of the early Church as "a concealed republic within the empire" and wrote, in terms again pre-figuring Gibbon, that "Two scourges at length destroyed this great colossus [the Roman empire]: barbarians and religious dispute" (*BR 2*, pp. 94, 122).

Yet Voltaire's project seems to evoke no answering approval in Pocock: religion features in his pages as a language of discourse whose content is to be understood and whose incidence is to be measured, not as a natural ally or barbarism or an inherent enemy of politeness.[36] This is evident, too, in Pocock's treatment of key figures of the Scottish Enlightenment. Hume features as an investigator of "the historical conditions which underlie modern commercial society and its government," drawn backwards in time from the Stuarts to Julius Caesar to explain the historical preconditions of the Hanoverian regime (*BR 2*, pp. 197, 200). Robertson appears as a member of the 'Moderate' party, that Scots latitudinarian attempt to soften the edges of Calvinism, an historian preoccupied with

---

36. Pocock protests that "Since we are all liberal agnostics, we write whig histories of liberal agnosticism" (*BR 1*, p. 9). It is open to doubt whether that is what Pocock himself has written here.

the question of how Scotland might become "a polite and cultivated commercial society, such as the Union with England was intended to make it." The answers had to do with martial virtue (the militia) and manners (the repression of 'enthusiasm') (*BR 2*, pp. 268, 270), not, it seems, the rejection of religion as such. Much of this was Scotland-centred: Robertson's *Charles V*, a history of the European state system in which Scotland hardly featured, was nevertheless "a history needed for the understanding of Scottish history" (*BR 2*, p. 275).

Adam Smith is dealt with as the archetypal author in an emergent "species of 'natural' or 'conjectural' history of civil society in general," written by men like Smith, Ferguson and Millar who did not call themselves historians but produced accounts of "morality, sociability and… history as systems intelligible in themselves" and in which the divine did not feature: Gibbon "was to proceed in this way when writing the history of the Christian church" (*BR 2*, pp. 310–14). Ferguson himself appears as a justification for Gibbon's regarding the prehistories of Greek and Roman society as "founded in barbarism, but never in savagery" (*BR 2*, p. 355). Yet, given that Gibbon in 1751 read William Howel's *General History* and the continuation of Laurence Echard's *Roman History*, which carried the story to the fall of Constantinople in 1453, why did Gibbon himself much later take the same dates and become an historian of Byzantium, an empire with a history that hardly exemplified stadial transitions from feudalism to commerce, rather than of the medieval West? It may be that the influence of Scottish 'conjectural history' was not so strong.

These questions return us to issues of method. Discourses, in *Barbarism and Religion*, become contexts, but with a key qualification. Having reconstructed a variety of plausibly relevant contexts, Pocock is candid about the difficulty of bringing this rich scholarly culture to bear in explaining exactly how the project of the *Decline and Fall* was formulated (*BR 1*, pp. 275–308; 2, pp. 397–402): "As Gibbon's history moved outwards it became also a multifaceted history of barbarism; and it is hard to find even the germ of this on 15 October, 1764," or even to explain the work's development towards being an ecclesiastical history (*BR 1*, p. 288; 2, pp. 378–79, 382). Pocock gives priority to his observation that Gibbon did not fully anticipate where his work would lead him when he published its first volume in 1776 (*BR 1*, pp. 2–3), and even the reconstruction of so many discourses does not dispel that element of underdetermination.

This may be more a qualification of 'contextualist' studies: positing a context of texts is one thing; proving it to have shaped the work in question as we think it ought to have done is quite another. In one way, of course, languages of discourse provide just such problematic contexts; but there are differences, and helpful ones, if the relevance of a language of discourse can be shown by parallel usages rather than needing to be established by acknowledged acceptances.[37]

A close tying of this intellectual background to the processes of composition of the *Decline and Fall* is, remarkably, prevented by the absence of any of Gibbon's journals for the decade before the publication of the first volume. Hence Pocock offers "an ecology rather than an etiology" (*BR 1*, p. 10). Historians who expect tight chains of causation may be frustrated; others may be rewarded by the rich and diverse texture of the backgrounds that Pocock invokes. Some question remains, however, as to exactly what features of Gibbon's narrative are explained by this approach.[38]

With *Barbarism and Religion*, it may be that contextual history has diffused into a truism.[39] No longer does it aim to recast our understanding of authorial intention or the impact of the text; rather, it now paints a broad and varied picture which the text in some sense inhabits. In Pocock's method, even 'the Enlightenment,' formerly a specific thing to be characterized and explained, has diversified into 'enlightenments,' as many as there were able thinkers, none of them a dominant, context-setting, force. As Pocock himself remarkably concludes, "It will follow that there is no key to the development of the *Decline and Fall* but the text of the *Decline and Fall* itself; the secondary documents do not offer it" (*BR 2*, p. 401).

It is always easy to say that the substantive results of enquiries which follow programmatic statements do not embody the principles of method announced at the outset.[40] It has been asked of Pocock's method in general

---

37. Yet how far can this be taken? Pocock devotes a chapter to Pedro Mexía, author of *Historia imperial y Cesarea* (1551), although acknowledging that there is no evidence that Gibbon knew of it (*BR 3*, p. 240).

38. Pocock presents *Barbarism and Religion* as "intended to exhibit Edward Gibbon and his *Decline and Fall of the Roman Empire* in historical contexts to which they belong and which illuminate their significance" (*BR 3*, p. 1); the key term here is "illuminate."

39. For a movement in Pocock's direction, see Skinner, *Liberty before Liberalism*, p. 101: "intellectual historians will do well to focus not merely on a canon of so-called classic texts, but rather on the place occupied by such texts in broader traditions and frameworks of thought."

40. Bevir argues that when Skinner and Pocock write histories of change, "their account of change cannot be based on the theories of meaning they avow" (*Logic of the History of Ideas*, p. 49). This may interpret those theories too rigidly

whether it reduces historical actors to mouthpieces for languages of discourse, and whether it can accommodate an account of change. These objections deserve consideration.

First, the alleged dominance of discourses. Pocock's relative lack of appeal to etiologies suggests, on the contrary, that the subject matter of his history of ideas is less overdetermined than radically underdetermined people.[41] Less texts, existing in a context of other texts, than people, living in a discursive setting in which conventions of speech limit and describe what they can do but do not limit it to the point of predictability. And yet these two options overlap, and no clear resolution of this question seems yet to be proposed by either 'discursive' or 'contextualist' sub-schools.[42]

Barbarism and religion emerge in Pocock's work as bound in no necessary unity by the method he has chosen, that of seeking a context in surrounding discourses. If so, change (in this case, the changes in the Roman empire that we sum up with the word "decline" is locked into no simplistic logic, and Pocock reconstructs those changes instead by elaborate accounts of their historiography. Is barbarism's problem that it cannot establish itself as a discourse? Not every practical activity yields such a language: we should not be surprised at the absence of discursive connections between apples and oranges, even if they function as each others' contexts in a still-life made up of well-painted texts.

Does Pocock's method end in antiquarianism, unable to account for change? It may be that this charge was provoked by his earlier atten-

---

although, as is suggested here, their consequences are somewhat different; nevertheless, it is open to question how far the work of either Pocock or Skinner has yet given sufficient attention to the historical phenomenon of conceptual innovation, a process to which Gibbon did not (unlike his contemporary Bentham) contribute. For Pocock in 1962, and to some degree later, the historian "will tend to approach the history of political thought through studying the regular employment of relatively stable concepts" ("The History of Political Thought," p. 195).

41. For a contrary argument that Pocock's method reduces individuals to "mouthpieces of the script-writing paradigms which constitute their conceptual frameworks," see Bevir, *Logic of the History of Ideas*, pp. 35, 49, and here and there; for differences between Pocock and Skinner, see p. 41. Bevir's argument, published in 1999, may now be compared with Pocock's volumes on Gibbon.

42. This distinction between methodologies is the present author's. For Pocock, "contexts consist largely though not wholly of discourses, of which there are several defining the context in different ways" (private communication).

tion to a writer who did not raise the issue (as Gibbon prominently did): "Pocock's Harrington…is less interested in ultimate historical causes of the changes to which he draws attention than he is in the prospect they offer for constitutional reconstruction." The charge of producing a static analysis might be more telling against Skinner's method than Pocock's.[43] We may indeed bear in mind at this point the political agendas that have been attributed to Skinner, although not necessarily ones that Skinner himself has avowed or repudiated.[43]

Given the presentist agendas often seen in the historical arena, it is important that Pocock and other 'discursive' historians of ideas have been drawn critically to the subject of national identity or identities within the British Isles.[45] Before this debate emerged, Pocock had pioneered a cognate area of scholarship, 'British history' understood as the relations and dynamics of Britain's component parts.[46] There is a contrast here between the 'contextualist' variant of a shared endeavor, which has issued in a programmatic republicanism and secularism, allegedly revived with too little regard for the very different settings in which those historic doctrines

---

43. Hampsher-Monk, "Political Languages in Time," p. 96—consult also p. 104: "Skinner's outspoken criticism of ideas as possible historical subjects, and his methodological insistence on a full understanding of the contemporary linguistic context of a particular 'utterance'…pushes in the direction of history as a series of static 'snapshots' or 'thin sections.'"

44. Fred Inglis's review of Skinner's *Reason and Rhetoric in the Philosophy of Hobbes*, *The New Statesman*, 29 March 1996, insists that "Skinner's work has consequences for politics," delighting in his appointment as Regius Professor at Cambridge despite Thatcherism and the "punctual way" in which the "great Matron and her stooges rewarded the hordes of toadies in scholarly life." Skinner believes, argues Inglis, that "key concepts (expressed in no matter what words) carry veins of radical energy laid down as residue in stored meanings. The historian may retrieve these meanings so that their residue flows back into the energies of the living." The reviewer concludes: "This is the revenge of historical thought all right"; (pp. 30–31). For a similar perception of a presentist agenda in Skinner's work, although with an opposite evaluation of it, see Maurice Cowling, "A Three-faced Historian," *The Spectator*, 31 January 1998, which argues that Skinner's method "has prevented scrutiny by others of assumptions at which Professor Skinner has merely hinted" (p. 38).

45. For skepticism of presentist uses of history in this setting, see Pocock, "Gaberlunzie's Return," *New Left Review* 5 (2000): 41–52.

46. For example, see Pocock, "British History: A Plea for a New Subject," in *DI*, ch. 2 and his "The Limits and Divisions of British History: In Search of the Unknown Subject," *American Historical Review* 87 (1982): 311–36.

were formulated in the seventeenth century,[47] and Pocock's 'discursive' variant, which has illuminated rather differently the historiography of the various communities of discourse that compose the constantly changing polities of the British Isles.[48] In this most momentous of current British political debates, discursive analysis has founded a school that is preoccupied by constitutional and discursive change; contextual analysis has contributed in other ways. Neo-Roman themes may have some impact on present-day British politics, but the rival discourses of barbarism and religion seem set to occupy our attention for some time to come. For the United States in particular, these two concepts now assume an unwelcome contemporary relevance.

47. As is argued by Worden, "Factory of the Revolution." Skinner's *Liberty before Liberalism*, linking 1742 and 1776, deserves serious thought; especially on what the present-day impact might be of reviving in a normative manner principles that once inspired such episodes. Skinner disavows any such forceful intention, identifying continuities only at "a deeper level" (pp. 117–18).

48. Reviewed in Pocock, "Contingency, Identity, Sovereignty," in *Uniting the Kingdom? The Making of British History*, ed. Alexander Grant and Keith J. Stringer (London, 1995), pp. 292–302, and in his "The Union in British History," in *DI*, ch. 10. This may be compared with Pocock, "The Historian as Political Actor in Polity, Society and Academy," *Journal of Pacific Studies* 20 (1996): 89–112.

8. Property, Liberty and Valour: Ideology, Rhetoric and Speech in the 1628 Debates in the House of Commons

Prepared for a Conference on the Petition of Right held at Washington University, 1978

J.G.A. POCOCK

Introduction

i

This essay has a history of its own, and may even make a minute contribution to the history it is part of. It was written in 1978 for a conference
organised by the late J.H. Hexter at Washington University in St. Louis,
with the aim of celebrating two occurrences: the 350th anniversary of the
Petition of Right in seventeenth-century England, and the publication
in 1977 by Yale University Press of the *Commons Debates: 1628*,[1] in which
the formation and presentation of the Petition could be traced. The proceedings of that conference were not published, and this paper (as it
then was) remained forgotten, even by its author, until recently, when
the curiosity of some and the serendipity of others have brought it back
to light.[2] It is here published after very light editing, designed to lessen
its character as a spoken lecture; no changes in its argument or vocabulary have been attempted.

There are two sets of reasons why it may be worth publishing today.
In the first place, there seems to have been no attempt to explore the rhetoric and conversation of the 1628 House of Commons on a scale comparable to this, though certain moments and interventions have been pre-

---

1. See below, n. 13.
2. I would like to thank Perry Anderson, Richard Davis, Derek Hirst, and
Linda Levy Peck for their parts in this recovery. A summary of some points in
this essay appeared in *ACFL*, pp. 289–305.

sented by historians. It is evident that there was a parliamentary style of
rhetoric, unlike that taught classically in the schools, and that this can be
resurrected, for the further reason that shorthand permitted it to be recorded and there were conventions governing the conversion of shorthand into longhand manuscripts that were distributed and have sur-
vived. The editors of the 1977 Yale volumes (four in number) worked
from a number of manuscript and printed sources, and it is argued below that these support one another. From the record of debate they sev-
erally supply, it is possible to select an often dramatic narrative, and
this is attempted in the following essay. Certainly, the moments of which
it consists have to be isolated from a background in which parliamentary business is proceeding as usual, and this must not be forgotten; but
there are moments at which drama emerges from the background and
takes over. The Debates of 1628 are the narrative of a political happening as well as a documentation of parliamentary culture.

The narrative takes place in the politics of speech. The orators and de-
bators (no doubt a fraction of the members present) are declaring their
distress and anger, and arriving at a spoken consensus as to what the anger
is about. At the same time they are trying, on the whole unsuccessfully,
to use speech so as to get the king and his ministers to meet them in speech
and use language which will permit a union of minds. In a kingdom governed by counsel, even in part, this is a serious matter, and there is room
to suppose that the parties are in earnest and mean what they say. The
nature of the record, furthermore, is informal, and speech is recorded in
informal situations. The gap between rhetoric and conversation narrows.
It follows, to look further still, that there is a case for studying rhetorical speech itself, language in which speech is conducted. From this we
may learn, not only what the speakers meant to say, but what they meant
without saying it and said without meaning to.

Rich patterns of meaning and coherence may therefore emerge, and
in this essay are organised around the notion of property, spelt as "propriety" for reasons that will appear; there are complex perceptions of human society and English history, of which some speakers are aware while
others take them for granted. It is valuable to study mentalities at different levels of articulation and sophistication; and this the *Commons Debates*
of 1628 permits us to do, while tracing the narrative of a crucial and ca-
lami-tous political negotiation in the medium of speech. Here is the first
set of reasons for publishing this essay.

The second set is historiographic. Re-read after nearly thirty years,
this essay opens a window into the mental world inhabited by histori-

ans of England in 1978, a world with which some readers will not be acquainted. The resolute constitutionalism of Jack Hexter—who shortly afterwards initiated at Washington University a Center for the History of Freedom[3]—did not make him a Whig historian, but had yet to encounter the often vehement revisionism that was soon to come. The late Conrad Russell was a participant in the 1978 conference, and will have presented the view that Charles I and his ministers may have found it as hard to meet the Commons in shared speech as the Commons found it hard to meet them. The conference did not (as I remember) adopt the position that there were two incompatible views of government in collision; it was nearer saying that something had gone profoundly wrong with a hitherto profound consensus. There will be found in this essay the premise that the Commons desperately wanted the King to meet their anxieties, and were as desperately frustrated by his refusal to do so.

Subsequent revisionisms have reached the point of denial that there was anything profound happening at all. In retrospect, what is perhaps most striking about the conference of 1978 is not the presence of Conrad Russell, but the absence of the late Geoffrey Elton, whose basic position was that the Civil War ought not to have happened, and who therefore denied its significance in every way a powerful intelligence could suggest. There are other ways in which this essay opens windows into the past of historiography; it was clearly written at the end of the era in which it had been generally believed that economic realities, whether of interest or of class, lay behind all assertions of thought or action and should be used to explain them. I found myself at issue with the late Brough Macpherson, for whom the concept of "property" and "bourgeoisie" lay too close together. In reply I engaged, in what was to be called the "Cambridge" manner, in an investigation of how the term property/propriety was used and how it stirred the depths of self-perception.

ii

There is one way in which this essay may be said to link a historiographic past with a present: the time of Hexter and Russell, Elton and Macpherson, with the time of Quentin Skinner. Here, it will be said with as-

---

3. Under his direction and that of R. W. Davis, it published a number of volumes from the Stanford University Press, of which series title was *The Making of Modern Freedom*.

surance, are the "democratical gentlemen" of the House of Commons, voicing their "neo-roman" concept of liberty as freedom from domination, to which Thomas Hobbes was to take such memorable exception perhaps fourteen years later.[4] Hobbes, indeed, published his translation of Thucydides—which he later described as a warring against democracy—in 1629, and it has been suggested that he was moved in doing so by the parliamentary disorders of that and the preceding year.[5] It is quite possible that one or more of the manuscript diaries on which the Yale editors relied come his way as a circulated copy; and as we read the debates we hear voices calling loudly for liberty as non-domination. Without property (spelt propriety) in their lands and goods, they say, they are slaves without legal existence; without a law built round such property, there is no kingdom and no England; without proprietors in this sense, the king can have no soldiers who are truly his subjects. The whole thrust of the Petition of Right is toward persuading King Charles to confirm the law as the structure of his kingdom. But to what extent is this rhetoric neo-roman? Writing this essay in 1978, three years after publishing *The Machiavellian Moment* and one year after publishing *The Political Works of James Harrington*, I had reason to think I was still operating in the medieval world of *The Ancient Constitution and the Feudal Law*. Sir Edward Coke and John Selden were leading figures in this parliament—the former exuberantly and ubiquitously so; the law to which they appealed for their social being was the common law; the whole issue of arms and soldiers came down to that of the common law's supremacy over martial law and "law of state"; and if there is any writer exercising authority in the speakers' minds, he is probably not Machiavelli, but Sir John Fortescue.

Quentin Skinner has pointed out that, though the law whose failure would render Englishmen slaves is the common law, the doctrine that the law's failure would have that effect is Roman and civilian;[6] the point

---

4. Quentin Skinner: "A Third Concept of Liberty," *Proceedings of the British Academy*, 117:237–68; "Classical Liberty, Renaissance Translation, and the English Civil War," in *Visions of Politics: Renaissance Virtues* (Cambridge: Cambridge UP, 2002), 2:308–43; "Classical Liberty and the Coming of the English Civil War," in *Republicanism: A Shared European Heritage: The Values of Republicanism in Early Modern Europe*, ed. Martin van Gelderen and Quentin Skinner (Cambridge: Cambridge UP, 2002), 2:9–28.

5. This suggestion was made by Miriam Reick, *The Golden Lands of Thomas Hobbes* (Detroit: Wayne State UP, 1971), pp. 36-52. See Noel Malcolm, *Aspects of Hobbes* (Oxford: Oxford UP, 2002), pp. 8–9.

6. See Skinner, "Classical Liberty, Renaissance Translation, and the English

is part of his argument that this concept of liberty is neo-roman. Selden and Coke, however, insistent that Roman law obtained in England only by the common law's permission, would not see their position as a retreat from common to civilian. They will have couched their whole argument in common-law terms, finding in Bracton the dictum that "there is no king where will rules and not the law," and in Fortescue the doctrine that it is immemorial customary law which binds king to kingdom, creating both a *dominium regale et politicum* and a mystical body of which the king is head.[7] In the 1628 debates we find Pym arguing that Manwaring has pushed the independence of *regale* from *politicum* so far as to make the king a ruler by conquest and divorce him from his kingdom.[8] The repudiation of any conquest occurring in 1066 was long rooted in English argument. Alongside the neo-roman, then, there stood unshaken a palaeogothic.

However, this is the parliament of 1628. It was in 1642 that Thomas Hobbes, according to his account many years later—an account on the whole accepted by Skinner—perceived that an argument based in Roman law, to the effect that prerogative was threatening all property, was at the point of leading to an argument based in the Roman republic, tempting every proprietor to rely on his virtue as a citizen.[9] It is a long stride from imperial law to republican virtue, and we must see the concept of the "neo-roman" as undergoing a profound transformation. Would the "democratical gentlemen" of 1642 have accepted Hobbes's account of themselves? There is evidence of a republican component in their thinking,[10] which gathered strength during the years of civil war; nevertheless, what was in the making in 1642 was not a republic but a civil war, unimaginable in 1628, but now undertaken against the king in the king's name. Charles I, said his opponents, was threatening a dissolution of his own government; misled by evil counselors, he was acting in his natural person so as to destroy the political person which he embodied

---

Civil War" and "Classical Liberty and the Coming of the English Civil War," for his reading of the debates of 1628.

7. For a reading of Fortescue in the context of my own works, see *MM*, pp. 9–30.

8. For details, see *ACFL*, pp. 299–300.

9. Skinner, "Classical Liberty and the Coming of the English Civil War," p. 15.

10. David Norbrook, *Writing the English Republic: Poetry, Rhetoric and Politics, 1627–1660* (Cambridge: Cambridge UP, 1999).

only when at unity with his parliament.[11] The latter could therefore act against him in his own name, and by 1649 had reached the brink of charging him with treason against himself. The brink they crossed, however, was that between executing a king and abolishing monarchy.

The doctrine of the king's two bodies — crucial for James I and John Pym alike — had roots in the Roman-law concept of incorporation and the Christian concept of incarnation,[12] but the name of Fortescue is enough to show us that it was entirely compatible with the common law and the ancient constitution; contained within it, the latter might even outlast it. A consequence, only immediately paradoxical, is that no lasting concept of English government as other than monarchical ever was or has been formulated. James Harrington, coming at a moment when it seemed that one might be necessary, lived on as the author of a historical scheme, stating the conditions necessary for either monarchy or republic, but foreseeing some convergence between the two. The gentlemen of 1628 — whom Hobbes may have considered democratical — were in fact defining property as rooted in the common law, and acting rightly, in these terms, when they called aloud for monarchy to redefine itself as immemorially rooted in the law of tenure.

* * *

The parliamentary session of 1628 was in many ways a disaster; at least, the disasters with which it was big began to come to monstrous birth in the following year; but it has two characteristics which seem to me to justify study of its records of debate. In the first place, it is a principal episode in the evolution of parliamentary political culture: what was said by the speakers who dominated debate in the Commons remained in their minds and in due course became part of the historical record — though that is a story, from Rushworth to yesterday, which I shall not attempt to tell — and the later words, actions and mentalities known to us by such labels as Court and Country, Whig and Tory, Presbyterians and Independ-

---

11. For the genesis of these arguments, traced by an astute but neglected contemporary, see my "Thomas May and the Narrative of Civil War," in *Writing and Political Engagement in Seventeenth-Century England*, ed. Derek Hirst and Richard Strier (Cambridge: Cambridge UP, 2000), pp. 112–44.

12. The classic treatment remains that of E. H. Kantorowicz, *The King's Two Bodies: A Study in Medieval Political Theology* (Princeton: Princeton UP, 1957).

ent, were in various ways really shaped by what happened in the 1628 debates. Since it is a fixed rule that men's speech reveals more to us than their intentions in speaking, and tells us much concerning their unspoken assumptions and perceptions concerning the world they live in, we may of course study it not only as recorded speech act but also as a social document or archaeological layer. I shall make some attempt to do this, and the word "ideology" which forms part of my title can appropriately be used here; though in using it I do not hope to find in the speech of debate evidence of a process of social change which can in turn be used to explain the history of the period. What we shall see, I believe, is not a record of how speech changed to deal with changing social and political realities, nearly as much as how modes of speech which we may think archaic even in 1628, and which their users would unhesitatingly describe as "ancient," were apparently found entirely satisfactory as means both of describing social reality and of performing political acts. This is of course central to the meaning of the Petition of Right itself: it was an attempt to get the King to subscribe to an affirmation of ancient language as a means of rectifying the relations of government and society. In using the term "ideology" to denote the social assumptions and perceptions which may be extracted from the records of debate, we must then use it in a way that emphasises effective archaism a good deal more than innovation and adaption. There will be exceptions, but they will prove this rule. Out of the old fields did old corn come, and a great deal of it seeded harvests that were fully expected. It is not at all clear that the disastrous failure of this parliament was a failure of language on the ideological level.

The word "rhetoric" also forms part of my title. One reason for its inclusion is that the diaries and other sources contain an invaluable wealth of speech at varying levels of formalisation, ranging from the purely ritual orations of the Lord Keeper and Speaker at the opening of Parliament[13] to interjections such as Sir James Perrott's "I would have women Jesuits put in,"[14] and somewhere in between Sir Edward Coke's remark: "He hath read Quintilian, and God forgive me, so have I."[15] Speakers reveal themselves differently at different levels of rhetoric and conversa-

---

13. *Commons Debates: 1628*, ed. Robert C. Johnson, Mary Frear Keeler, and others, 4 vols. (New Haven: Yale UP, 1977–78), 2:3–7, 9–10, 14–24. All future references to the *Commons Debates* of 1628 — hereafter *CD* — will be given with the source (in italics in notes) for each quotation.

14. *CD*, 2:257 (*Newdegate*, 27 March).

15. *CD*, 2:195 (*Stowe*, 29 March).

tion, and therefore this diversity is of evidential value in the study of ideology; but they also perform speech acts of varying character at varying levels of formalisation. Here we move to the study of rhetoric, not merely as speech at a certain such level, but as speech in action, designed to achieve results. I have in mind Derek Hirst's late reminder—peculiarly applicable to the study of this parliament—that it is well to pay attention to the steady conduct of private business as well as to "the often passionate, sometimes fruitless rhetoric of debate."[16] He will, I know, be the first to agree that, in 1628 especially, it is important to know why the rhetoric was passionate and why it was fruitless; reminding us to keep business and rhetoric in their due relation to each other. We are dealing with men who debated and orated in the spoken word, who drafted, presented and recorded the written word, in the passionate if fruitless expectation that thereby they would perform political acts and achieve political results of a highly specific if sometimes misconceived nature. We may decide that they failed because they were confused; but even so, it is highly important to discover what they failed to do—if only because that helps us understand what they did next—and we cannot discover that without discovering what they thought they were going to do, part of the secret of which must lie in what they told each other they were doing. This, incidentally, explains why Sir Benjamin Rudyard has attained immortality through his gift for the sudden revealing phrase, though the upshot of his speeches is usually timid and procrastinatory. Speech both acts—or intends to act—and reveals.

There is one final point before I leave off speaking of the study of speech in general. An informal (and hitherto unpublished) record of debate is a different kind of document from one composed for publication and printed by its author. The Putney Debates differ from the *Leveller Tracts* as regards both intention and effect; and there is the further point that in an informal record of an oral speech act or conversation we may have only what one man thought he heard another say, or could get down on paper as a record of his impressions. In the case of 1628, it is true, we are not uniformly on this level. The *Proceedings and Debates*, as the editors remind us,[17] may have been both compiled and circulated by a group including some of the principal speakers, with all that this implies for and against their reliability; and it is with relief that I record an overall impression that the Stowe reporter, Newdegate, Grosvenor and the rest

---

16. *Journal of Modern History* 50 (1978): 51.
17. *CD*, 1:8–20.

seem to supply fragmentary and approximate reinforcements to the *P&D* record, rather than radically different accounts. Nevertheless, there are a great many variations, and we have to resist according a kind of canonical status to the most striking version of some remark by Rudyard, Phelips or Coke, unless there is independent evidence that this is what he really said or desired to go on record as saying. On the other hand, every word in the published *Debates* of 1628 (footnotes excepted) is a seventeenth-century document; and should we ever suspect that diarist rather than speaker was the creative author, the creative speech act will still have been performed though communicated to fewer persons. It seems legitimate, therefore, to analyse all these fragments of seventeenth-century language in search of what they may reveal, while exercising greater caution with respect to what they may have performed; and the most necessary precaution is that our references must always include source as well as speaker — the words must be given as those of Eliot in *P&D*, or of Rudyard in Stowe, and we must be punctilious about the existence of variants if we are to avoid constructing canonical fiction. In taking these precautions, however, we are not indexing different levels of reliability so much as non-identical happenings between the speaker's voice, the diarist's ear and the latter's paper; and there is considerable overlap between these happenings, while some events are recorded and enrolled to the point where these considerations approach irrelevance. It is only as the speech act becomes more complex — as we move from what speaker said and diarist wrote towards what happened in St. Stephen's Chapel or the Painted Chamber as an outcome of the utterance — that our demands in respect of reliability must increase. It is one thing to analyse what Newdegate thought he heard, another to establish what the House or the Lords or the King were told formally, publicly and politically — assuming, that is, that it was possible to tell King Charles anything: an assumption so often, so necessarily and so tragically made.

Moving now to some considerations of ideology and significant verbal usages, I must begin by explaining the way in which the word "property" is spelt in my title. It is well known that in 17th-century English the spellings "property" and "propriety" are used without apparent distinction, though to us they denote different words and concepts; and it is not easy to decide whether to ignore this ambiguity.[18] To say "propri-

---

18. The writer confronted this problem in editing the works of James Harrington, and opted for making "property" the uniform spelling. He would now justify himself by arguing that for Harrington "property" — a word he uses less

ety" with the long I would be to use a word which has now nothing to do with possession, let alone with economics; yet to adopt the opposite alternative, and say simply "property," is to step directly into one of the cloudier streams of the historiographic tradition. There is [1978] among historians a well-founded but still treacherous practice of assuming that the way in which individuals or groups own or possess objects which involve them in the processes of production and concomitant social relationships has much to do with their political behaviour, language and consciousness. I am not proposing to attack this practice—perhaps I should call it a sub-practice—of writing as if the economic component in political language and behaviour (a) was always concealed, (b) always contained the true key to speech and action, so that when we have established that men who talked about liberty were also talking about property, we believe we have uncovered the secret explanation in the writings of historians who do not even believe it. But in the debates of 1628, the association between liberty and property-propriety is not concealed and is not unconscious. The two are constantly and insistently connected if not identified; speaker after speaker hammers away at the relations between them, and expounds it in a highly technical and even theoretical language with which the House is evidently well acquainted. If this is ideology, it is not a latent fabric of mentality; it is ideology articulated in a sophisticated and active rhetoric, whose content and effect we have to study.

A second sub-practice, not yet extinct among historians, is that of behaving as if the word "property" were always implicitly preceded by the word "private," and as if this association carried with it connotations to which the words "middle-class" and even "bourgeois" might appropriately be applied. There are of course known to be many forms of property ownership besides this one, but we still give a kind of priority to the emergence of the latter. You will be familiar with the "possessive individualism" thesis put forward by C.B. Macpherson,[19] according to which a notion of property entailing the ownership of goods circulating upon a market, and permitting the owner an increasing liberty of appropriation and accumulation, gained ground steadily from the middle of the seventeenth century. Macpherson has not to my knowledge applied his thesis to the 1620s, and has shown some signs of a willingness to leave

---

commonly than we might expect—had moved significantly into a sociological context, whereas the debaters of 1628 used it in a legalistic.

19. C.B. Macpherson, *The Political Theory of Possessive Individualism* (Oxford: Clarendon, 1962).

the seventeenth century to be debated by others; wherefore there is no need to dispute with him further today. But there is a long tradition disposing us to associate the very notion and word of "property" with private ownership in its capitalist or pre-capitalist form; and it is because we still have this unexamined habit, and because I think the language and rhetoric of the 1628 debates do not in any way entail the association, that I have resolved to bridge (while emphasising) the gap between the two versions of the crucial word by pronouncing it "propriety" with the short i sound. Whatever the spoken word in 1628 may have sounded like, the usage I propose will challenge our mental habits and will enable me to explore the possibility that the contemporary notion of propriety did not rest upon a notion of marketability, and even had less to do with one of ownership than might seem to be the case.

It is commonplace that the House met in a mood to assert the liberty of the subject and the propriety of goods, and were chiefly moved to this by the imprisonment of subjects who had refused to pay loans and by billeting of soldiers under martial law. The floodgates of debate were opened on March 22, and I shall start by analysing the rhetoric of Eliot in the *Proceedings and Debates* report (the Stowe and Newdegate versions are non-identical but not inconsistent). This report runs:

It is not for monies, or the manner how to be levied, but the propriety of goods, whether there be a power in the law to preserve our goods. This I defend and prove not by fears or necessities, but by law that shall speak. The law gives everyone his own. Rights of all sorts must be kept. Justice is but distribution of law. Execution gives her motion; that ceasing, all propriety ceaseth. The ancient law of England, the declaration of Magna Carta and other statutes, say the subject is not to be burdened with loans, tallages or benevolences. Yet we see them imposed. Doth not this contradict the law? Where is law? Where is *meum et tuum*? It is fallen into the chaos of a higher power.[20]

Need I repeat that we are not here analysing Eliot's motives or establishing his inmost feelings, but analysing the force of a piece of rhetoric written down in 1628? The first point to be noticed is that "propriety" is distinct from "goods": it denotes not the object of possession — the "property" as we use the term — but something more like the possessor's right to or in the object; as the formal language of resolution was later to put it, "it is the ancient and undoubted right of every free man that

---

20. *CD*, 2:57 (*Stowe*, pp. 67–68; *Newdegate*, p. 72).

he hath a full and absolute propriety in his goods and estate."[21] Eliot says "the law gives everyone his own," and "*meum et tuum*" obviously implies that the business of law is to establish who owns what; rights of possession are by both common and civil law vested in individuals (though this is not what participants in the Macpherson debate mean by possessive individualism), and it is perfectly possible to summarise the passage quoted in the phrase: "if no law, then no *meum et tuum*." But the equally possible formula "if no *meum et tuum*, then no law" is not a mere converse of the first. "Rights of all sorts must be kept. Justice is but distribution of law. Execution gives her motion; that ceasing, all propriety ceaseth." *Meum et tuum* is both final and efficient cause of justice; certainly the end of justice is to preserve to each individual that which is his own,[22] but without the individual's propriety in that which is his own the entire nexus of legal, social and moral relations between individuals which the words "law" and "justice" summarise would not exist. What this meant to the poor, the female, the servile and the barbarous is obvious enough, but not yet relevant to the history of the parliament of 1628. At the centre of the words attributed to Eliot lie the relations between freemen—men of propriety—and two other entities termed "law" and "state"; and not only Eliot, but every other speaker on March 22, reiterates the point that "propriety" defines the individual in terms of what is "his own" and at the same time in terms of all the legal, social and moral relations in which he is properly involved and to which he may properly lay claim in law and justice. This is the bridge over which we pass in journeying from "property" in the economic sense to "propriety in the ethical and moral; and the social reality expressed in the language is that of common-law England, in which a law which was essentially a law of tenures had become the main regulating, identifying and describing device whereby both the propertied individual and the kingdom knew themselves to exist.

This idea of the essential character of propriety is voiced by a series of speakers in the debates of March. We are all familiar with Rudyard saying: "This is the crisis of parliaments; by this we shall know whether parliaments will live or die," and "Men and brethren, what shall we do?

---

21. *CD*, 2:78-79 (Hakewill, reporting from the grand committee, *P&D*, 3 April; compare *Newdegate*, p. 284); 450 (text of the petition against billetting, 14 April).

22. See Margaret A. Judson, *The Crisis of the Constitution: An Essay on Constitutional and Political Thought in England, 1603–1645*, Rutgers Studies in History, no. 5 (New Brunswick: Rutgers UP, 1949), pp. 26, 40–42, 50.

Is there no balm in Gilead?" But between the two utterances, in *Proceedings and Debates* (supported by Stowe and Newdegate, though the latter missed the "crisis of parliaments") lies the following:

> The cause why we are called hither is to save ourselves, and self-preservation is a thing as natural as sin. No man needs to be persuaded to it. Mr. Speaker, we are not now upon the business of the kingdom. We are upon the very *esse* of it, whether we shall be a kingdom or no. When we have made it sure that England is ours, then may we have time to prune and dress it.[23]

Rudyard's ringing phrases conclude, as usual, in a rather feeble call to action;[24] but on March 24, Newdegate heard Sir Robert Phelips say:

> …as the patron of the law [Coke? It could hardly be Rudyard] said, we must first know whether we have a being before we go to the maintaining of our well being…For my part I have nothing that I know to think of, if our estates be subject to arbitrary discretion, but this carcass, which I care not what becomes of it, for if we be subject to perpetual imprisonment we have neither our lives nor our bodies free, but the essence of both called in question and hazard.[25]

Newdegate's notes run together the issues of propriety in estates and liberty of the person, which would not stay apart; the next day it had to be ordered that

> We shall begin with the liberty of the person, and next the propriety of the goods, and that we should not speak to one before the other be ended.[26]

But a day later still we find Digges, in *Proceedings and Debates*:

> The fundamental liberty is now in debate. I would hear any say or give any reason why we should not have that propriety.[27]

---

23. *CD*, 2:58 (*P&D*; *Stowe*, p. 60: "We are not now upon questions of our *bene esse*, but of our *esse* only"; *Newdegate*, p. 72, ditto).

24. So much so that Harold Hulme took him to be playing, on occasions, the role of a courtier; *The Life of Sir John Eliot, 1692–1632: Struggle for Parliamentary Freedom* (New York: New York UP, 1957), pp. 215–16, 218.

25. *CD*, 2:92.

26. *CD*, 2:113 (*Harleian MS. 1601*, 25 March).

27. *CD*, 2:123–24 (*P&D*).

And Phelips:

It hath been acknowledged by all writers that the goods of the subjects of England are their own and cannot be taken away without their consents, and that in parliament. Such is the liberty of England and hence is ascribed the great victories in war.[28]

The commonplaces are becoming clear. Propriety, liberty and legality are distinguishable terms, but it is self-evident that their interconnectedness is such that they cannot be spoken of apart. Together they define not only the *bene esse* but the *esse* of both subject and kingdom;[29] and law is the medium, or the tissue of modalities, through which property becomes the extension of personality into the universe of social reality. It is possible to draw a sharp distinction between the participatory and the so-called liberal ideals of liberty—in the former the individual's liberty is his capacity for public action, in the latter his freedom to enjoy his goods under law[30]—and to fault the latter for denying him the *vita activa* of politics. But one suspects that to these gentlemen magistrates of 1628, these men of substance and gravity, the world of courts and assemblies in which propriety involved them through law provided an entirely satisfactory forum of public action. They were not exactly strangers to the *vita activa*.

There are two directions in which we might proceed from the point reached in the last citations. One is indicated by some words of Coke, recorded in *Proceedings and Debates* for the 25th of March:

No other state is like this. *Divisos ab orbe Britannos.* We have a national appropriate law to this kingdom...I will say somewhat, and I will speak with reverence; and I would not speak were it not that my gracious King I hope shall hear it. It is not I, Edward Coke, that speaketh it. I shall say nothing, but the records shall speak.[31]

---

28. *CD*, 2:124 (*P&D; Stowe*, p.130; *Newdegate*, p. 135; neither mentions "victories").

29. See n. 21 above, and *CD*, 2:122 (Phelips, *P&D*, 22 March: "our liberties, which are our very essence").

30. Compare Archbishop Abbot, quoted by Judson, *Crisis of the Constitution*, p. 42: "There is a *Meum* and *Tuum* in Christian Common-wealths, and according to Laws and Customs, Princes may dispose of it, that saying being true, Ad Rege potestas omnium pertinet, ad singulos proprietas."

31. *CD*, 2:101 (*Stowe*, p. 107).

The rhetoric—and coming from Coke it is rhetoric—unites the theme of legality as the *esse* of the individual with that of English law fundamental because autochthonous and therefore immemorial, and the only natural and proper medium of communication between the King and his people represented in parliament. This was to be the dominant theme of the Petition of Right, of this parliament and its failure; but before we pursue it, we should look in the second direction, indicated by a speech of Sir Nathaniel Rich, based in part upon citations from James I himself and recorded in much the same form by nearly every source for March 26. Here is the Stowe version:

...if there by no property, no *meum* and *tuum*, then there is no justice. When there is no justice, what is there left to establish a King's throne? Those that pull it down [he probably means Montagu and Maynwaring] pull down the King. No propriety, no industry; no industry, all beggars; no propriety, no valour; no valour, all in confusion. You may enlarge and add to these as you please.[32]

And the Newdegate:

If there be no propriety of the subject, there must be needs a confusion; and if there be no *meum* and *tuum*, there must be no justice; if so, no industry, and then there will be a kingdom of beggars; if so, no valour, for no man will fight for that that is not in some sense his own.[33]

You may recollect that valour was the third term in the revised version of my title. In linking it here with a series of tropes with which we are already familiar, Rich—like Phelips and many another—was in effect citing one of the favourite authors of this parliament: Sir John Fortescue, the fifteenth-century author of *De Laudibus Legum Angliae*. Fortescue not only supplied speakers in 1628 with a paradigm concept of monarchy *regale et politicum*; he has a good claim to be thought of as a sort of English Machiavelli, interested in the social foundations of military virtue. Together with Bacon and others, he was an author of the potent myth that English yeomen fought better than French peasants because

---

32. *CD*, 2:130.

33. *CD*, 2:135. See also 2:124 (*P&D*) and n. 37 (the *James I* source); 138 (*Harleian MS. 2313*); 141 (*Nicholas*); 142 (*Harleian MS. 1601*); 4:104 (Pym, *Braye*, 4 June); Judson, *Crisis of the Constitution*, p. 40, quotes a draft statement drawn up by Laud for Charles: "Without those two be maynteyned, Liberty and Properiety, no care, courage, or Industry will be found among any people."

the latter were ground down by seigneurs and despotic kings;[34] and in the passage quoted, Rich is integrating this—as did Phelips and many other speakers[35]—into a theory of the social function of propriety and legality. Without a system of justice grounded on *meum* and *tuum*, the husbandman will not labour for his holding—the word "industry" bears no technological and need bear few entrepreneurial implications—nor will he display valour, since men will neither labour nor fight for that which "is not in some sense their own." In petition and remonstrance, as well as in oratory and debate, the House of Commons was therefore able to couple the image of propriety with that of bygone English military glory—a theme of peculiar resonance when Wallenstein was on the Baltic and Buckingham had been disgraced at the Isle de Rhé. The Fortescue motif thus leads into the theme of propriety and fundamental law, and at the same time helps supply the sociology of military service prominent when the House debates the grievance of the billetting of soldiers.

Before exploring the last-mentioned matter, I will go into the aspect of this parliament's behaviour which has figured most prominently in my own work and that of others. What ultimately became the Petition of Right was, as we know, intended as a declaration and re-enactment of the fundamental ancient law of the kingdom.[36] The liberty of the subject and his propriety in his goods and estate were not merely cardinal points in the law; they were, for reasons we have looked into, its essence—all justice was *meum* and *tuum*, as all common law was law of tenure, and for the same reason all liberty was to be spoken of as inheritance. Therefore liberty and propriety could best be vindicated by affirming legality itself, and by prevailing on the King to join in the affirmation. But to affirm the common law was to affirm it in the form of its antiquity, and there now arose those mechanisms of thought and language once described as characteristic of "the common-law mind."[37] The law was said to be custom,

---

34. Fortescue, *De Laudibus*, c. 36.

35. *CD*, 2:62 (Phelips, *P&D*—compare *Stowe*, p. 69; *Newdegate*, p. 73); 362, (Hakewill, *P&D*, 8 April; compare *Stowe*, pp. 366–67; *Nicholas*, p. 370); 450 (Speaker, *P&D*, 14 April).

36. Frances H. Relf, *The Petition of Right*, Studies in the Social Sciences, no. 9 (Minneapolis: U of Minnesota P 1917); Faith Thompson, *Magna Carta: Its Role in the Making of the English Constitution, 1300–1629* (Minneapolis: University of Minnesota P 1948); Herbert Butterfield, *The Englishman and His History* (Cambridge: Cambridge UP, 1944).

37. Pocock, *ACFL*.

and custom was immemorial; the law now to be affirmed had been confirmed (but never made) by Edward the Confessor, by William the Conqueror (who had been no conqueror), in Magna Carta and 30 times since, and now required to be confirmed again. This assertion was from one point of view—to which we shall return—a strategic choice; but it has also been the argument of historians that it was the outcome of thought-processes so deeply rooted in the common-law mind that the authority of Sir Edward Coke rather arose from them than was needed to enforce them, and that it was virtually impossible to conceive of English law and history in any other way. Twenty years and more after completing my own formulation of this argument, I am beginning to wish I could see it re-examined; and though I would rather leave the task to others than perform it myself, I read the *Commons Debates* of 1628 with an eye to seeing what confirmation or criticism the interpretation receives.

John Selden—that mind-boggling combination of pedant and *libertine* who was by far the most sophisticated legal-historical thinker in parliament and all England—quite clearly wants to see Magna Carta, and all other confirmations before it and after, as acts of parliament rather than misty artificial reason.[38] This, however, is rather an elaboration than a criticism of the doctrines we associate with Coke—I would love to know more of the relations between these two extraordinary men—because it is axiomatic with Selden that the function of statute may be to declare, refine and reinforce custom, and the concept of custom—however much his intellect refined it—continues to shape his image of English legal history. Coke himself—garrulous with age, but inclined rather to reminiscence than to missing the point—attacked on April 26 the Lords' proposal that

his Majesty would be pleased graciously to declare that according to Magna Carta and the statutes...every free subject...has a fundamental propriety in his goods and a fundamental liberty in his person.[39]

---

38. *CD*, 2:154 (*Stowe*, 27 March); compare *Newdegate*, p. 158; *Harleian MS. 2313*, p. 161, and *Harleian MS. 1601*, p. 164; 3:96 (*P&D*, 26 April; compare *Stowe*, p. 101; *Grosvenor*, p. 105; *Newdegate*, p. 110; *Harleian MS.*, 2313, p. 115; *Nicholas*, p. 117); 439 (*P&D*, 16 May; compare *Grosvenor*, p. 438: "an act of parliament may alter any part of Magna Carta").

39. *CD*, 3:74 (*P&D*, 25 April).

and rather strikingly declared (according to *Proceedings and Debates*):

I know not what "fundamental" is. It is Holborn Latin. I understand not fundamental liberty or propriety. We gain nothing by all those.[40]

But in the same version of his speech we read a little later:

I would never yield to alter Magna Carta…Never yet was any fundamental law shaken but infinite trouble ensued.[41]

Coke, in fact, knew perfectly well what "fundamental law" meant — or at least saw no objection to this blockbuster of a phrase — and objected only to the adjective being detached from the noun "law" and attached to "liberty" and "propriety" as isolated phrases. It was the Commons' strategy to oblige the King to confirm the whole body of the common law as the only remedy for the kingdom's grievances, and to operate wholly within the linguistic and procedural universe of the law as the medium of communication with his people. In this enterprise — unsuccessful, as it turned out — the myth of Magna Carta and immemorial custom might well seem a linguistic necessity, and there is little or no sign that even Sel-den was operating outside it. Yet it is noteworthy that in the conference with the Lords of April 7, when the Commons' grant strategy was made known to the Upper House, the exposition of the historical myth was left, by decision of the Commons, to the legally educated but not yet professional Sir Dudley Digges, while Littleton, Selden and Coke adopted other approaches. Digges did not omit to mention

that *meum* and *tuum* that is the nurse of industry and mother of courage, and without which there can be no justice, of which *meum* and *tuum* is the proper object.

But after extolling in set terms out of Glanvill, Bracton and Fortescue, the antiquity of the common law, we find him concluding this part of the speech:

But, my good Lords, as the poet said of fame, I may say of our common law: *ingrediturgue solo caput inter nubila condit.* Wherefore the cloudy part being mine,

---

40. *CD*, 3:95 (*P&D*, 26 April; compare *Stowe*, p. 100; *Grosvenor*, p. 104; *New-degate*, p. 109; *Harleian MS. 2313*, p. 114; *Nicholas*, p. 117).

41. *CD*, 3:95.

I will make haste to open the way for your Lordships to hear more certain arguments, and such as go on more secure grounds.[42]

It is hard to know how much we should make of this deprecatory language. The reference to cloudiness may affirm the law's antiquity rather than suggesting the uncertainty of the doctrine, and Digges may be apologising for his own limited learning rather than for anything in his case. But as his more erudite colleagues speak after him, each justifies the Commons' assertion that liberty and propriety are part of the fundamental law by the use of strictly and technically professional arguments, which in no way negate the affirmation of antiquity but in no way rely upon it. Littleton's charge is to argue the Commons' case out of existing and ancient statutes, which takes up seven pages[43] in our modern edition; Selden's is "matter of record and judicial precedents," and occupies fourteen pages.[44] As for Coke, it had been decided that he was "to show these acts of parliament and precedents to be but affirmations of the common law. To show the reasons hereof, and that the showing of cause of imprisonment not against reason of state."[45] In the event he confined himself wholly to cause of imprisonment and legal reason, alleging nine maxims of the common law supportive of the doctrine that cause should be shown and making no direct reference whatever to "reason of state" (of which more hereafter).[46] This may tell us something about Coke's role among professional lawyers in the closing years of his life; but the incident as a whole may suggest that the great myth of the Ancient Constitution belonged rather in the speeches and writings of gentlemen and others trained at the Inns of Court than in the technicalities of legal argument, and that even before the House of Lords its function was rhetorical rather than forensic. There is no sign in the Commons records that anyone attacked it.

On the day following this conference (as earlier on April 2)[47] there occurred a lengthy debate concerning the billetting of soldiers, a good

---

42. *CD*, 2:334 (composite text, 7 April).

43. *CD*, 2:334–42.

44. *CD*, 342–56. For the words quoted, see following note.

45. *CD*, 2:234 (*Commons Journal*, 7 April); compare *Nicholas*, p. 331, where "regione di stato" is used.).

46. *CD*, 2:356–58: "…by manifest and legal reasons which are the grounds and mothers of all laws."

47. *CD*, 2:252–55, (*P&D*); 259–60 (*Stowe*); 263–65 (*Newdegate*); 268; (*Harleian MS. 2313*) p. 72; (*Harleian MS. 1601*).

deal of whose matter found its way into the Petition of Right. To historians of ideology, this is informative in a number of ways. It becomes part of the theme of propriety and legality: Fortescue is quoted to the effect that billetting is known in France but not in England, and we hear in so many words from Christopher Sherland that "a man's house (is) his castle to preserve his person" (*Proceedings and Debates*) and "What use is there of my house when the property is gone?" (Stowe).[48] But the debate is also part of the history of English anti-militarism, studied by Lois Schwoerer in *No Standing Armies!*,[49] and presents some interesting features in that connection. The standing army as later rhetoric was to depict it is still a good way off; rhetoric is focused on that familiar figure of the earlier 17th century, the footloose, destructive and anti-social mercenary, dangerous both because there is no money to pay him and because he has no home to go to—in Machiavellian terminology, *la guerra è la sua arte*, and he is foreign to all propriety. One cannot exaggerate the social fear which the age felt for this figure, or the number of occasions on which public authority collapsed in the face of violence between country-people and soldiers; but one would like to know more of the facts concerning this kind of disorder in England in 1628. Is it true that—as more than one speaker averred—tenants left their farms and hid in towns to avoid the soldiers, so that landlords could not collect their rents?[50] Worse things happened in Germany. What is noteworthy from our point of view is that barbarous assaults upon the person, together with assaults on the relations between gentlemen and their social inferiors, are complained of without recourse to the rhetoric of propriety and legality. An offence against propriety was an offence against justice by those who should maintain it, as when the householder was obliged by warrant to accept soldiers into his home. The soldiers were bad enough, but the warrant was an offence of a different order—one complained of in the name of legality, whereas the soldier was a phenomenon outside all law and society, a potential enemy within the realm. He was assumed to be a social danger more or less by

---

48. *CD*, 2:361, 366.

49. Lois Schwoerer, *No Standing Armies!: The Anti-Army Ideology in Seventeenth-Century England* (Baltimore: Johns Hopkins UP, 1974).

50. *CD*:253 (Rich, Digges, Giles, *P&D*, 2 April; compare Digges, *Stowe*, p. 260; also Rich, *Newdegate*, p. 264, and *Harleian MS. 2313*, p. 268; Rich, *Harleian MS. 1601*, p. 272). The petition of 14 April speaks (2:452) of the danger that the soldiers and the poor will join in insurrection. This had not been mentioned in debate and seems to have been inserted in committee.

definition, and the assumption was reinforced by the belief that a great many of Buckingham's returning troops were not merely mercenaries, but Gaelic into the bargain. "If we spend many days," says Secretary Coke as early as March 25,

There will be an enemy rise up in our own bowels. I mean the Irishmen in Essex, who have lately mutinied

on St. Patrick's Day, according to a footnote;[51] and on April 8 Sir Henry Wallop is reported:

The Isle of Wight is now pestered with 1500 Scots and Redshanks, a barbarous people.[52] Murder is ordinary with them (he adds in the Stowe account). In the Isle of Wight they attempted to geld a scholar.[53]

Very likely that got a laugh, but it would be a nervous laugh. "Redshanks" may mean Highlanders or Hebrideans, if anyone knew the difference; the Scots in the Isle of Wight were the Earl of Morton's regiment,[54] and I am told he was more likely to recruit from the Douglas lands than from the Outer Isles; but it is noteworthy how soon the phrase "Irish and Redshanks...fit only to die in ditches" enters the record of debate—one probably papist and certainly propertyless Celt was as bad as another. The speaker here[55] was Richard Knightley of Northamptonshire, as reported in *Proceedings and Debates*, and in the Nicholas diary we have him striking a familiar note with:

This kingdom is not to trust to any for defence of it but the trained bands, who have estates and wives and children, and will fight for us and may be trusted, and not such vagabonds and idle soldiers.[56]

What would later be called the militia of the kingdom—the embodiment in arms of liberty, property and deference—had a long life before it as the antithesis in political rhetoric of the 18th-century standing

---

51. *CD*, 2:105, (*Stowe*; see p. 97n4).

52. *CD*, 2:361, (*P&D*).

53. *CD*, 2:365.

54. Lindsay Boynton, "Billeting: the Example of the Isle of Wight," *English Historical Review* 74 (1759).

55. *CD*, 2:363.

56. *CD*, 2:371.

army;[57] but the scenario in 1628 was not so simple, since the fundamental problem before the debaters was how to devise an armed force obedient to common law. Ralph Baber, the Recorder of Wells, who was expelled from the House for billetting soldiers in his city, gave the Stowe reporter a vivid account of his predicament:

> About January the soldiers came, and they came in great numbers, and their suddenness surprised us, little looking for them. The council of the city joined together in these warrants, for we were all circled in with soldiers — poor, beggarly, unfortunate men. They were all English, and nature commanded me to yield to necessity rather than law.[58]

But this, Baber found, was his offence: soldiers might be menacing, but the use of warrants was intolerable. He seems to have acted under instructions from the deputy lieutenants of Somerset (against whom the House took no measures[59]), and it does not seem that martial law played a part in the business. But debate very soon focused on the use of martial law to hang soldiers within the kingdom, always with the implication that the free-born subject might find himself liable to martial law in his dealings with soldiers or in military emergencies; and we see it developing two themes — the relation of martial law to common law, and the ways in which the character of an armed force might determine its relation to law of either kind. Selden is a leading speaker on both subjects: his erudition permitted him to argue that martial law was not a mere drumhead procedure in the field, but an ancient if obscure branch of the civil law, and for this very reason of no force in England except as common law permitted its presence;[60] while his grasp of feudal history enabled him to tell the House that kings in past time had raised men first through the obligations of tenure, later through "covenants" — which seems to mean indentures — with great men, and last of all:

> For pressing, a man may guess from whence it came, when these covenants were in use with great men. When their greatness ended, then great officers

---

57. The only use (a very specific one) of Machiavelli as an authority on the evils of mercenaries is attributed to Sir John Maynard, a supporter of Buckingham: *CD*, 4:188–89 (*Grosvenor*, 7 June).

58. *CD*, 2:383 (*Stowe*, 9 April; compare *Newdegate*, p. 387; *Nicholas*, p. 392).

59. *CD*, 2:384 (Sir Edward Rodney; compare *Stowe*, 2 April, p. 254).

60. *CD*, 2:462–65 (*P&D*, 15 April; compare *Stowe*, pp. 467–79; *Harleian MS. 2313*, pp. 470–73; *Nicholas*, pp. 473–74; *Harleian MS. 1601*, pp. 475–76).

began to press men…But in all these statutes there is not a word of any soldiers pressed or sent away under compulsion, and so the law then knew no pressing.[61]

This plainly alarmed the House. If pressing had no foundation in law, said a string of speakers, then the less said about it the better;[62] "and let us, I beseech you," said Digges in Newdegate's report,

rather cover the power the subjects have than let it be openly spoke abroad, that mean men may not know it, which perhaps if they should would be inconvenient.[63]

It was one thing to establish that Sir Peter Heyman could not be ordered into foreign command by way of political harassment;[64] quite another to let Mouldy and Bullcalf get it into their heads that they needn't accept press money if they didn't want to. But in ordering a committee to draw up an act for impressment,[65] the Commons were not merely ensuring the legitimacy of pressing men for foreign service; they were trying to ensure that authority over armed forces should be rooted in *lex terrae* and act of parliament. In the debates over martial law it is repeatedly affirmed that offences by soldiers within the realm can be dealt with by oyer and terminer,[66] and that the problem is to establish armies on a foundation of common-law authority. Selden points out that when all men owed military service by reason of tenure, there could be no martial law independent of common law;[67] but what is to be done now that arms no

---

61. *CD*, 2:279–80 (*P&D*, 3 April; compare *Newdegate*, pp. 286–87; *Harleian MS. 1601*, p. 292).

62. *CD*, 2:281 (Solicitor, Phelips, Pryor, Wentworth, *P&D*).

63. *CD*, 2:287.

64. *CD*, 2:103 (*P&D*, 25 March; compare *Newdegate*, p. 111); 2:287 (Digges, *Newdegate*).

65. *CD*, 2:288 (*Newdegate*); 291 (Wentworth, *Harleian MS. 2313*).

66. *CD*, 2:363 (Coke, *P&D*, 8 April); 413 (Eliot, Edmondes, Erle, *P&D*, 11 April); compare *Stowe*, pp. 416–17, *Newdegate*, pp. 420–21); 460–79 (all sources, committee of the whole, 15 April); 481 (Bankes, *P&D*, 16 April); compare *Stowe*, pp. 484–85; *Newdegate* p. 486; *Harleian MS. 2313*, pp. 487–88; *Nicholas*, pp. 489–90); 541–61 (committee of the whole, 18 April); 567–77 (committee of the whole, 22 April; 3:23–39 (committee of the whole, 22 April).

67. *CD*, 2:465 (Selden, *P&D*; compare *Harleian MS. 2313*, p. 472; *Nicholas*, p. 474).

longer have that basis? "If the king will have soldiers," says the Northumbrian member (and future crown lawyer) John Bankes,

he must give money and condition with gentlemen, and they are to condition with soldiers. That is the ancient usage.[68]

But Selden has already shown this to be obsolete outside northern society, and there are many references to the Tilbury camp of 1588[69] to show that new forms of mobilisation are coming in. Eliot (in Harleian 1601) is made to say that "he finds little difference between these soldiers (the billettees) and the ancient standing camp of the Romans,"[70] and his later speeches contain invective against "praetorians";[71] but we find one speaker remarking "admit there be a standing army, there may be a commission of oyer and terminer...if any disturb or betray it...it is treason."[72] The term "standing army" had not yet taken on its full post-Restoration resonance. The difference is that between an army which may escape parliament's control and serve as a means to its corruption—this is the later usage—and an army which may be subject to another form of law than that which it concerns parliament to uphold. Debate in 1628 moves steadily away from the depredations of soldiers, and towards the issue of martial law and its status with respect to common law and parliamentary authority. On April 18 the civil lawyer and admiralty judge Sir Henry Marten argued that soldiers and sailors must be subject to a law not identified with that of oyer and terminer;[73] but here, from the Stowe MS.,

---

68. *CD*, 2:465 (*P&D*, 3 April; compare *Stowe*, p. 368).

69. *CD*, 2:287 (Digges, *Newdegate*, 3 April); 3:25 (Hoby, *P&D*, 22 April); compare *Stowe* p. 28; *Grosvenor*, p. 33; *Harleian MS.* 2313, p. 37; *Harleian MS. 1601*, p. 39.

70. *CD*, 2:272 (2 April; compare *P&D*, p. 253).

71. *CD*, 4:117 (*P&D*, 5 June; compare *Grosvenor*, p. 128); 145 (*P&D*, 6 June; compare *Grosvenor*, pp. 157–58, [no reference]; *Newdegate*, p. 164; *Rich*, p. 170).

72. *CD*, 2:544 (Ball, *P&D*, 18 April; compare *Grosvenor*, p. 554; *Newdegate*, p. 557; *Harleian MS. 2313*, p. 559). Note the confusion arising on April 22 between Digges and Secretary Coke concerning the words "militia" and "trained bands" (3:32–33, *Grosvenor*, *Newdegate*, p. 35; *Harleian MS. 2313*, p. 37; *Harleian MS. 1601*, p. 38–39).

73. *CD*, 2:542–43 (*P&D*; compare *Stowe*, p. 548–49; *Grosvenor*, p. 555–53; *Newdegate*, p. 556–57; *Harleian MS. 2313*, pp. 558–59; *Nicholas*, p. 560).

is Coke's characteristic reply:

> Good sir, keep your circle; next mine own profession I love yours very well. Our common law bounds your law martial. Tell me of this or that or what or what you will, but show me such a law as the common law; no nation hath any like it. We are *toto divisos*, etc.[74] (*Divisos ab orbe Britannos.*)

It had happened the day before, in a conference with the Lords, that Serjeant Ashley — whose views on the problem of prerogative and law Margaret Judson found admirable[75] — incurred the censure of the Upper House (which saved him from the wrath of the Lower) by arguing

> Every imprisonment which is lawful is not within Magna Carta. As there is a common law, so there is an ecclesiastical law which is the law of the church. So also there is a law of state.
> There is a martial law which may be used in time of invasion of hostility, but not in time of peace. 23 E. 4, 9 and 10, a merchant alien complains of wrong done to him. It is there said that an alien is to be tried according to merchants' laws, which is according to the law of nature. So in the law of state their acts are bounded by the law of nature. The common law doth not provide for matters of state, and if they have jurisdiction of matters of state they ought to have power coercive.[76]

Ashley's offence in the Commons' eyes was that he seemed to be inventing a new branch of law — the "law of state" — with no function but to justify the Council's power to imprison for reasons of state. But in addition he was turning Fortescue against the common lawyers, and seeking to expand the *regale* component in the compound *regale et politicum;* he was multiplying into several modes of jurisdiction that power which Fortescue's king possessed to govern of himself according to the law of nature, itself not formalised into the procedures of common law. It had become the strategy of Selden and Coke and the rest to insist that martial law and any other such jurisdiction existed in England only in so far as the common law allowed; and the implication must be that England existed in the world of nature exclusively through the mediation of her peculiar and autochthonous customs. Hence the importance to Coke of

---

74. *CD*, 2:550 (*Stowe;* compare *P&D*, p. 545; *Grosvenor*, p. 555; *Newdegate*, p. 558; *Harleian MS. 2313*, p. 559; *Nicholas*, p. 561).

75. Judson, *The Crisis of the Constitution*, pp. 120, 124, 135, 251.

76. *CD*, 2:528–29 (composite text, 17 April).

the tag *divisos ab orbe Britannos*, it made the same point as Selden's far more sophisticated historicism. And since the common law, the law of tenures, was the law of *meum* and *tuum*, propriety — important enough in itself — became a means of asserting the uniqueness of England and the supremacy of *politicum* over *regale*.

Marten the civilian joined with Glanville the common lawyer in persuading the Lords to give up their intention of presenting the Petition to the King with a "saving" clause safeguarding his sovereignty and prerogative.[77] The Commons were plainly glad to have him on their side, and we should remember that the common and other laws were not engaged in an adversary relationship so much as a contest over precedence. The existence of non-common modes of jurisdiction was clearly only part of what King Charles meant when he spoke of his prerogative, and as we know, the Commons thought they were not trying to limit prerogative so much as to secure assurances of its exclusive relation with and commitment to the law of *meum* and *tuum*, the only law which defined their liberties and essence as Englishmen. Here of course we reach the brink of that unending misunderstanding which was to precipitate crisis after crisis in the 17th century, and it may seem to you that I have said little enough about its inner nature. Nearly everything which may be found concerning propriety, liberty and valour in the ideology of the 1628 parliament comes from the period down to late May, during which the Petition was in gestation and underwent what some might cynically call a breech presentation; and this is what one might expect, since it was the attempt to formulate a declaration of fundamental law which made men reveal and assert most of what they felt about themselves and their society. The pursuit of ideology does not lead one to explore the later developments: the growing uneasiness with the King's responses, the first gusts of the storm against Buckingham, the traumatic sitting of June 5, when everyone was in tears, the grand remonstrance against the Duke and the Arminians, and the final unsuccessful tactic over tonnage and poundage. But, as my title indicates, speech may both reveal ideology and perform (or attempt to perform) actions; and I should like in conclusion to say something

---

77. *CD* 3:572–80 (*P&D*, 23 May). Having asked in a review of this volume (*Journal of the History of Ideas* 39 (1978), p. 331) how well it had been known that Coke's words on this matter had been "Magna Carta... will have no saving," not "sovereign" (3:495 — *P&D*, 20 May; for the whole debate, see pp. 494–503), the writer is glad to report that Margaret Judson gives the correct text in *Crisis of the Constitution*, p. 261.

about the rhetoric of this parliament considered as a series of attempts to say and do things, and to get the King to say and do things. This is the point at which ideology becomes action; we shall not be asking how far it was the motive force behind the Commons' actions, so much as how far it was the medium through which they attempted to act.

The whole strategy that led to the Petition of Right—that of a general rehearsal of the fundamental law and its principles—was arrived at partly spontaneously (nothing could have stopped these grievances being expressed in this language), but also as the result of a conscious decision (we almost know by whom and when)[78] to proceed in this way instead of striking direct at Buckingham. After the Rhé disaster, the Duke may have looked expendable, and yet it would be known that the King would be stubborn about him. The problem which continues to vex historians is how far what became the Petition of Right is to be thought of as legislative—an attempt by statute or other means to set limits to the exercise of the prerogative—and how far declaratory: an attempt to get the King to commit himself, by the performance of certain approved speech acts, to certain principles and courses of action. It is not entirely a *question mal posée*, since the latter interpretation lays greater emphasis on the ritual need for communication between the King and his subjects —which was known to be a large part of the purposes for which parliaments were held—and may be preferred for that reason. Looked at in this way, the strategy of declaring fundamental law and inviting the King to confirm it displays two characteristics. It was undertaken at some psychological cost, since the impulse to attack Buckingham direct was very strong and difficult to repress; much of its energy went into the asseveration of fundamental law and reinforced the powerful emotional charges which propriety and liberty generated anyway. As the King's answers to the Petition give increasing dissatisfaction, feeling against Buckingham breaks surface in Eliot's speech of June 3; and the tearful and fearful scene of two days later, precipitated by a royal message forbidding further attacks on ministers, is clearly occasioned in part by a feeling that the Petition, with all its symbolic and actual importance, has been a failure and has proved a strategic mistake. After that propriety and liberty disappear from the rhetoric, not because they are unimportant but because they can no longer channel emotion towards constructive action; nothing is heard for some days except denunciations of popery, Arminianism and treason, and bitter remarks about "with what moder-

---

78. *CD*, 4:66n42; Hulme, *Life of Sir John Eliot*, p. 184n2.

ation we have proceeded."[79] All Buckingham's soldiers, by the way, now appear as Irish and foreign mercenaries, papists and enemies within the realm;[80] martial law is forgotten, except as a threat of Roman dictatorship.[81] The obsession with the image of the evil favourite—the Haman or Sejanus, very characteristic of the age—had been of course implanted in the Commons' mind by the events of 1626. Now it becomes obsessive; there not only is, but must be an evil counselor to account for the King's falsity on *meum* and *tuum*, on parliamentary right, on propriety and liberty; and perhaps this helps explain why, when Buckingham was dead, the session of 1629 turned into an attack on Weston, that of 1640 into an attack on Strafford. Neither man was another Buckingham, but the role had to be played by someone.

In the second place, the entire strategy of declaration and petition, the rhetoric and ideology of liberty, propriety, Magna Carta and fundamental law, now take on the character of a gigantic frustrated speech act: a tissue of overtures to the King, to which he was invited to reply with the degree of generosity and formality which the House would have found satisfactory—to answer lovingly, to answer in a parliamentary way, to answer in writing and as matter of record.[82] It does not settle all questions; yet it is hard to avoid the feeling that what the Commons wanted the King to do was to make a golden speech in the manner of Elizabeth I, and that if he had all questions of prerogative and even Buckingham—Arminianism is perhaps another matter—might have been resolved

---

79. *CD*, 4:113 (Phelips, *P&D*, 5 June); compare *Stowe*, p. 118; *Grosvenor*, p. 122), 114 (*Rich*, *P&D*); compare *Grosvenor*, p. 123; 115 (Coke, *P&D*; compare *Stowe*, p. 119; *Grosvenor*, p. 124; *Newdegate*, p. 129), 121 (Selden, *Stowe*; compare *Grosvenor*, pp. 126–27).

80. *CD*, 4:120 (Sherland, *Stowe*, 5 June); compare *Grosvenor*, p. 125; *Newdegate*, p. 130; *Lowther*, p. 132); 120 (Knightley, *Stowe*; compare p. 125); 143 (Rich, *P&D*, 6 June); 145 (Strangways, *P&D*); 146 (Coxe, Waller, Erle, *P&D*; compare *Grosvenor*, p. 158; *Newdegate*, p. 164; *Rich*, p. 170; *Lowther*, p. 173); 147 (Bulstrode, Denys, *Strode*); compare *Grosvenor*, p. 159; *Newdegate*, p. 164; *Rich*, p. 170); 168–69 (Pym, *Rich*); 170 (Annesley, *Rich*). For Eliot on "praetorians," see n71 above.

81. *CD*, 2:159 (Stuart, *Grosvenor*, 6 June; compare *Rich*, p. 171); 254 (Long, *Stowe*, 11 June; compare *Grosvenor*, p. 259; *Newdegate*, p. 265). These are the occasions on which "dictatorship" is specifically mentioned.

82. For example, 3:228 (Coke, *Harleian MS. 1601*, 2 May); 238 (Marten and Erle, *Stowe*, 3 May); 272 (Coke, *P&D*, 6 May; compare *Grosvenor*, p. 283; *Newdegate*, p. 286; *Harleian MS. 5324*, p. 289; *Nicholas*, p. 293; *Harleian MS. 1601*, p. 296); 407 (Wentworth, *P&D*, 14 May; and Pym, *P&D*); 630 (Phelips, *Stowe*, 27 May).

in a transformed climate. Certainly, even after repeated experiences of Charles' remarkable capacity for coldness, for snubbing, for weaseling and letting it be seen that he was weaseling, they persisted in believing they had got the answer they wanted. "I am half dead for joy," declared Coke on June 7.

Laugh not at my French, gentlemen, for I have gotten as much by it as some of you[83] ... *Soit droit fait comme ils desirent.* We could never have had a better answer[84] ... there is no doubtfulness or shadow of ambiguity.[85]

But King Charles had not finished with his subjects yet. The whole point of the Petition of Right, and of the ideology of liberty and propriety, had been to get him to talk the language of the common law, of *meum* and *tuum*, the language used to assure freemen that they were not villeins, without ambiguity; and there were reasons of personality as well as of history why this unambiguity was not in him. This is a highly quotable parliament, and I might conclude with something Marten let fall on June 3:

All men are taken with respect of persons, and if the King like not our persons all is in vain.[86]

A good deal of the truth is there. But perhaps the last words should be those of Sir Francis Nethersole's dream, recounted (he said) to cheer the House as far back as April 22, when an early taste of the King's style had produced an unhappy silence.

All knowledge is but as a dream, and I will tell you what I dreamed last night. Methought I saw two fair and goodly pastures. The one an enclosure, the other a common. The common had a fair flock of sheep in it. The enclosure had only a goodly bellwether. I found there was a division between these grounds by a great deep ditch, and a narrow, narrow bridge to join them together. I saw the bellwether hasting to the common to invite the sheep to eat with him, but the narrow bridge hindered his passage. Whereupon a poor sheep said,

---

83. *CD*, 4:185 (*Stowe*, 7 June).

84. *CD*, 4:182 (*P&D*).

85. *CD*, 4:185. Compare 3:630 (*Stowe*, 27 May): "what both Houses do agree upon, no judge of England dare oppose. If they do, let me speak no more."

86. *CD*, 4:67 (*P&D*; compare *Stowe*, p. 70; *Grosvenor*, p. 75; *Newdegate*, p. 78).

"There is no means for him to pass. Let us all lie down on our bellies, that the bellwether may pass over us."[87]

The Speaker had been trying to stop Nethersole; and Coke now rose and said there were phlegmatic dreams,[88] fantastic dreams and prophetic dreams, and perhaps they'd better leave it at that. Nethersole's was a prophetic dream. Twenty years in the future we can hear a voice saying, with greater sincerity, "We have laboured to please a King, and I think, except we go about to cut all our own throats, we shall not please him."[89]

---

87. *CD*, 2:434 (*Stowe*; compare *P&D*, p. 431; *Harleian MS. 2313*, p. 438).

88. *CD*, 2:435: "*somnia divinationis, somnia phlegmatica* and *somnia fantastica*, and so much for dreams. I pray let us fall to our business." Compare pp. 431, 438.

89. Edward Sexby, at the opening of the Putney debates in 1647.

Index

Abbot, George, Archbishop of of Canterbury, 244*n*
Acton, Emerich Edward Dalberg, Lord, 183–84
Addison, Joseph, 88. 91
Agnew, Jean-Christophe, 79*n*
agrarian politics, 87, 92–93*n*
Alford, Edward, MP, 204
American Revolution, 5, 108
ancient constitutionalism, 2, 6–7, 11, 14–19, 23, 25, 175–208 (ch. 6), 222, 236, 246–49, 252–56. *See also* constitutionalism; *con sult also* English common law
Anglo, Sydney, 182*n*
Anglo-Scottish Union, 6, 187–208
Annesley, Sir Francis, MP, 258*n*
anti-aristocratic critique, 82–83
anti-militarism, 98, 250, 254
anti-popery, 75, 77, 146, 169, 170, 257–58
antinomianism, 69, 218*n*
Apocalypticism, 5, 68–69, 71, 171
Appian, 221
Appleby, Joyce, 18*n*, 116
Arendt, Hannah, 16*n*
aristocratic ideology, 82–83, 95
Aristotle, 23, 36, 67, 68, 194–95
Arminianism, 256, 257, 258–59
Ascham, Anthony, 80
Ashley, Sgt. Jacob, 255
Asian despotism, 150–51, 154
Atwood, William, 145*n*
Augustine of Hippo, St., 44
Augustus, Emperor, 31

Austin, J.L., 14, 17*n*, 24, 41, 54
'autocentric' historiography, 183–8. *Vs.* 'heterocentric historio- graphy

Baier, Kurt, 17*n*
Babbitt, Irving, 3
Bacon, Sir Francis, *later* Lord Verulam, 191, 192, 197, 201, 202–3, 204, 206, 245
Bailyn, Bernard, 115*n*, 117
Bankes, Sir John, Attorney- General, 253*n*, 254
Bannet, Eve Tavor, 31*n*
Baron, Hans, 5
Barthes, Roland, 38, 40. *Consult also* French post-structualist theory
Basagne, Jacques, 223
Bayle, Pierre, 223
Baxter, Stephen, 144*n*
Beardsley, Monroe, 38, 40. *Consult also* 'intentional fallacy'
Becker, Carl, 117*n*
Begriffsgeschichte, 28, 29, 45, 47–50, 214–15. *See also* 'Geschichtliche Grundbegriffe'
Bell, Daniel, 17*n*
Benn, Stanley, 16*n*
Bentham, Jeremy, 227*n*
Berkowitz, Peter, 123*n*
Berlin, Sir Isaiah, 13, 17
Bevir, Mark, 127*n*, 219*n*, 226–27*n*, 227*n*
Beza, Theodore, 199
Bill of Rights, 146

Billetting Controversy, 241–42, 249–54

Biondo, Flavio, 44, 221

Blackmore, Sir Richard, 135*n*

Blue Guards, 139–40, 151

Bodin, Jean, 198, 199, 200

Bolingbroke, Duke of Hereford, *later* Henry IV, King, 147

Bolingbroke, Henry St John, Lord, 31*n*, 66, 87, 98, 111

Bolton, Edmund, 93

Bossche, Geert van den, 52*n*

Bouchard, Telesphore D., 121*n*

Boucher, David, 124

bourgeois order, the, 69–71, 76, 78, 233. *See also* capitalism

Bowyer, Allen D., 189*n*

Boynton, Lindsay, 251*n*

Bracton, 235, 248

Brady, Dr. Robert, 2, 21, 133, 141, 143, 145–47, 183–84, 211

Brandt, Richard, 17*n*

Brecht, Arnold, 16*n*

Brooks, Christopher, 188

Brown, Peter, 167*n*

Bruni, Leonardo, 44, 221

Bruti, the, 154

Brutus, Marcus Junius, 190

Buckingham, George Villiers, 1st Duke of, 83, 246, 251, 252, 256, 258

Buel Jr., Richard, 33*n*

Bulstrode, Sir William, MP, 158*n*

Bunyan, John, 70–71, 81

Bunzl, Martin, 18*n*

Burgess, Glenn, 6–7, 12*n*, 181*n*, 214*n*, 215*n*

Burgh, James,

Burke, Edmund, 5, 14, 15*n*, 22, 53, 183–84

Burnet, Gilbert, Bishop of Salisbury, 135*n*

Burns, J.H., 200*n*

Burrow, J.W., 184*n*

Burtt, Shelley, 95*n*, 109*n*, 111

Butler, Samuel, 145

Butterfield, Sir Herbert, 3, 4*n*, 183*n*, 184*n*, 211, 218*n*

Calvinism, 5, 70, 81, 223, 224. *Consult also* Protestantism

Carhart, Michael C., 43*n*

Caesar, Julius, 150, 151–52, 153, 224

Calvin's Case, 207–8

Cambridge, University of, 3, 12, 13, 211, 228

'Cambridge School,' 4–7, 11–14, 15–18, 27–28, 39, 41, 47, 54, 101, 122–28, 213–14, 233. *Consult also* history of ideas, intellectual history

Cambrio-Britons, 136–38

Canterbury, University of, 3, 4

capitalism (early), 63, 69–71, 76–77, 78, 79, 81, 86–87, 92. *See also* bourgeois order; *consult also* 'commercial ideology'

Carr, E.H., 16

Case of Monopolies, 199

Cato, 110–111, 114, 128

Cavaliers, 152, 164

Champion, Justin, 211, 216

Charles I, King, 83, 97, 165, 234, 235–36, 237, 248, 256–60

Christianity, 2, 6–7, 64, 67–73, 81, 179, 214–15.

See also Protestantism

Christianson, Paul, 184–85, 201

Church of England, 223

civic humanism, 1, 4, 6, 34, 29–99 (ch. 3), 101–28 (ch. 4), 129–73 (ch. 5), 219. *See also* 'Country' ideology, neo-Harringtonianism; *consult also* humanism, Renaissance humanism, republicanism

Clarges, Sir Thomas, MP, 136

Clark, Jonathan, 7, 131*n*, 162*n*

classical republicanism. *See* civic humanism, republicanism

Claydon, Tony, 135*n*, 136*n*

Clive, John, 184*n*

Cocks, Sir Richard, 172–73

Coke, Sir Edward, 2, 21, 24, 51, 183–84, 189*n*, 189–90, 196, 206, 207, 234–35, 237, 239, 244–45, 247–48, 249, 251, 254*n*, 254–56, 257*n*, 258*nn*, 259, 260. *Consult also* ancient constitutionalism, English common law

'commercial ideology,' 62, 76, 78

Commission of Public Accounts, 136, 138*n*

Commons Debates of 1628, 7, 231–60 (ch. 8)

Confucius, 154

conquest theory, 187, 191–96, 204

constitutionalism, 2, 6–7, 11–28 (ch. 1), 74, 131–32, 138–39, 157–58, 160, 162, 166, 168–73, 175–208 (ch. 6), 222, 233, 236, 246–49, 252–56. *See also* ancient constitutionalism, parliamentary patronal sovereignty; *consult also* '*divisos ab orbe Britannos*,' '*meum et tuum*,' '*nolumus leges Angliae mutare*,' '*regale et politicum*'

contextualist historiography, 6, 28, 32, 37, 51–55, 115–29

Corbet, John, 93

Cotton, Sir Robert, 204–5*n*

'Country' ideology, 6, 49, 74–75, 120, 125, 129–73 (ch. 5), 236–37. *See also* civic human-

ism, neo-Harringtonianism

Country Party politics, 75, 129–73 (ch. 5)

Cowling, Maurice, 228*n*

Coxe, William, MP, 258*n*

Craig, Sir Thomas, 200–1

Cromwell, Oliver, Lord Protector, 149–50, 151–53, 165

Crouchback, Richard, 147

Crousaz, Jean-Pierre de, 223–24

Cowper, William, 189*n*

customary legality, 180–81, 182, 186–87, 193, 194–95, 235, 246–48, 255. *Consult also* ancient constitutinalism, English common law

Darby Sr., John, 148

Davenant, Charles, 82, 84, 113, 130, 132–33, 137*n*, 141, 142–45, 162

Davies, Sir John, 21, 156

Davis, J.C., 109

Davis, R.W., 233*n*

Decemvirs, 163

Defoe, Daniel, 82, 86, 87–88, 90–92, 94, 132, 161, 167–73

Deloney, Thomas, 76–77

Denham, Sir John, 79, 133*n*

Denys, Sir Edward, MP, 258*n*

Derrida, Jacques, 38, 40, 41

Desmaizeaux, Pierre, 154–55

Dickson, P.G.M., 86–87

Digges, Sir Dudley, MP, 206, 243, 248–49, 250*n*, 253, 254*nn*

Disbanding Bill, 139–40, 141, 160

divine-right kingship, 170–73

Divisos ab orbe Britannos, 244, 255. *Consult also* constitutionalism

Doddridge, Sir John, 193

Dorchester, Dudley Carleton, Viscount, 204

Downie, J.A., 136*n*

Drake, Dr. James, 160*n*

Dray, William, 16*n*

Dryden, John, 36, 90–91, 133, 137*n*

Dugdale, Sir William, 3

Dunn, Brian R., 191*n*

Dunn, John, 4, 12, 14, 110, 117, 211, 216. *Consult also* 'Cambridge School'

Dworetz, Steven M., 115

ecclesiastical history, 223, 225

Echard, Laurence, 223, 225

Edmondes, Sir Thomas, MP, 253*n*

Edward I, King, 145–46, 197, 204, 247

Edward II, King, 138

Edward III, King, 146

Ehrenstein, Christoph von, 42*n*

Eliot, Sir John, MP, 239, 241–42, 254, 257, 258*n*

Enclosure Movement, 89

Engagement Controversy, 5

English civil law, 24, 185*n*, 234–35, 242, 252. *See also* Roman law

English Civil Wars, 6, 15, 22, 64, 97–98, 163–64, 165, 233

English Commission Act, 201–2

English common law, 19, 24, 64, 89, 180–81, 185–87, 203, 208, 234–36, 242, 246–49, 252, 252–56, 259. *Consult also* ancient constitutionalism, customary legality, immemorial legality

English national identity, 208. *Con-cult also* 'new British history'

Enlightenments, 11, 32, 44, 52, 220–21, 223, 224, 226

Erle, Sir Walter, MP, 253*n*, 258*nn*

erudite historical learning, 2, 224

European Union, 176–77

Fall of Constantinople, 225

Fenlon, Dermot, 182*n*

Ferguson, Adam, 22, 221, 225

feudalism, 2, 51, 62–63, 88*n*, 152–53, 167, 180, 225

feudal tenures, abolition of, 87, 88, 98

Filmer, Sir Robert, 15*n*, 21*n*, 183–84, 211, 214, 216

Financial Revolution, 62, 76, 86–87, 92, 98

Flanagan, Eugene, 186*n*

Fleming, Sir Thomas, Chief Baron, 199, 206

Foerster, Norman, 3

Foley, Paul, 136

Forbes, Duncan, 113, 183*n*

Fortescue, Sir John, 188, 189, 234–36, 245–46, 248, 255

Fortescuean politico-legal thought, 188–97, 246. *Consult also* ancient constitutionalism, constitutionalism, English common law

fortuna, 74, 81–82, 90, 92, 113, 179

Foster, Elizabeth Read, 185*n*

Fountain of Favor, 162, 171

Fountain of Justice, 162, 171

French poststructuralist theory, 38–41, 231, 215

Fuller, Nicholas, MP, 204

'fundamental law,' 22, 197–205, 247–48, 249, 257–58. *Consult also* ancient constitutionalism, constitutionalism, English common law, Fortescuean politico-legal thought

Galway, Henri de Massue of Ru-vigny, Earl of, 140

Galloway, Bruce, 192*n*, 193*n*, 196*nn*

Gardiner, Stephen, Bishop of

Winchester, Lord Chancellor, 182*n*

Garter, Order of, 146

Gaveston, Piers, 138, 146

Gellner, Ernest, 14*n*

George III, King, 97

George of Denmark, Prince, 140

General Election of 1698, 139

Gentili, Alberico, 196, 206

Geschichtliche Grundbegriffe, 47–50. *See also Begriffsgeschichte*

Ghosh, Peter, 43*n*

Giannone, Pietro, 44, 221, 224

Giannotti, Donato, 104, 105

Gibbon, Edward, 2, 31–32, 39, 43–45, 151, 152, 179, 180, 214, 220–28

Gilbert, Felix, 113*n*

Giles, Edward, 250*n*

Glanville, Sir John, MP, 248, 256

Glorious Revolution, 89, 112, 134–35, 150, 169, 170, 216, 222

Goldie, Mark, 211

Goodale, Jesse, 108–9

Goodfield, June, 19*n*

Gordan, Thomas

Gough, J.W., 16*n*, 198–99, 203

'Gracchan explanation,' 44, 151–52, 221

Gracchi, the, 151, 164–65

Grand Remonstrance, 256

Grants Controversy, 129–73 (ch. 5)

Greenberg, Janelle, 184*n*, 187*n*

Guicciardini, Francesco, 104

Guilhaumou, Jacques, 45*n*

Gunn, J.A.W., 6, 76*n*, 77*n*, 102, 107*n*, 111–112, 212*n*

Hakewill, William, MP, 242*n*, 246*n*

Halifax, Charles Montague, Earl of, 141, 158

Hall, John, 148, 156–57

Hammond, Paul, 137–38*n*

Hampshire, Stuart, 17*n*

Hampshire-Monk, Iain, 33*n*, 213*n*, 227–28

Hand of Providence, 162, 167

Hanowy, Ronald, 110*n*

Harley, Edward, 164

Harley, Robert, *later* Earl of Oxford, 136, 164

Harpham, Edward J., 114

Harrington, James, 2, 28, 34, 37, 96, 105–8, 110, 128, 130, 143, 147–58, 162, 180, 213, 216, 218*n*, 221, 222, 228, 236, 239–40*n*. *Consult also* neo-Harringtonianism

Hart, H.L.A., 16*n*

Hartz, Louis, 16*n*, 115*n*

Haversham, John Thompson, Lord 159

Hayton, David, 130–31*n*, 139*n*

Hayward, Sir John, 190, 196, 202

Hedley, Thomas, 184–88, 195–96, 202

Hegel, Georg Wilhelm Friedrich, 175

Helgerson, Richard, 19*n*

Hellmuth, Ekhart, 42*n*

Herzog, Donald, 118*n*, 121*n*

'heterocentric' historiography. *Vs.* 'autocentric' historiography

Hexter, J.H., 7, 44*n*, 105, 231, 233

Heylin, Peter, 146*n*

Heyman, Sir Peter, 253

Higham, John, 18*n*

Hill, Christopher, 16*n*, 213*n*

Himmelfarb, Gertrude, 184*n*

Hirsch, E.D., 38

Hirst, Derek, 238

historical semantics, 50

'history of ideas,' 27, 28, 30, 33, 34, 35*n*, 36–37, 39, 42–43, 50, 72,

history of ideas (cont'd)
101, 122–28, 211–29 (ch. 7).
Consult also 'Cambridge School,'
intellectual history
Hobart, Sir James, MP, Attorney-
Gen., 204
Hobbes, Thomas, 5, 21, 24, 34,
35–36, 80, 179, 234, 235–236
Hoby, Sir Thomas, MP, 254*n*
Holt, Sir John, Chief Justice, 204
Hont, Istvan, 113*n*
Höpfl, Harro, 123*n*, 199
Houston, Alan Craig, 107*n*
Howe, John Grobham, MP, 163
Howel, William, 223, 225
Huguenot diaspora, 223–24
Hulme, Harold, 243*n*, 257*n*
humanism, 3, 4, 19*n*. *Consult also*
civic humanism, Renaissance
humanism
humanistic study, 2, 3, 4
Hume, David, 22, 112–14, 183*n*,
224
Hume, Robert D., 6, 28, 35*n*, 36*n*,
221
Hurd, Richard, 31*n*
Hutcheson, Francis, 22
Huyler, Jerome, 110*n*, 111*n*
Hyde, Lawrence, 204

illocutionary meaning, 38, 40, 53.
Consult also speech-act theory
imagination, discourse of, 90–99
immemorial legality,
245, 246–49. *Consult also* ancient constitutionalism, English
common law
Impeachments of the Four Lords,
141, 158–59, 161, 164–65,
168–69
inflation of honors,' 83
Inglis, Fred, 228*n*

Impositions Debate, 184–85, 187,
206
Instrument of Union, 203–4
intellectual history, 27, 30, 42,
73–74, 122–28, 226*n*. *Consult
also* 'Cambridge School,' 'history of ideas'
'intentional fallacy,' 38
intentionalist reading, 29*n*, 38–41,
51
intertextuality, 52
Ireland, Robert de Vere, Duke of,
146
Irish Reports, 208
Isaac, Jeffrey C., 114*n*

Jacob, Margaret, 18*n*
Jacobitism, 137, 140, 143, 144–45,
147, 149–50, 152, 222
James I, King, 83, 156, 189, 198,
199–201, 202, 206, 207, 236,
245
James, II, King, 140, 146, 169, 170,
173
janissaries, 129, 150
Janssen, Peter L. 42*n*
Johns Hopkins University, 4, 133
Jones, David Martin, 217*n*
Jordan, David, P., 43*n*, 44
Jouvenal, Bertrand de, 16*n*
Judson, Margaret, 242*n*, 244*n*,
245*n*, 255, 256*n*
Jurieu, Pierre, 223
jus privatum, 203, 206
jus publicum, 203, 206

Kantorowicz, E.H., 236*n*
Kelley, Donald, 19*n*
king-in-parliament, 15, 185–86
king's two bodies, doctrine of, 171,
236
Kirk, Russell, 3

Klein, William, 205n
Kloppenberg, James T., 115n
Knightley, Richard, 251, 258n
Knolles, Richard, 198n
Knowles, Ronald, 75n
Koselleck, Reinhart, 47, 50, 214n.
    Consult also 'Begriffsgeschichte,'
    'Geschichtliche Grundbegriffe'
Kramnick, Isaac, 111n
Kristeller, Oscar, 5
Kuhn, Thomas, 16, 18n, 33n, 123,
    121–13. Consult also paradigm
    theory

labor discipline, 69–73, 77, 93.
    Consult also 'Protestant ethic'
Ladd, John, 17n
Lady Justice, 162, 167
Lady Liberty, 154–55
Lancaster, John of Gaunt, Duke of,
    147
'landed interest,' 76, 78. Vs. 'mon-
    ied interest'
Laslett, Peter, 3, 4, 12, 13, 15n,
    16nn, 16, 16–17n, 21n, 211, 214,
    216, 220. Consult also 'Cam-
    bridge School'
Laud, William, Archbishop of
    Canterbury, 245n
'law of state,' 234, 255
Le Clerc, Jean, 223
leges imperii, 199, 200, 201n
Levack, Brian, 190–91, 194n
Leyden, Wolfgang von, 16n
liberalism, 63, 65, 76, 107, 117–18,
    119, 120, 220, 224n, 244
libertarianism, 170, 200, 220,
    221, 229, 234. See also 'negative
    liberty,' neo-Roman libertari-
    anism, political liberty, 'positive
    liberty'
Lilly, John, 88

Littleton, Sir Edward, later Baron,
    206, 248, 249
Locke, John, 5, 12, 13, 35–36, 63,
    64, 80, 110, 114, 115, 117,
    125–26, 211, 216, 220, 223–24
Lockyer, Andrew, 106n
Loevesteiners, 157
Loftus, Lady Mary, 163
Long, Sir Robert, 258n
Lonsdale, John Lowther, Viscount
    164–65
Lovejoy, A.O., 34, 35, 37, 123
Ludlow, Maj.-Gen. Edmund, 148
Lycurgus, 154

McIlwain, C.H., 198
McIntire, C.T., 211n
McKeon, Michael, 6, 76n, 77n, 81n,
    83n, 85n, 93n, 95n, 133
Macaulay, Thomas Babington,
    Lord, 183–84
Macfarlane, Alan, 88
Machiavelli, Niccolo, 5, 28, 34, 35,
    44, 67, 68, 74, 81, 90, 101, 104,
    106, 107, 115, 120, 179, 221,
    234, 252n
MacInnes, Allan I., 200n
Mackworth, Sir Humphrey, MP,
    160–61, 168
Macpherson, C.B., 12, 89n, 101,
    121, 233, 240–41, 242
Magna Carta, 187, 196, 241,
    247–48, 255, 258
Malcolm, Noel, 234n
Manwaring (or Maynwaring),
    Roger, later Bishop of St.
    David's, 235
Marshall, John, 211, 216
Marshall, Paul A., 217n
Marten, Sir Henry, MP, 254–55,
    256, 258n
martial law, 234, 252–54, 258

Marvell, Andrew, 74–75, 79, 80
Mary II, Queen, 134–35, 163
Marx, Karl, 70
Marxism, 70, 76, 118
Mary Tudor, Queen, 156, 182
Maori, 177–78. *Consult also* New Zealand political history
Maynard, Sir John, 252*n*
megalopsychic man, 67, 68
mentalité history, 36, 46, 47
Messianism, 171
meum et tuum, 241–42, 244*n*, 245, 246, 248, 256, 258, 259. *Consult also* ancient constitutionalism, constitutionalism, property
Mexía, Pedro, 226*n*
Middleton, Conyers, 223
military valour, 245–46, 248, 251
Millar, John, 225
Milton, John, 71–73, 148
Miner, Earl, 135*n*
Misselden, Edward, 77
modernization theory, 213*n*
monarchy, 22, 64, 81*n*, 153*n*, 154, 156–57, 170–72, 199, 215, 236
'monied interest,' 76, 78. *Vs.* 'landed interest'
Montague, Sir Henry, *later* Earl of Manchester, 204–5, 245
Montesquieu, Charles-Louis de Secondat, Baron de, 67–69
Moore, James, 113*n*
Moral Reform Movement, 135–36
Morton, William Douglas, 8th Earl of, 251
Moses, 154
Munslow, Alun, 19*n*
Musgrave, Sir Christopher, MP, 136

Nadon, Christopher, 36*n*
narrative historiography, 205

Nassau, House of, 153. *See also* William III *and other individual royal members*
National Debt, 86–87
natural law, 92, 207, 255. *Consult also* philosophical-juristic ideology
Naturalization Debates, 200, 206, 207
'negative liberty,' 96–98, 244. *Vs.* 'positive liberty'; *see also* political liberty; *consult also* liberalism, libertarianism
neo-Harringtonianism, 34–35, 74, 108–9, 120, 129–73 (ch. 5)
neo-Roman libertarianism, 220, 221, 229, 234. *See also* civic humanism, 'Country' ideology
Nethersole, Sir Francis, MP, 259–60
Neville, Henry, 148
'new British history,' 7, 53, 228–29
New Criticism, 38, 133–34
Newdegate reporter, 242–43
New Zealand political history, 177–78
Nine Years War, 135
nolumus leges Angliae mutare, 194, 205. *Consult also* ancient constitutionalism, constitutionalism
Norbrook, David, 106*n*, 235*n*
Nordic Conquest, 152–53
Norman Conquest, 165, 187, 191
Numa, 154

Oakeshott, Michael, 14, 17
oligarchy, 130, 142–43, 163
Orford, Edward Russell, Earl of, 141, 158
Orkney, Elizabeth Villiers, Hamilton, Countess of, 140, 172–73
Orosius, 44, 221

Otto, Bishop of Freising, 44, 221
Owen, Sir Roger, MP, 204
owl of Minerva, 176–77

pakeha, 178. *Consult also* New Zealand political history
Palonen, Kari 50
Pangle, Thomas, 111*n*
paradigm theory, 33*n*, 46, 60–61, 84–85, 92, 123, 124, 127–28, 205, 212–13, 227*n*
parliamentary patronal sovereignty, 131–32, 138–39, 157–58, 160, 162, 166, 168–73
parliamentary reporters of 1628, 232, 238–39. *Consult also* Newdegate reporter, Stowe reporter
Partition Treaty, 159
pastoralism, 93*n*
patriotism, 62, 75*n*
Patterson, Annabel, 184*n*
Pawlisch, Hans, 186*n*
Peck, Linda Levy, 167*n*
Pelham, Henry, 112
Peltonen, Markku, 185*n*
Perrott, Sir James, MP, 237
Peters, Richard, 16*n*
Petition of Right, 7, 231, 234, 237, 245, 250, 256–59
Pettit, Philip, 18*n*, 119–20, 222
Petty, Sir William, 80
Phelips, Sir Edward, MP, 194, 239, 243, 244, 245, 246, 253*n*, 257*n*, 258*nn*
Philip II of Spain, King, 182
philosophical-juristic ideology, 65–66. *Consult also* natural law
Philp, Mark, 221–22*n*
Pincus, Steven, 157*n*
Pitt, James, 95*n*
Plamenatz, J.P., 20*n*

Plant, Raymond, 17*n*
Plantagenets, 145–47. *See also* individual royal members
Plato, 194–95
Pocock, J.G.A. references to writings:
"Appeal from the New to the Old Whigs?, An";
Ancient Constitution and the Feudal Law, The," 1, 2, 6, 11–28 (ch. 1), 51, 59, 175–208 (ch. 6), 211–12*n*, 218, 219, 220, 234, 235*n*, 246*n*;
Barbarism and Religion, 1, 7, 27–29, 31–32, 35, 39, 43–45, 47, 51–52, 59, 152*n*, 212, 213, 214, 215*n*, 220–28;
"Between Gog and Magog," 102, 126;
"Book Most Misunderstood since the Bible (The): John Adams and the Confusion about Aristocracy," 125;
"British History: A Plea for a New Subject," 182*n*, 228*n*;
"Burke and the Ancient Constitution," 183–84;
"Concept of Language and the *métier d'historien*, The," 125, 212*n*;
"Concepts and Discourses," 48, 213*n*;
"Contingency, Identity, Sovereignty," 229*n*;
"Deconstructing Europe," 176*n*, 176*n*;
Discovery of Islands, The, 1, 176*n*, 178, 182*n*;
"Early Modern Capitalism — the Augustan Perspective," 112*n*;

"Empire, Revolution and the End of Early Modernity" (in *Varieties of Political Thought*, Pocock [ed.]), 119;

"Enlightenment and Counter-Enlightenment," 176*n*;

"Gaberlunzie's Return," 228*n*;

"Historian as Political Actor, The," 229*n*;

"History and Sovereignty," 176;

"History of Political Thought,The," 14, 122, 212*n*, 227*n*;

"Ironist, The," 2;

"Languages and Their Implications," (in *PLT*), 4–5, 29, 33–34, 39, 60–61, 63, 65, 84, 122, 133, 212*n*, 212–13, 216, 219*n*;

"Law, Sovereignty and History in a Divided Culture," 178;

"Limits and Divisions of British History, The," 182*n*, 228*n*;

"Machiavelli and the Rethinking of History," 179, 182;

Machiavellian Moment, The, 1, 2, 5, 6, 27, 31, 35, 36*n*, 37, 44*n*, 47, 51, 59–99 (ch. 3), 101–28 (ch. 4), 129–73 (ch. 5), 184*n*, 213*n*, 218*n*, 219, 222, 234, 235*n*;

"*Machiavellian Moment* Revisited, *The*," 35*n*, 117–18, 219*n*;

"Modernity and Anti-Modernity in the Anglophone Political Tradition," 125*n*;

"Myth of Locke and the Obsession with Liberalism," 118*n*, 131*n*, 220*n*;

"Negative and Positive Aspects of Locke's Place in Eighteenth-Century Discourse," 126*n*;

"New Bark Up an Old Tree, A" 29–31;

"New British History in Atlantic Perspective, The," 182*n*;

"Notes on an Occidental Tourist I," 176;

"Notes on an Occidental Tourist II," 176, 177, 183;

"On the Non-Revolutionary Character of Paradigms," (in *PLT*), 129, 175;

"Origins of the Study of the Past," 177;

"Owl Reviews his Feathers, The," 4, 175;

"Political Ideas as Historical Events," 212*n*;

Political Works of James Harrington, The, 1, 37, 143, 148, 162, 213*n*, 219, 234;

Politics, Language, and Time, 1, 29, 31, 37, 39, 46, 60–61, 63, 65, 84, 124, 129–31, 162, 175, 179, 183–84, 212*n*, 216, 219*n*;

"Present at the Creation," 212*n*;

"Problem of Political Thought in the Eighteenth Century, The," 126*n*

"Quentin Skinner," 7;

"Reconsideration Impartially Considered, A," 109*n*

"Reconstructing the Traditions," 212*n*;

"Reconstruction of Discourse, The," 40*n*, 124, 212*n*, 219*n*;

"Robert Brady: 1627–1700," 143, 211;

"Some Europes in Their History," 176*n*;

"States, Republics, and Empires," 114*n*

"Texts as Events," 126*n*, 133–34, 212–13*n*;

"Third Kingdom, The," 182–83;

"Thomas May and the Narrative of Civil War," 236*n*;

"Time, History and Eschatology in the Thought of Thomas Hobbes," (in *PLT*), 179;

"Time, Institutions and Action," 179;

"Treaty between Histories, The," 176*n*, 178, 179, 180;

"Uniqueness of Aoteoroa, The," 178;

"Union in British History, The," 229*n*;

Varieties of British Political Thought, Pocock, (ed.) 22, 49, 119;

"Varieties of Whiggism from Exclusion to Reform," (in *VCH*), 183*n*;

Virtue, Commerce, and History, 1, 32*n*, 45, 62, 65–66, 76, 78, 86–87, 88–89, 95–99, 134, 183*n*, 212*n*;

"Verbalising a Political Act," 212*n*;

"*Vous autres Européens*," 176*n*;

"What is Intellectual History?" 29;

"Working on Ideas in Time," 177, 205

Polanyi, Michael, 18*n*

political corruption, 62, 71, 73–75, 77, 83, 92–93*n*, 104, 106, 108, 110, 111, 112, 135, 142–43, 144–45, 170, 213*n*, 222

political liberty, 25, 96, 98, 170, 200, 231–60 (ch. 8). *Consult also* liberalism, libertarianism, neo-Roman liberterianism

political resistance doctrine, 168

political tyranny, 97, 149–51, 154, 166–67, 168–172. *See also* Asian despotism

Pope, Alexander, 133*n*

Popham, Sir Francis, MP, 196

Popper, Karl, 4

populist politics, 64, 168–72

Portland, Hans Willem Bentinck, 1st Earl of, 136–38, 140, 141–42, 146–47, 158

Portland, Richard Weston, 1st Earl of, 258

'positive liberty,' 96–98, 244. *Vs.* 'negative liberty'; *consult also* civic humanism, libertarianism, political liberty, neo-Roman libertarianism

Price, Polly, J., 207–8*n*

Price, Robert, MP, 136–38

Prosch, Harold, 18*n*

property, 7, 65–66, 67, 73–75, 80, 86–99, 112, 203, 206, 208, (or, propriety) 231–60 (ch. 8). *Consult also* tenure, law of; feudal tenures, abolition of

Protectorate, 149–50, 165

Protestantism, 64, 67–73, 77, 81, 92. *See also* Calvinism, Puritanism

Protestant ethic,' 62, 69–73, 77, 93

Providentialism, 134–35, 162, 167

public credit, 78, 81–84, 86–87, 112, 221*n*

Puritanism, 67–73, 83. *Consult also* Calvinism, Protestantism

Putney Debates, 238

Pym, John, 64, 66, 197, 206, 236,

Pym (cont'd)
    258*nn*
Quiller-Couch, Sir Arthur, 3
Quintilian, 237

Rahe, Paul A., 112*n*
Ralph, James, 151
Rape of Lucrece, 163
Rastell, John, 188–89
Rawls, John, 16*n*
'reason of state,' 249
Redworth, Glyn, 182*n*
Reformation, the, 72
regale et politicum, 235, 245, 255.
    Consult also constitutionalism
Reick, Miriam, 234*n*
Relf, Frances H., 246*n*
Renaissance humanism, 3, 5, 81,
    83–84. *See also* humanism; *con
    sult also* civic humanism
republicanism, 2, 11, 28, 36, 59–99,
    (ch. 3), 101–28 (ch. 4), 149, 152,
    154, 156–57, 221, 221–222*n*,
    228, 235–36. *Consult also* civic
    humanism, 'Country' ideology
Resumption Bill, 140, 141, 143–44,
    152, 164
Rich, Sir Nathaniel, MP, 245–46,
    250*n*, 258*n*,
Richard II, King, 146–47
Richter, Melvin, 45–46, 47, 48, 50,
    214*n*. *Consult also Begriffs-
    geschichte*
rights-based politics, 25, 65–66, 89,
    98. *Vs.* virtue-based politics;
    consult also philosophical-
    juristic ideology
Robbins, Caroline, 16*n*, 117
Roberts, Lewes, 77
Robertson, John, 43*n*, 113*n*
Robertson, William, 221, 224–25
Rodgers, Daniel T., 116*n*, 126*n*

Rodney, Sir Edward, MP, 252*n*
Roman Catholic Church, 75, 77
Roman Republic, 152
Roman Empire, 221, 224, 227
Roman law, 24, 185*n*, 187–88, 217,
    234–36. *See also* English civil
    law
Romulus, 165
Rose, Craig, 138*n*
Rosenheim Jr., Edward, 131*n*
Rossiter, Clinton, 16*n*
Roundheads, 164
royal patronage, 83, 129–73 (ch. 5)
royalist absolutism, 21, 98, 185*n*
Rudyard (or Rudyerd), Sir Ben-
    jamin, MP, 238, 239, 242–43
Runciman, W.G., 17,
Rushworth, John, 236
Russell, Conrad, 207*n*, 233
Ryan, Alan, 120
Ryle, Gilbert, 17*n*
Ryswick, Treaty of, 135, 167

Sabine, George, 16*n*
Salic Law, 200
Sallust, 221
Salmon, J.H., 16*n*, 215*n*
Sandys, Sir Edwin, MP, 191–92,
    203–4, 207
Schochet, Gordon, 6, 22, 212*nn*,
    220
Schwoerer, Lois G., 135*n*, 220
Scott, Jonathan, 106
Scott, Thomas, 78–79, 80, 83
Scottish Commission Act, 203
Second World War, 2–3, 4, 17
secularization, 63, 67–73, 74, 92
secularist historiography, 217, 228
Selden, Sir John, 21, 181*n*, 234–35,
    247, 248, 249, 252, 253–56,
    258n
Selim, 150

Sergeant, John, 137–38*n*

Settlement, Act of, 163

Sewell, Keith C., 183*n*, 211*n*

Sexby, Edward, *later* 'Cpt.,' 260*n*

Shapiro, Ian, 116*n*

Sharp, Andrew, 215*n*

Sharpe, Kevin, 133

Sherland, Christopher, MP, 250, 258*n*

Sidney, Algernon, 106–7, 128, 148

Skeel, Caroline, 188

Skinner, Quentin, 4, 7, 12, 14, 27, 29, 33, 35–36, 38, 39, 40, 41, 42–43, 46, 47, 48, 50, 51, 52, 54, 119–20, 122–28, 132, 139*n*, 211, 212, 213, 215, 217*n*, 218–19, 221, 221–22*n*, 233–35. *Consult also* 'Cambridge School'

Smith, Adam, 22, 114, 221, 225

Smith, Bonnie, 18*n*

Smith, David, 23*n*

Smith, Sir Thomas, 189

social mobility, 81*n*, 92–95

Solon, 154

Somers, John, Lord, 141, 158, 164

speech-act theory, 28, 40–41

Speck, W.A., 78*n*

Spelman, Sir Henry, 3, 21, 192–93

'spirit of capitalism,' 69–71

Stallybrass, Peter, 97*n*

Spedding, James, 202*n*

St John, Sir Oliver, 191

Stephen, Leslie, 217*n*

Stone, Sir Lawrence, 83

Stowe reporter, 242–43, 252

Strafford, Thomas Wentworth, 1st Earl of, 163, 258

Strangways, Sir John, MP, 258*n*

Strauss, Leo, 13, 16, 110, 213–14

Straussianism, 118, 213–14, 215, 220

Strawson, P.F., 17*n*

Stuart, Sir Francis, MP, 258*n*

Suleyman the Magnificent, 150

Sulla, 151–52

Sullivan, Vickie B., 104*n*

Summerville, J.P., 187*n*

Swift, Jonathan, 84–85, 90–92, 98, 132, 161–68, 171

Tacitean narrative history, 44, 221

Tacitus, 221

tangata whenua. See Maori

Tanner, J.R., 206*n*

Tarlton, Charles, 127

Tarcov, Nathan, 103*n*

Tarquins, 154, 163

Tawney, R.H., 71*n*

tenure, law of, 7, 186, 206, 236, 242, 246, 252–53, 255. *Consult also* ancient constitutionalism, English common law, property

Tercheck, Ronald J., 105*n*

Thompson, Martyn P., 197*n*, 199

Thompson, Faith, 246*n*

Thornborough, John, Bishop of Worcester, 192

Thucidides, 234

Tillotson, John, Archbishop of Canterbury, 135

Toland, John, 130, 133, 141, 142, 147–58, 160, 161, 162, 164

Toryism, 143, 145, 149, 169–70, 236–37

Toth, Kathleen, 106

Toulmin, Stephen, 19*n*

Toews, John E., 123*n*

Trenchard, John, MP, 109, 110

Tubbs, J.W., 19*n*, 180–81, 185*n*

Tuck, Richard, 211

Tucker, Josiah, 119

Tulloch, Hugh, 184*n*

Tully, James, 117

Turner, Stephen, 18*n*

Tutchin, John, 134, 141–42

US Constitution, 24
Union Commission, 201

Venturi, Franco, 223
Vernon, James, Secretary-of-State, 139
Virgil, 31
virtù, 51, 62, 67–68, 72, 90, 92, 222
virtue-based politics, 65–66, 89, 98. *Vs.* rights-based politics
vocationalism, 70–72, 77, 93. *Consult also* 'Protestant ethic'
Voltaire, Francois-Marie Arouet de, 44, 221, 224
vox dei, 170, 171
vox populi, 25, 170

Waitangi, Treaty of, 178. *Consult also* New Zealand political history
Wallace, John, 4
Wallenstein, Albrecht von, 246
Waller, Edmund, MP, 258*n*
Wallop, Sir Henry, MP, 251
War of the Spanish Succession 158
Warren, Austin, 3
Warrender, Howard, 16*n*
Wasserman, Earl, 133
Weaver, Richard M. 3
Weber, Max, 70. *Consult also* 'spirit of capitalism'
Weldon, J.D., 16
Wentworth, Thomas, 253*n*, 258*n*
Wesley, Samuel, 135*n*
Weston, Corinne C., 12*n*
'Whig interpretation of history,' 3, 63, 118, 180–81, 183
Whiggism, 2, 3, 23, 81, 149, 168, 183–84, 219–20, 222, 224*n*, 233

Whitelocke, James, MP, 206
Wilders, John, 145*n*
Willem II, Prince of Orange, Stadholder, 157
William I, King, 187, 247
William III, King, 130, 132–73
Williams, Raymond, 50
Williamson, Arthur H., 198*n*
Wimsatt, William K., 38, 40. *Consult also* 'intentional fallacy'
Winch, Donald, 114
Winch, Peter, 16*n*
Winstanley, Gerrard, 218*n*
Wittgenstein, Ludwig, 16, 54
Wolsey, Thomas, Cardinal, Lord Chancellor, 77
Woolf, D.R., 19*n*
Wood, Gordon, 115*n*, 117
Wootton, David, 212*n*
Worden, A.B., 148*n*, 219*n*, 229*n*
Wordie, J.R., 89*n*

Yelverton, Sir Henry, MP, 204
Yolton, John, 16*n*

Zagorin, Peter, 16*n*
Zuckert, Michael, 54*n*, 118–19, 127
Zwicker, Steven N., 133